C0-BIK-567

THE ARCHITECTURE OF
HIGH POINT
NORTH CAROLINA

To Donna Blakely —

Thank you for everything you have done for High Point's history! I hope you will enjoy learning about the architecture of our home town!

THE ARCHITECTURE OF
HIGH POINT
NORTH CAROLINA

A History and Guide to the City's Houses,
Churches and Public Buildings

BENJAMIN BRIGGS

Charleston · London
History PRESS

Published by The History Press
Charleston, SC 29403
www.historypress.net

Copyright © 2008 by Benjamin Briggs
All rights reserved

Cover design by Marshall Hudson.

First published 2008

Manufactured in the United Kingdom

ISBN 978.1.59629.326.7

Library of Congress Cataloging-in-Publication Data

Briggs, Benjamin.
The architecture of High Point, North Carolina / Benjamin Briggs.
p. cm.
Includes bibliographical references.
ISBN-13: 978-1-59629-326-7 (alk. paper)
1. Architecture--North Carolina--High Point. 2. High Point
(N.C.)--History. I. Title.
NA735.H52B75 2007
720.9756'62--dc22
                                        2007038696

Notice: The information in this book is true and complete to the best of our knowledge. It is offered without guarantee on the part of the author or The History Press. The author and The History Press disclaim all liability in connection with the use of this book.
All rights reserved. No part of this book may be reproduced or transmitted in any form whatsoever without prior written permission from the publisher except in the case of brief quotations embodied in critical articles and reviews.

The survey on which this book is based was financed in part with federal finds from the National Park Service, Department of the Interior. The contents and opinions here do not necessarily reflect the views or policies of the Department of the Interior, nor does the mention of trade names and commercial products constitute endorsement or recommendation by the Department of the Interior.

"We who today are enjoying the comforts and privileges that are ours should feel justly proud of the generations that have made it possible."

–A.M. Briggs, 1932

CONTENTS

Preface
Acknowledgements — 9
Introduction — 13
— 15

Part I. History of High Point

Early Settlement and Development, 1750–1852
The Village of High Point, 1852–1888 — 19
The Rise of Industry, 1889–1905 — 27
Hosiery Manufacturing and High Point's — 37
 Growth as a City, 1905–1930
Modern Period and Civil Rights Era, 1930–1975 — 45
— 73

Part II. Inventory of Historic Properties

Introduction
Sites Built Prior to the Civil War, 1750–1861 — 91
Downtown High Point — 93
Western and Southern Neighborhoods — 107
Eastern Suburbs — 139
Midtown and Western Suburbs — 151
Northern Suburbs — 167
— 221

Glossary of Architectural Terms
Preservation Resources — 237
Notes — 245
Works Cited — 247
Index — 251
— 255

PREFACE

High Point's existence, like that of many cities, is a result of geography and the advantages afforded it through transportation. Early Piedmont transportation routes included the ridge-hugging Great Western Plank Road and the gentle incline-bound North Carolina Railroad, both of which traversed the future site of High Point. Transportation lines not only allowed for raw materials such as lumber and cotton to be brought easily into the city, but also aided in delivering processed goods to faraway markets.

High Point's conception is not solely linked to transportation; it is also tied to religious freedom, beginning as early as the mid-eighteenth century as a refuge for Pennsylvania Quakers who came to the region in search of affordable land, good climate and an opportunity to create a principled and ordered community. Members of the Society of Friends held beliefs that many thought were heresy in the late eighteenth century. Central to these core convictions were values of community and equality, which led to the development of specialized trades and early educational systems that were the foundations for future growth of the region.

Since its incorporation in 1859, High Point has been an ambitious city. Whether rallying around Union carpetbaggers in the 1870s and textile barons in the 1910s or planning public parks in the 1930s, the city has always been forward-looking in its prospects. City historians such as J.J. Farriss, Stephen C. Clark, Frank Sizemore and Holt McPherson have proudly documented the city's past as if writing a user's guide for building a model city. Memorialized in numerous successful businesses and family fortunes, this ambition is also recorded in the city's architecture.

Though High Point attained great wealth as one of North Carolina's leading industrial centers, it is unusual in that it was not dominated by one industry or industrialist. Unlike the Reynoldses of Winston-Salem, the Cones of Greensboro or the Dukes of Durham, no single name stands synonymous with High Point's past. This diversity is embodied in the city's architectural environment by numerous large residences, notable churches and civic structures that brought recognition to their patrons through tangible architecture instead of implied social

Preface

status. As a result of this practice, notable architects from the city and beyond were called in to make strong statements using exuberant designs that incorporated superior materials and sumptuous landscaping.

Reflecting the city's growth and influence is an architectural inventory epitomizing High Point's increasing civic pride and cultural sophistication. Since the city's early settlement, hotels and merchant houses have presented fashionable façades to visitors and discerning shoppers. Later, wealthy industrialists had ambitious residences and churches erected in popular styles that illustrated the growing town's sense of style. Finally, civic projects such as schools and parks utilized modern designs that spoke to High Point's progressive spirit and quickening pace. By the middle of the twentieth century, High Point had amassed an impressive collection of architecture representing nearly every popular style since the city was founded, including designs by nationally recognized architects and planners.

Awareness of the value of the community's architectural resources began relatively early, stemming from an appreciation of early Quaker history. The first concerted act of preservation in the city took place in 1927, when members of the Springfield Friends Meeting decided to preserve their 1858 meetinghouse as a museum upon the completion of their new meetinghouse nearby. Under the banner of the Museum of Old Domestic Life, the Springfield Memorial Association began to display artifacts of early Piedmont material culture in 1933, with guidance from historian and meeting member John J. Blair.

Additional conservation initiatives followed, including preservation of the Mendenhall Store and Jamestown Indulged Meeting House in 1934, when High Point's City Lake Park was constructed. In 1934, a photographer with the Historic American Buildings Survey paused in Jamestown long enough to photo-document these two buildings as part of a project to survey the remarkable architecture of the American South. A few years later, in 1946, Ruth Coltrane Cannon, pioneer North Carolina preservationist and president of the North Carolina Society for the Preservation of Antiquities (now Preservation North Carolina), assisted in the restoration of the 1848 Allen Jay House in Springfield. This Quaker home, then in poor repair, was restored for use as social space by Springfield Friends Meeting.

A startling loss of early housing stock throughout the city, especially in early downtown neighborhoods, spurred the organization of the High Point Historical Society in 1967. Immediately, the society commenced restoration of the John Haley House, a notable brick residence built in 1786 and the earliest documented structure on its original foundations in Guilford County. The Haley House was purchased by the City of High Point from Capus Waynick for $30,000, and the initial phase of restoration began in the summer of 1968, continuing under the supervision of Mary Lib Joyce and John Bivens. The building holds the distinction of being the first in the city to be placed on the National Register of Historic Places, having been listed in May 1971.

Adaptive use of historic properties, made popular in larger cities in the 1960s, was introduced to High Point as a tool for preserving historic places in 1976 with the conversion of the H.A. Millis House on North Main Street to Millis Square, a collection of upscale boutiques. Initially threatened with demolition in order to make way for the city's first McDonald's franchise, this important house began a long and successful run of high-profile adaptive-use projects.

Foremost among these ventures was the adaptive use of the Tomlinson Manufacturing Company as Market Square in 1980. Fresh off their first successful project, the conversion of the North Side Hose Co. Number 1 (the Old City Hall) in 1979, Jake Froelich and designer Pat Plaxico teamed with other investors to blend the charm of the turn-of-the-twentieth-century brick industrial complex into furniture showroom space. The result was an instant success that contrasted with the predictable interiors of High Point's newer furniture showrooms. Market Square was the first project in the city to take advantage of federal and state rehabilitation tax credits; later the project also utilized local historic property tax deferrals.

In 1984, the High Point Preservation Society was established to support the historic architecture of the city. In 1986 the City Council established the High Point Preservation Commission

Preface

to govern the city's first locally zoned historic district, which encompasses the residences of the Johnson Street neighborhood. The effort began in the early 1980s as the neighborhood was threatened with street widening and rezoning. Approval of the district was narrowly won, but it soon witnessed positive results as several key houses were restored within five years of designation.

The Oakwood neighborhood was awarded High Point's first National Register Historic District listing in 1990, followed a year later by Sherrod Park. Additional preservation projects have continued this momentum into the new millennium, most notably the restoration of the J.H. Adams House in 2000 and the Southern Railway Passenger Depot in 2001–03. Both projects illustrate renewed interest and excitement over historic preservation in a city that continues to value its historic architectural environment.

As High Point matures, additional properties cross the fifty-year threshold often used in determining a site's importance and value to history. Other factors, such as social history, designer or function, may contribute to the importance of a site as well. High Point's preservation community will continue to meet challenges in gauging social value and defining what is important to the city. Consequently, this book is not the final inventory of city historic sites. On the contrary, this book should be viewed as a starting point to encourage community dialogue to recognize, record and protect that which makes High Point's architectural environment unique. History is never static, and further research is needed to expand, update or correct this body of knowledge. In short time, new stories will be gathered and new sites will cross the fifty-year threshold, requiring further investigation and inventory of historic sites.

ACKNOWLEDGEMENTS

This publication stemmed from two major initiatives. First, its author was raised in an environment that cultivated a deep appreciation of old places and architecture. Special recognition goes to my mother, Doris Briggs, for teaching me to be curious about places and to recognize the soul of things that are careworn and that hold a rich patina. Gratitude is also extended to my father, Roy Briggs, who taught me to appreciate history, analyze the past and understand architectural forms and concepts (such as the classical orders!).

Secondly, this project stemmed from a series of articles published in the *High Point Enterprise* from 1997 through 2003. This effort resulted in over one hundred articles ranging in topic from urban planning to architecture, history and landscapes specific to High Point. Dozens of citizens contributed to my understanding of High Point's history during that public vetting process, and a great deal of background information was secured. Thanks to *Enterprise* editor Tom Blount for accepting the idea to publish the column, as well as the staff of the newspaper for their encouragement, expertise and patience. Appreciation is also extended to individuals who contributed information and images to me for use in the column—their spirit of sharing has enriched us all.

Lastly, the catalyst for this publication grew from an initiative from the High Point Preservation Commission, which sought in 1999 to compile a comprehensive survey of the historic resources of central High Point. In partnership with the North Carolina State Historic Preservation Office (Division of Archives and History, Department of Cultural Resources), this survey included photo documentation, research and personal interviews over a one-year period in order to develop a working understanding of the city's resources. Claudia Brown, staff contact for the state, provided helpful direction and insights on architecture and history, as well as editorial comments and proofreading. Catherine Bishir, statewide architectural historian, supplied advice and ideas liberally throughout the composition of this book. Chandrea Burch was invaluable in assisting with research files, and Bill Garrett was generous and enthusiastic in lending his skills to take photographs of key buildings. Locally, gratitude

Acknowledgements

is extended to the High Point Historic Commission members: Geneva Adams, Dan Allen, Anne Andrews, Betty Price-Burris, Kathy Carter, Terri Cartner, Dennis Forbis, Marilyn Fowells, Lawrence Graves, A.B. Henley, Clayton Mays, David Oden, David Parsons, Carlvena Pettiway, Abigail Pittman, Pat Plaxico, Pat Rizzo, Josef Walker and Norman Zimmerman.

Specifically, I would like to thank the City of High Point Planning and Development Department staff for their leadership, perseverance, creativity and patience. Lee Burnette provided guidance and approval of this project, and Bob Robbins supplied leadership and foresight. Carmen Cannon focused primarily on developing maps and recording information to city systems. Finally, Leslie Wagle acted as point person, bringing together city, state and private resources to bring the project to fruition.

In addition to the above-mentioned contributors, numerous citizens have been active participants in this publication. I am indebted to Mary Lib Joyce, who graciously opened access to her detailed files containing information related to Emerywood, growth of the city and topics recorded by her father, Stephen C. Clark. Dorothy Gay Darr shared her interest in High Point history, her recollections of interviews with leading citizens and her analytic approach to history. Barbara Taylor of the High Point Museum proofread the manuscript and supplied comments. Jackie Hedstrom and staff of the North Carolina Collection at the High Point Public Library provided invaluable guidance with research. Brenda Haworth, historian of Quaker heritage, provided guidance and advice on topics related to Springfield and members of the Society of Friends. Mac Whatley of Randolph County assisted with insights on early High Point settlement and industrial heritage. Lee Dowdy provided insights on early buildings and their locations throughout the city.

Too many citizens to mention contributed through interviews and observances. Specific names include Florence Allen, Anne Andrews, Sonny Blair, Ruth Briles, Mary Browning, Lib and Bob Conner, Glenn Chavis, Bill Freeman, Lawrence Graves, Hallie Meyers and Katherine and Pete Peyton, all of whom contributed to my knowledge and understanding of High Point's architecture and history.

Additional appreciation is extended to the High Point Community Foundation, the City of High Point and others who have contributed to make this publication a reality. I am sure that this gift to the future citizens of High Point will be valued for decades to come.

INTRODUCTION

High Point stands among the youngest of North Carolina's largest municipalities, having been founded in 1859. The city was born from the crossroads of two of the state's major transportation improvement initiatives of the nineteenth century: the Fayetteville and Western Plank Road and the North Carolina Railroad. The crossing of these thoroughfares within the industrializing Piedmont section of the state was a magnet for trade and manufacturing, and the crossroads village quickly grew, becoming a city by the turn of the twentieth century. Sustained growth, especially in the furniture and hosiery industries during the first half of the twentieth century, led to the city's distinction of holding high rank among industrial centers in the American South. By 1950, as the city prepared to celebrate its centennial, civic boosters had confidently named the city "the Furniture and Hosiery Capital of the World."

PART I.
HISTORY OF HIGH POINT

EARLY SETTLEMENT AND DEVELOPMENT, 1750–1852

Settlement

High Point is located on a high ridge that separates the Deep River basin on the east from the Yadkin River basin on the west and rises to become the Uwharrie Mountain range just ten miles south of the city. The region enjoys a temperate climate, with even distribution of precipitation, including occasional winter snows. Its gentle climate has provided for the development of a temperate mixed forest of oak, hickory, poplar and pine since the Pleistocene era—a resource that would contribute to the economy of High Point and surrounding cities in the nineteenth and twentieth centuries.

Little remains of early Native American civilization in the region except for place names such as Totera [*sic*], Uwharrie, Carroway and Sapona. Archaeological remains of campsites, town sites, hunting grounds and burial sites can be found across the region. Legends record the existence of the Woccon tribe, which is said to have maintained a camp on the banks of the Deep River, an area now flooded by City Lake. Many arrowheads and "relics" were found at the site before the lake was built.[1]

English explorer John Lawson passed just south of present-day High Point in the winter of 1701 and observed the region before European settlers arrived. He crossed the area on his way from South Carolina northeastward via the Yadkin River—near the Trading Ford, roughly along present-day U.S. 64—west toward Caraway Mountain in Randolph County. Of his passage through modern-day Randolph County, Lawson wrote,

> *Next day, we had 15 Miles farther to the Keyauwees. The Land is more mountainous, but extremely pleasant, and an excellent Place for the breeding Sheep, Goats, and Horses; or Mules, if the English were once brought to the Experience of the Usefulness of those Creatures. The Valleys are here very rich. At Noon, we pass'd over such another stony River, as that eight Miles from Sapona. This is call'd Heighwaree*[2]*…Five Miles from this River, to the N.W. stands the Keyauwees Town. They are fortify'd in, with wooden*

Puncheons, like Sapona, being a People much of the same Number. Nature hath so fortify'd this Town, with Mountains, that were it a Seat of War, it might easily be made impregnable; having large Corn-Fields joining to their Cabins, and a Savanna near the Town, at the Foot of these Mountains, that is capable of keeping some hundred Heads of Cattle. And all this environ'd round with very high Mountains, so that no hard Wind ever troubles these Inhabitants. Those high Clifts have no Grass growing on them, and very few Trees, which are very short, and stand at a great Distance one from another. The Earth is of a red Colour.[3]

Although the large "Corn-Fields" remain a common site in the region today, the grassless mountains have long since been reforested.

Contact with Europeans and their accompanying diseases nearly eradicated all native populations before intensive resettlement occurred. Surrounding tribes and villages were depopulated, forcing the small collection of survivors to band together. In time, colonials relocated these assembled groups to Catawba Town in South Carolina.[4]

Early European settlers came to the area from eastern North Carolina, the Tidewater and the Philadelphia area in search of affordable and open land. King Charles II established the colony of North Carolina in 1663, when eight Lords Proprietors were granted the rights to administer, govern, partition land and tax its residents. Seven of the original proprietary shares were sold to King George II in 1729, making North Carolina a royal colony. Only John Carteret, second Earl Granville, chose not to sell the share he owned.

The Granville District, an area that encompassed the upper half of present-day North Carolina, was created and partially surveyed in 1744 for the Earl Granville. Unlike the early Proprietors, Granville owned all unsettled lands but had no right to govern the area. Earl Granville appointed agents there as representatives to grant land, collect rents and conduct his business through a land office that was opened in 1748.

By 1753, the area known today as High Point found itself on the border between Orange County to the east and Rowan County to the west. In 1771, Guilford County was established, with its first seat and court located in the northern environs of the city. The landscape was largely undisturbed, with grassy ridgeline savannahs interspersed with hardwood bottomlands.[5] Narrow dirt roads connected places of worship, residences, mills and trading centers, following ridgelines in order to reduce the need for bridges over streams and rivers. Aside from occasional travelers using the Petersburg to Salisbury stage road that passed through the territory, the region was largely insulated from outside influences until well into the nineteenth century.

Quaker settlers were among the first Europeans to select land in these fertile hills and bottomlands of North Carolina's Piedmont in the mid-eighteenth century. Seeking affordable land and religious freedom, members of the Society of Friends arrived in the Piedmont from many areas, including the Tidewater of northeastern North Carolina and the Lowcountry of South Carolina. The greatest number of Quakers came to the region from the crowded Philadelphia area, where the growing population forced young families southward in search of land and good climate.[6] They joined numerous national, ethnic and religious groups that settled within the region, including the English, Moravians, Germans and Scots-Irish. Quakers were the

Early Piedmont landscape. *Courtesy of the Briggs Collection.*

Early Settlement and Development, 1750–1852

primary group to settle in and around what would later become High Point. In contrast to the contemporary Moravians, who quickly set about establishing planned villages in present-day Forsyth County, Quaker settlers valued land ownership, which resulted in dispersed settlement across this region.

The first landowning Friends came to the area around 1752 and quickly formed a network of friends and family that organized a meeting for worship at Deep River in 1754, a congregation that remains active today.[7] More Quaker meetings followed, including Springfield in 1780, and soon the area was thickly settled with Friends representing a broad range of socioeconomic backgrounds, skills and traditions. Several early structures related to Friends remain scattered in and around the region, and Quakers remain a high-profile sector of the community. Quaker influences ran deep, manifested in a dedication to education, a disdain for slavery and a penchant for industry.

Evidence suggests that the earliest residences in the region were constructed of logs and were often intended to be only temporary. Corner-timbered houses were built in a variety of floor plans, including a single pen (room), two rooms of differing dimension side by side (hall and parlor) or two equal-size rooms with a chimney in between (saddlebag). Selection of early homesites was done with great care and scrutiny. Early High Point historian A.M. Briggs reported that "a bubbling spring seems to have been their first objective as wells were an unknown quantity for water supply. Their houses were built either with clapboards or logs chinked with clay according to the financial ability of the builder. Glass windows, brick chimneys and plank floors were not in evidence. A chest, a table, a bed or two, and two or three rude stools completed the furnishings of most homes."[8]

The Hoggatt House at High Point Museum remains an example of residences from this period of settlement. Members of the Hoggatt family moved to central North Carolina from Virginia around 1754, though their home was erected around 1801.[9] Originally a single-room residence near the intersection of Rotary Drive and Phillips Avenue, the Hoggatt House features a stone foundation, a loft and a wood shingle roof. Some time after the one-room structure was completed, a second room was added to the side. For both rooms, roughly dimensioned logs are laid horizontally and joined at each corner using a V-notch technique. Corner joinery represents a familiar and often-used fastening technique in the Piedmont that traces its roots in America to the mid-Atlantic region. Logs were "chinked" using a combination of wood shims, slabs of tree bark and native clay, sometimes mixed with grass and twigs. The rudimentary log form of shelter characterized the norm in residential housing in the High Point area until economic strides associated with improved transportation led to higher construction standards around 1850. Other attributes of the original structure, including a large cooking fireplace, small window openings and hand-manufactured hardware such as hinges and nails, remained popular in isolated examples until well after the Civil War.

Like houses, early religious buildings were also simple and utilitarian in appearance. The first Deep River Friends Meeting House was erected in 1758 of timber frame construction. Set

1758 Deep River Friends Meeting. *Courtesy of the North Carolina Friends Historical Collection, Guilford College, Greensboro, North Carolina.*

upon a fieldstone foundation, the clapboarded structure featured a wood shingle roof and two rooms separated by a partition, but lacked a chimney. The interior was heated by stoves "whose pipes, extending through the overhead ceiling, discharged their contents into the space beneath the rafters. The smoke finally escaped through the cracks between the shingles."[10] This building was destroyed in 1877.

In the decades after initial settlement, development of a system of specialized tradesmen allowed for improved standards of building construction. Briggs relates,

> *Saw mills were in production, brick made of the finest clay known, black smiths turning out forged nails or "home-made" nails, enabled the settlers to build more commodious homes, some of them brick, but mostly wooden construction with rock chimneys topped with brick. Some were quite elaborate for that period. A few at this date [1932] are still standing as evidence of the durable mechanical and architectural ideas entertained by promoters and builders of the finest industrial section in our Old North State.*[11]

The Quakers' strong sense of place and permanence led to construction of several brick residences located north and east of the city, such as the Phebe and John Haley House of 1786, the Phebe and Isaac Beeson House of 1825 and the Holton House of circa 1835.[12] Like many early houses, these were arranged in the three-room Quaker plan, a tradition likely brought to the region from central Great Britain by way of Philadelphia. In North Carolina, the Quaker plan is most often found in the central Piedmont, where it became associated with "weighty Friends" of influence and stature. The region around High Point contains an unusually high concentration of Quaker-plan houses due to the number of Friends in the area. The house type possibly represented solidarity among Friends in the context of a broader antebellum culture that contrasted dramatically with Quaker values.[13]

The ambitions of early Quaker settlers who erected permanent brick houses soon gave way to the deep isolation experienced by those who lived in the Piedmont "backcountry." Though a well-developed community of artisans and specialized tradespeople had evolved in southwestern Guilford County by the early nineteenth century, local farmers and craftsmen had few nearby markets in which to sell their crops and goods. The cost of shipping goods to places such as Charleston or Philadelphia, where higher profits could be realized, often exceeded the sales profits.[14] The result of this isolation was economic stagnancy that gripped the region for more than fifty years. Though Friends began to vacate the South, including the High Point area, in the 1830s to escape the poor economy as well as the unpalatable practice of slavery, several small mercantile communities had developed in the region, including Jamestown (1812), Westminster (circa 1830), Browntown (circa 1791), Bloomington (circa 1830) and Pennfield (circa 1820).[15] Browntown was centered on the 1756 Abbott's Creek mission church and Pennfield near Brummel's Inn, both in nearby Davidson County. The other communities were all within Guilford County. Specialized trades developed in the forms of millers, rifle makers, tanners, furniture craftsmen, potters, weavers and even hatters.[16]

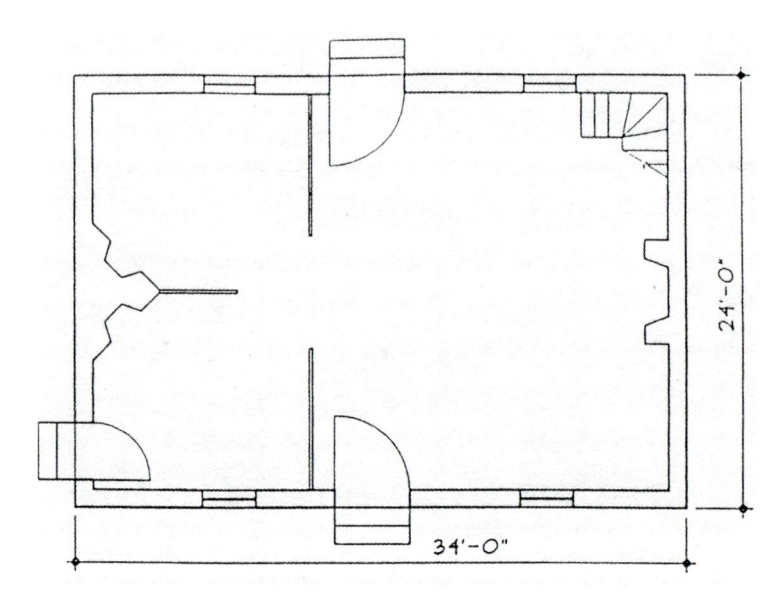

Haley House floor plan. *Courtesy of the High Point Museum, High Point, North Carolina.*

Early Settlement and Development, 1750–1852

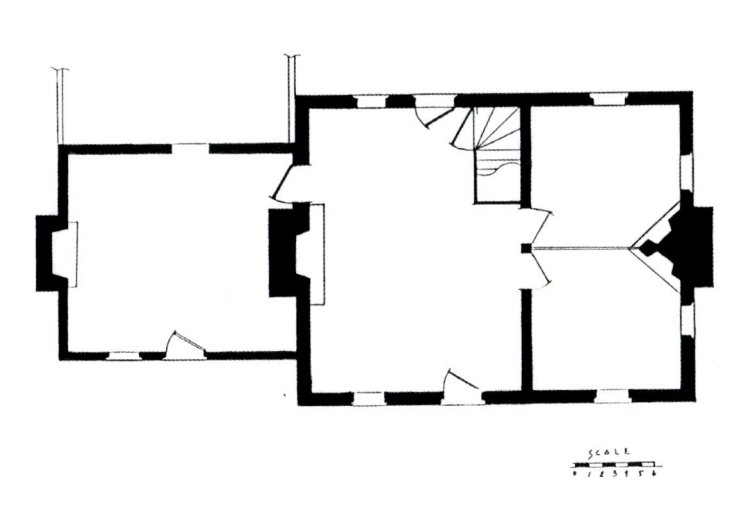

Beeson House plans. *Courtesy of the Briggs Collection.*

Chestnut Hill. *Courtesy of the Briggs Collection.*

Nineteenth-century Architecture

During the early nineteenth century, a general improvement of housing stock continued, though not at the pace enjoyed by earlier generations. Both the hall and parlor– and Quaker-plan houses were often constructed using techniques more modest than masonry, such as log or timber framing. Brick construction was often reserved for commercial structures, meetinghouses and schools. Several sturdy timber frame residences survive from the period, including Chestnut Hill of circa 1843 to the north of the city and the Zelinda and David Marshall House of 1846 near Springfield.[17] The Marshall House is a good example of the period, featuring a Quaker-plan form, heavy timber framing and a side-gable roof. Heavily renovated in the 1870s as the residence of prominent Quaker Allen Jay and restored in the 1940s by preservationist Ruth Coltrane Cannon, the house retains its wide board interior sheathing, pine floors and simple mantels and surrounds, all characteristic of the period.

A few examples of antebellum brick stores and churches can be identified in and around High Point, including the Mendenhall Store of 1824, the Jamestown Indulged Meeting House of circa 1825 and the Beard Hat Shop of circa 1825 (destroyed). The finest of these structures is the Mendenhall Store in central Jamestown (in today's High Point City Lake Park). The two-story, side-gable building features Flemish bond brickwork, a corbelled cornice with a distinctive "mouse-tooth" brick pattern and native stone sills and lintels. Traditionally associated with the early village of Jamestown but annexed into High Point in the 1920s, the Mendenhall Store stands as the earliest commercial structure within the city limits of High Point. The Jamestown Indulged Meeting House is set upon a stone foundation and features Flemish bond brickwork, segmental arches and a corbelled cornice. Interior appointments are simple, with plastered walls, a small fireplace and wooden ceilings with exposed joists. Photographs of the Beard Hat Shop depict similar construction standards, including segmental arched windows and doorways, Flemish bond brickwork and a high gabled roof.[18]

An unusual remnant of the antebellum industrial landscape was constructed in 1832 as a support service to the local gold milling operations that peppered the region. Charles McCulloch erected an imposing granite rock engine house to grind and extract gold from the milk quartz in which it was often embedded. Modeled on tin mine engine houses of Cornwall in England, the

The Architecture of High Point, North Carolina

Marshall House. *Courtesy of the North Carolina Friends Historical Collection, Guilford College, Greensboro, North Carolina.*

Mendenhall Store. *Courtesy of the Historic American Buildings Survey, L.R. Winslow, photographer, circa 1934.*

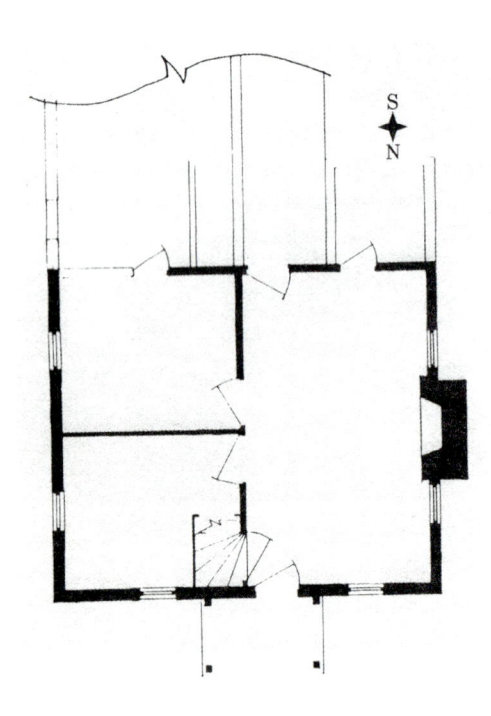

Beard Hat Shop. *Courtesy of the North Carolina Friends Historical Collection, Guilford College, Greensboro, North Carolina.*

Marshall House. *Courtesy of the Briggs Collection.*

building combines a tall chimneystack with a large hipped-roof block embellished by an unusual carved Gothic arch.[19] Perhaps an import to the Piedmont, this feature ranks the engine house among the earliest examples of Gothic Revival architecture in the state.[20]

In contrast to this stylish and sturdy industrial building, most early schools in the region were frugal frame structures that enabled financial resources to be diverted to teachers and books instead of architecture. An exception is the administration and classroom building of the Florence Female Academy of 1853, an excellent surviving example of brick construction during the antebellum period.[21] Located northeast of the city, the two-story brick building features English bond brickwork and a simple water table. The low roofline and wide, overhanging eaves mark the first application of the Romantic Revival Italianate style to the austere Quaker buildings in the Piedmont. The administration building and nearby dormitory of the academy are among the oldest documented educational structures in the county. Both buildings display simple details, but their low rooflines and double-panel doors suggest Romantic Revival influences.

THE VILLAGE OF HIGH POINT, 1852–1888

Formation of a Transportation Hub

In January 1849, historian Benson J. Lossing passed through the region on today's Lexington Avenue on his way from Jamestown to Lexington. His observations of the Piedmont's ridge-bound road system, topography and open treeless vistas were the stage on which High Point was established only four years later.

> *These ridge roads, or rather ridges upon which they are constructed, are curious features in the upper country of the Carolinas. Although the whole country is hilly upon every side, these roads may be traveled a score of miles, sometimes, with hardly ten feet of variation from a continuous level. The ridges are of sand, and continue, unbroken by the ravines which cleave the hills in all directions for miles, upon almost a uniform level. The roads following their summits are exceedingly sinuous, but being level and hard, the greater distance is more easily accomplished than if they were constructed in straight lines over the hills. The country has the appearance of vast waves of the sea suddenly turned into sand.*[22]

Central North Carolina saw the greatest changes since the Revolutionary War beginning in the 1850s, when new transportation routes opened trade with markets previously considered too distant. Nicknamed the "Appian Way of North Carolina," the Great Fayetteville and Western Plank Road that connected Fayetteville to Salem and Bethania passed through southwestern Guilford County in 1852. The road straddled the ridgeline that separates the Cape Fear River Basin to the east from the Yadkin–Pee Dee River Basin to the west, a natural thoroughfare that avoided marshy lowland crossings.

As surveyors were at work determining the future path of the Plank Road, politicians were lobbying for the construction of an alternative route to the interior of the state in the form of the North Carolina Railroad. The highest point along the proposed rail line happened to also be where the two thoroughfares intersected in southwestern Guilford County; hence, the location earned the name "High Point." Connecting Goldsboro in the east to Charlotte in the west by rail opened a vast section of the Piedmont, replacing muddy stagecoach trails as the chief method of communication and transit. Completion of the Great Fayetteville and Western Plank Road and the North Carolina Railroad through the region brought access to new markets and facilitated easier access to other areas of the state and beyond. As a result of this increased prosperity, farms were improved, schools were founded and a new era commenced. Guilford native Colonel W.A. Blair recalled,

The influence of the road upon the manners and customs of the people was striking and interesting. They were able to send produce, their dried fruit, beeswax and other commodities to the markets and people began to put on airs, dress better, move their pig pens back of their houses, fix up their homes, yards and garden, grease their boots and harness, curry their horses and quit using the old accustomed designation "meat sop" and called it "gravy"![23]

Exemplifying this period of reform was tanner and merchant Elihu Mendenhall. Mendenhall constructed a large addition to his house in the Deep River community north of High Point around 1855 and borrowed from both traditional and contemporary models. His house was a center of culture in the community, serving as a school for the children of freed slaves, a gathering place for young people and an accommodation for visiting Friends. Mendenhall embellished his grand two-story, five-bay, double-pile frame house with traditional Greek Revival details such as two-panel doors and post-and-lintel mantels. Simultaneously, the house displayed contemporary picturesque period porch lattice and exposed rafter tails that were popular in the region, due to architect A.J. Davis's design for Blandwood in 1846. In the Springfield community to the south, another Friends meeting enjoyed growth and witnessed the erection of a new meetinghouse in 1856. Constructed of brick, it coupled double-panel Greek Revival doors with picturesque period exposed rafter tails. These examples are but two of several from the period that reflect the Piedmont's progressive spirit,

Elihu Mendenhall House. *Courtesy of the Briggs Collection.*

Third Springfield Meeting House. *Courtesy of the High Point Museum, High Point, North Carolina.*

first demonstrated in Guilford County with Davis's influential designs in nearby Greensboro.

Despite over one hundred years of European settlement in the area, when the surveyor's stake was placed to mark the future route of the North Carolina Railroad in what is now downtown High Point, no structures stood within sight, and the land was used only for agricultural purposes. Recognizing the looming importance of the intersection as a convenient rail access for nearby Salem, land speculators began purchasing and subdividing property around the crossing. In 1853, longtime property owner Solomon Kendall subdivided a portion of his 231-acre farm into lots. This subdivision laid out streets in central High Point south of the railroad, such as Fayetteville Street (now South Main Street) and Factory Street (Commerce Avenue). Early resident Wyatt Armfield remembered the crossroads as it appeared when he was a boy:

> *My first recollection of High Point was just as the first real estate project was on foot. The railroad had not yet been completed but it had crossed the old Salem-Fayetteville plank road at this point. There was a well where Wright's Clothing store now stands* [101 South Main Street] *and a pile of lumber near it; these were the only indications of a town.*[24]

The "pile of lumber" would soon be used to construct the first residence at the crossroads: the home of Seborn Perry. The Italianate-style building was converted into the Jarrell Hotel soon after its construction, with new wings in the same style extending along South Main Street and West High Street. The L-shaped structure hugged a prominent village corner, just across from Depot Square, and featured a two-story veranda that wrapped around both street sides of the property. Latticework as well as tapered posts supported the low-hipped veranda roof. The building was destroyed around 1940.

The next year, Francis Fries of Salem, who held a position as a director and promoter of the North Carolina Railroad, purchased land north of the planned railroad from Kendall and subdivided the land for lots.[25] Fries was an industrialist who sought to cultivate an investment in High Point as a shipping point for his enterprises in Salem. The plank road north of the railroad took the name Salem Street, and the roadway south of the tracks took the name Fayetteville Street. Appropriate to a commercial crossroads, some of the earliest structures built took the form of general stores and inns. William Welch constructed the first store on Salem Street just northeast of its intersection with the railroad in 1854. Two parcels south, another establishment known as Farabee's was the finest store in the village for numerous years, selling "about everything from wooden shoe-pegs to grindstones."[26] The two-story brick building featured a three-bay upper façade with decorative window hoods and simple sills, an elaborate cornice and a traditional storefront spanning the first floor. While documentation is unclear, this two-story brick structure is generally believed to be the building that stands today at 104 North Main Street, though it has been recently covered by a false façade.

The first train arrived in the crossroads on November 22, 1855. In recognition of the growing stature of the hamlet, a United States Post Office was established that year in Welch's store, and

Jarrell Hotel. *Courtesy of the High Point Museum, High Point, North Carolina.*

the village became a magnet for businesses, many of which were hotels that catered to passing stage and rail traffic. Jeremiah Piggott erected the first building constructed specifically as a hotel around 1855. The substantial three-story brick building overlooking the railroad became a village landmark, known as an important stopover for travelers on the railway and plank road. It survived as the oldest building associated with early High Point before being destroyed in 1988.

When David Clark arrived in High Point during the snowy winter of 1856, he recalled that there were no local facilities for supplying lumber or building materials for his residence. "All the lumber for my buildings was procured at the Worth-Virdon mills, four miles south of Asheboro, and conveyed by wagons to High Point…and dressed by hand."[27] His remembrance illustrates that lumber at that time was procured in the forests of the Uwharrie Mountains, made easily transportable by the newly laid plank road north to High Point.[28]

High Point's one-hundred-foot-wide main street was established in 1859 with encouragement from Dr. A.J. Sapp, who moved to the village that year and urged its town commissioners to think big. Village leaders were not convinced of the need for such a wide thoroughfare, believing that the town would never grow to a great size on account of its close proximity to Greensboro and Salem. Dr. Sapp believed otherwise, stating, "We have the whole world in which to lay out this street, and I move that we make the street wide." Leading citizens were satisfied with his argument, and surveyors followed suit.[29]

Nathan Hunt Jr. moved his Hunt Hotel, an establishment originally in the Bloomington (today Springfield) community, to a new building at the corner of Fayetteville (South Main) and Factory (Commerce) Streets in 1857 to take advantage of stage and rail traffic. The new Hunt Hotel was an exuberant exercise in the Italianate style of architecture, featuring a double veranda, tall double-hung windows, wide bracketed eaves and a cupola. The frame building displayed a polychromatic paint scheme, keeping with national trends enabled by the availability of premixed paint brands shipped by rail.

Education was an important component of High Point life before the Civil War. The community's first temporary schoolhouse was erected on the east side of town. Constructed of logs, the building contained rudimentary facilities, including rough benches made of slabs of lumber where reading, writing, spelling and arithmetic were practiced. A more elaborate facility was the High Point Female Academy (destroyed), which was erected by Reverend M.I. Langdon just northwest of the depot on its namesake College Street (later Hayden Place) in 1858.[30] The structure was one of the most impressive in the village, "situated upon one of the highest hills in town, near the R.R. depot; yet in a retired and beautifully shaded place." The interior of the school contained twenty-five rooms with fireplaces and a dining hall.[31] With three full floors constructed of brick and wrapped on two sides by ornate verandas, this grand structure accommodating 138 young women was representative of similar initiatives of the period documented in Greensboro, Thomasville and Jamestown.[32]

Churches were among other important institutions of the time. Though Quakers had been long established in southwestern Guilford County, their meetinghouses remained

Hunt Hotel. *Courtesy of the High Point Museum, High Point, North Carolina.*

The Village of High Point, 1852–1888

rural, including Springfield Friends Meeting to the south and Deep River Friends Meeting to the north of town. Their buildings were brick with simple details, as exemplified by the side-gabled Springfield Meeting House of 1858, with modest Greek Revival detailing.

As the village that would become High Point grew, churches were quick to establish a presence in the community. Architecturally, many of High Point's early congregations developed within the format of a three-step process. The first period of church development was the founding of churches. Worshippers often met outside beneath an arbor or used another congregation's church. The second period was characterized by a simple frame structure that was used for a generation. The third phase involved replacement of the earlier frame building with a substantial masonry edifice. Socially, many early churches embraced both black and white congregants throughout this process of growth.[33]

The Methodists organized the first church in the village in 1855. Exemplifying the earliest period of church development, the congregation met in an arbor on Washington Street (Washington Drive) as early as 1836 and enjoyed sermons by circuit preachers.[34] Second-period churches are exemplified by the Methodist-Episcopal Church South, officially chartered in 1858 and housed in a simple frame building. This congregation was followed in 1859 by the First Presbyterian Church, which occupied a small frame building on English Street, with Reverend P.H. Dalton serving as the first pastor. The First Baptist Church was founded in Jamestown in 1832 and relocated to High Point in 1859.

Historic cemeteries in the High Point area date to the earliest occupation of non-indigenous people. Quakers, among the first settlers in the region, traditionally buried their deceased near their respective meetinghouses, as opposed to private family cemeteries. Such communal Quaker cemeteries are located both at Deep River Friends and Springfield Friends. The Deep River cemetery also admitted non-Quaker citizens of Jamestown after the Civil War.[35] Both cemeteries have areas of unmarked gravesites, representative of the early Friends' ideal of simplicity.

Following the death of Margaret Denny on January 16, 1859, just a few months before High Point was chartered, a committee gathered to identify a suitable municipal burying ground and selected a knoll north of town for that purpose.[36] Laid out in grid form, Oakwood Cemetery was important during the Civil War when the Barbee House (previously Piggott's Hotel) became a temporary military hospital.[37] In 1899, the Junior Order of Mechanics erected a Confederate Monument in Oakwood to commemorate local involvement in the Civil War. Victorian-era monuments are characteristically elaborate, featuring sculpture, obelisks and standing stones. By the turn of the twentieth century, increasingly monumental graves were being erected, including several stone mausoleums. The landscape of Oakwood Cemetery is equally rich, with feature plantings and trees situated with care among the numerous stone markers and monuments.

By the time High Point was chartered on May 26, 1859, the growing village boasted three doctors, one lawyer, two churches, two hotels, a steam sawmill, seven dry goods stores, a log schoolhouse and a female academy, with residential structures

1875 Deep River Friends Meeting. *Courtesy of the High Point Museum, High Point, North Carolina,* High Point Enterprise *Collection.*

erected along the railroad tracks as well as the plank road.[38] The village possessed seventy-five families, and its economic engine was its role as a depot for shipped goods from Salem as well as a processing center for dried blackberries, apples and peaches grown in surrounding locales.[39] The depot served towns along the plank road such as Salem, Bethania and Danbury in the north and Asheboro, Randleman and Cedar Falls in the south.[40]

Civil War and Recovery

Momentum and growth in High Point came to an abrupt halt with the Civil War in 1861. Resident David L. Clark remembered the period darkly:

> *Our fondest hopes blasted. Life energy paralyzed. Business suspended. The whole country in a state of tumult and uproar. Our bravest and best men, armed for the conflict, were rushing to the front. Battle after battle was being fought and the fearful tidings of some loved one who had fallen was flashed back upon the wires. There was weeping in our homes.*[41]

High Point residents did not unanimously embrace the idea of secession from the United States. Several leading citizens were Quakers who sympathized with the Union and actively sought to remain part of it. When North Carolina finally left the Union in May 1861, Camp Fisher was quickly established east of the village as a training ground for Confederate recruits.[42] As the war continued for months and then years, provisions grew thin and finances became increasingly scarce.

High Point enjoyed relative peace for most of the conflict, but the closing days of the war brought increased activity. Local hotels were filled with soldiers injured at the Battle of Bentonville, 120 miles to the southeast, who were delivered by train out of harm's way. Thousands were nursed back to health, although fifty casualties were buried in and around the village before being reinterred at Oakwood Cemetery some time later.[43] Union Colonel George W. Kirk led a band of raiders

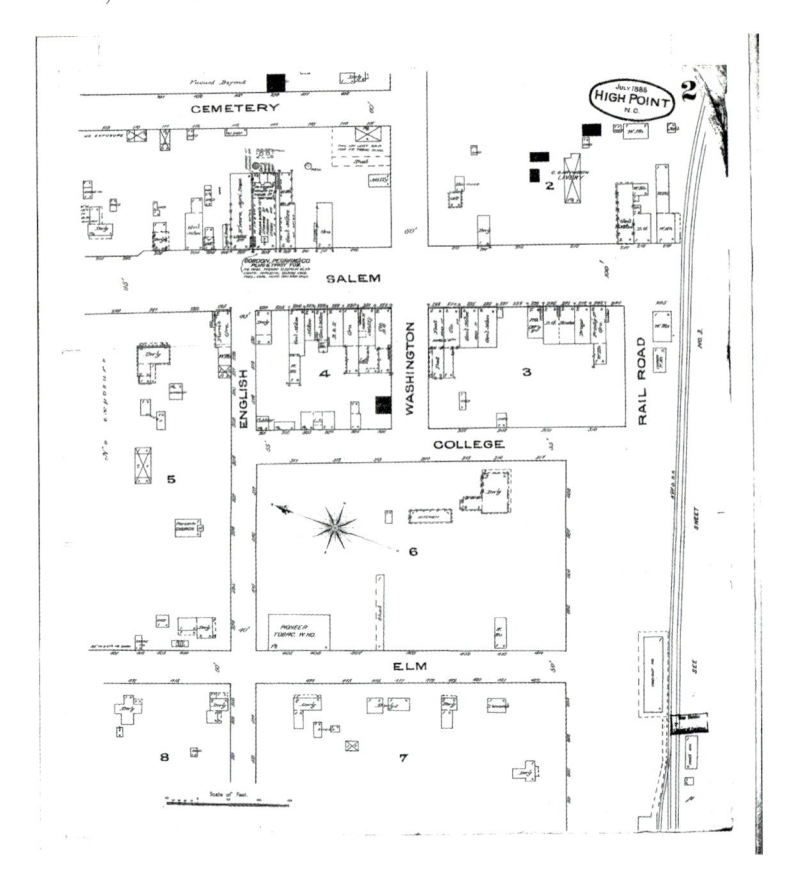

Sanborn Insurance Map, North Side High Point. *Copyright 1885 Sanborn Map Company, The Sanborn Library, LLC. All Rights Reserved. Further reproductions prohibited without written permission from The Sanborn Library, LLC.*

through the Piedmont destroying the railroad tracks, and in High Point burning the original frame depot, a freight car and the Fries Warehouse, which was filled with cotton.[44] Days later, Confederate President Jefferson Davis passed through High Point by horse, perhaps pausing at the Barbee House (formerly Piggott's Hotel) before continuing south.

After the war, the economy of the region was in shambles, and families had been separated by death and relocation. The burned shell of the depot stood as a solemn reminder of the war for years to follow. Although aid was brought to the region

The Village of High Point, 1852–1888

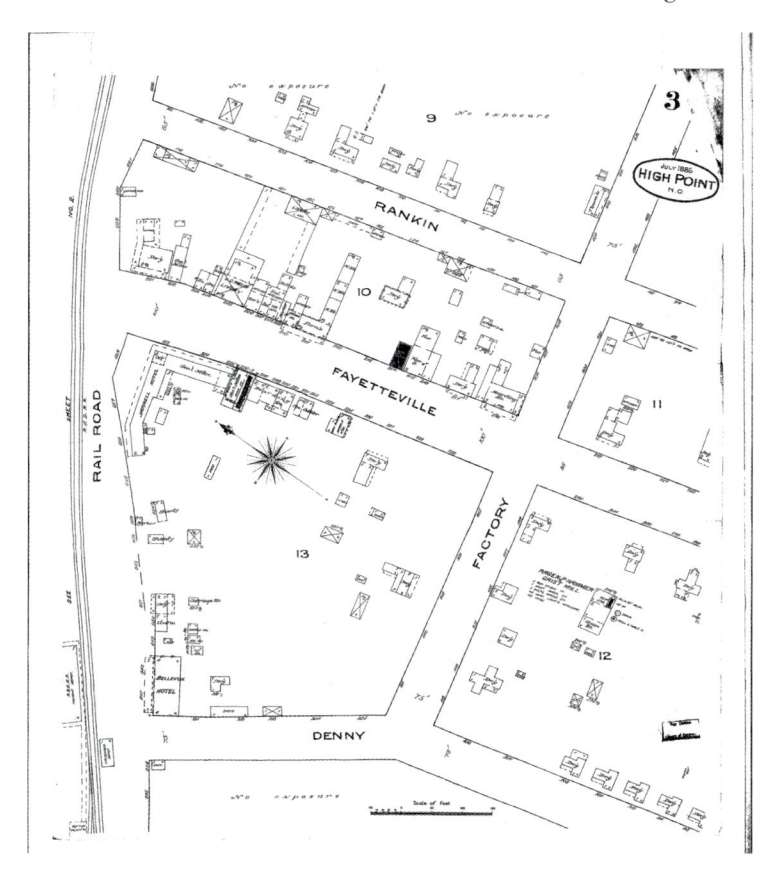

Sanborn Insurance Map, South Side. *Copyright 1885 Sanborn Map Company, The Sanborn Library, LLC. All Rights Reserved. Further reproductions prohibited without written permission from The Sanborn Library, LLC.*

through the efforts of Quakers both during and after the war, High Point's once energetic business climate cooled. With the reopening of the railroad within weeks of the surrender of the Confederacy in 1865, High Point resumed its position as a major shipping point for the central portion of the state, though it took years for freight volumes to resume prewar levels.[45] Commercial activity increased gradually throughout the remainder of the 1860s, to include sixteen merchants and two hotels by 1869. James Odell moved his general merchandise store to High Point from Randolph County in 1868, adding a wholesale department to his retail, but in 1874 he relocated to Greensboro, where his firm later became Odell Hardware Company.[46] Harrison Alexander opened a general merchandise store on North Main Street in 1870. Alexander's grew to become one of the finest stores in High Point.

A positive outcome of the Civil War was the introduction of Union Lieutenant W.H. Snow to the economic potential of the Piedmont. A native of Vermont, Snow became aware of the local timber resources during his military service in North Carolina.[47] He moved to Greensboro in 1867 to manufacture persimmon shuttle blocks for the textile industry, but soon relocated to High Point. Shuttle blocks had been made of apple wood prior to Snow's discovery that both persimmon and dogwood were suitable for use and were prolific in the Piedmont. His discovery opened a new market for lumber around High Point, and with the opening of a factory in the village in 1872, "Capt" Snow soon headed an industrial empire that manufactured spokes, axe handles and bobbins as well as shuttle blocks.[48] His industrial prowess continued with his co-establishment of High Point's first textile-related enterprise with O.S. Causey, the Willowbrook Cotton Mill in 1879.[49]

Although High Point's population had increased to only 991 by 1880, key industrialists were moving to the village to take advantage of transportation facilities and raw materials. A.A. Barker organized a plant to manufacture sash, doors, blinds and general millwork in 1880. J. Elwood Cox moved to the town in 1883 after purchasing Snow's spoke and handle factory, which was supplying 90 percent of the world's shuttle blocks. H.R. Welborn established his four-story tobacco factory on a site on North Main Street in 1884.

The Welborn factory was among the best-constructed buildings in High Point and stood as one of only two brick buildings north of the railroad for many years. Rising four stories above Salem Street, the building featured an elaborate façade, four window bays wide with decorative "jack-arch" lintels, flat pilasters and a heavy modillion cornice. Insurance records from the period document that numerous activities took place in the building, including "stems" on the fourth floor, "picking" on the third, "storage" on the second and "rolling and pack'g" on the first.[50] The Welborn factory remains standing at 212 North Main Street, serving as a mixed-use commercial and residential building.

Only one brick building, Farabee's Store, had been erected in High Point's business district by the Civil War, but by the 1880s, numerous brick commercial structures were being built along Main Street.[51] Among the street's most substantial buildings of the period, the two-story brick Dalton Building was constructed in 1881, the Best Building followed in 1884 and the Tate Building in 1887. African American entrepreneur Albert Miller operated a successful brickyard in the southeastern sector of the city from 1874 to 1877 and supplied materials for numerous residences and businesses, including the Harris Building of 1900 on North Main Street. John and Bill Robinson were prominent black brick masons credited with erecting most of the masonry buildings in the village from the close of the war to 1900. African American businessman Willis Hinton operated a café on South Main Street until he opened the Hinton Hotel in 1888 in the 600 block of East Washington Street, just east of an upper-income white neighborhood.

As the town's population increased, services and amenities followed. In July 1889, the High Point, Randleman, Asheboro and Southern Railroad was completed to Asheboro. Numerous enterprises were established along North and South Main Streets, including the Matton Drug Co. (1884), Beeson Brothers (1885) and the National Bank of High Point (1886). Other establishments, such as the Lyceum social club and the hometown newspaper *High Point Enterprise* (1885), began to promote the civic and social life of the community.

Schools and Churches

With an expanding population and increasingly strong economy, High Point developed greater needs in the areas of education and training. Major William Bingham Lynch was an early educator who founded Lynch's Select School for Boys in 1879 in a cruciform schoolhouse overlooking the railroad tracks west of town. The building remains standing at 106 Oak Street. The school quickly gained a strong reputation that attracted students from as far away as Virginia and South Carolina.[52] The school building's residential appearance, provided by sawn decorative window and door surrounds, double-hung windows and clapboard siding, represented the finest education money could afford in High Point at the end of Reconstruction.

At the other end of the financial spectrum, a "Free School" was established by the town in 1882 to provide educational opportunities for white children using public subsidies. Located at the corner of West Green and Centennial Streets, the school was run by William Allen Blair, a graduate of Haverford College and Harvard University.[53] The Oak Hill School near the corner of Burton and English Streets represents public educational facilities in High Point during the last quarter of the nineteenth century. It was constructed in 1879 by local residents to serve a county school district that extended from the Davidson County line into the working neighborhood of West End in westernmost High Point. The simple one-room frame building contained a platform opposite the front door that held the teacher's desk and

Oak Hill School. *Courtesy of the High Point Museum, High Point, North Carolina.*

chair. A blackboard extended across the entire wall behind the desk, and in front of the desk was a long bench from which the students recited their lessons. Each wooden desk was locally crafted and seated two pupils. Utilitarian in design and still standing, Oak Hill School is representative of primary public educational facilities in the late nineteenth century.

In March 1889, Dr. J.N. Stallings moved his Female College from Thomasville to the three-story frame structure on College Street that housed the High Point Female Academy before the Civil War.[54] The building was described as a "large brick edifice containing twenty-five well arranged rooms in good order, each with a fireplace."[55] Stallings, formerly a pastor at Abbott's Creek Baptist Church, administered the school until it closed in 1893. At that time it was sold for use as a private residence before being razed around 1900.[56]

In the years after the Civil War, additional congregations formed, including St. Mary's Episcopal Church in 1882. The congregation occupied a brick Gothic Revival–style sanctuary on College Place (Hayden Place), complete with pointed arches, pinnacles above the eaves of the high gable roof and a rosette window above the main entry. The building was destroyed after the congregation moved to a new site in 1928. By contrast, the Society of Friends erected a simple brick structure when they established a central High Point meeting in 1883.[57] Their brick meetinghouse, which inspired the name for nearby Church Street, stood two stories high and featured a broad front porch, hipped roofline and central gable.

Residential Architecture

Guilford County's black citizens constituted 22 percent of the population in 1860.[58] Many emancipated blacks came to High Point after the Civil War. They worked mostly in services and manufacturing, but some were artisans and professionals, and they settled along East Commerce Street, South Wrenn Street and South Main Street.[59] Documentary evidence from Sanborn Insurance Company maps illustrates that most residences of black citizens were frame and often one story in height. A small number of shotgun houses were constructed in the first two decades of the twentieth century, primarily north and south of Leonard Street, but none remain.[60] Occasionally blacks built brick houses for themselves. For example, Sallie and Bill Sawyer lived in a two-story house constructed of brick at the southeast corner of Wrenn and Commerce Streets.[61]

Residential development during this period was broadly scattered throughout the village. Moderate-income white residents lived in houses erected on quiet side streets, including West Green and South Wrenn Streets. Upper-income white residents chose prominent locations along major thoroughfares, including North and South Main Streets, East Washington Street, South Hamilton Street and West High Street. Most of these houses, whether modest or elaborate, were of frame construction and continued established building forms such as the I-house, sometimes embellished with popular Queen Anne detail.[62]

Residences in High Point frequently followed patterns that were well established throughout North Carolina. Probably the

Early housing in eastern High Point. *Courtesy of the High Point Museum, High Point, North Carolina.*

most popular nineteenth-century form was one room deep and one or two stories high, with a center hall plan. Many of these houses have a rear wing, or "ell," that usually contains a kitchen at the rear. Early examples are often frame constructions, sheathed with clapboards and topped by a gable or hipped roof. In some cases, a small pediment or gable centered over the front door augments a gable-end roof, lending the term "triple-A" to describe the one- and two-story, one-room-deep houses. This type was popular throughout the state in countryside and town alike during the late nineteenth and early twentieth centuries.

Perhaps the most notable triple-A house in High Point is the dwelling for the Model Farm, located west of Brentwood Avenue south of the village. In 1868, the Baltimore Association constructed a demonstration farm to educate North Carolina farmers about modern agricultural practices. Northern Quakers built the farm in a manner that was unusual and progressive in central North Carolina for its great assortment of agricultural buildings as well as the form and style of the main house, which resembled farmhouses typical of northeastern Maryland in its bold proportions. The frame house features the side gables and central forward-facing gable of the triple-A, and a full-width porch supported by attenuated posts across the five-bay façade. The farmhouse was a model for architectural as well as agricultural practices, and several houses in the High Point area reflect its design.

Another variation in single-pile houses presents a forward-facing gable located to the left or right of center. These gables top a forward projection, which creates an L-shaped plan. Nearly all of these houses sport a front porch, a simple and centered front door and double-hung windows. Across the city, many of these houses remain but have been altered with replacement siding, porch posts and windows.

Model Farm House. *Courtesy of the North Carolina Friends Historical Collection, Guilford College, Greensboro, North Carolina.*

THE RISE OF INDUSTRY, 1889–1905

With the incorporation of the High Point Furniture Company in 1889, a popular new industry arrived in the town. The manufacturer of affordable and medium-grade home furnishings led a parade of announcements from other furniture companies throughout the 1890s, including High Point Chair and Home Furniture (1890); Tate Furniture and Eagle Furniture (1893); Globe Furniture, Southern Chair and Alma Furniture (1896); and Myrtle Furniture and Union Furniture (1899). These announcements demonstrate the feverish pitch at which furniture manufacturers were taking advantage of abundant regional timber resources and local artisans' talents. By the turn of the twentieth century, High Point contained thirty-three factories and was poised to secure its place as the "Furniture Capital of the South."

Industrial and Commercial Development

High Point's industrial buildings constructed before the turn of the century were often of post-and-beam frame, resembling oversized barns. The furniture industry began to make the transition to factories with load-bearing brick walls around the turn of the century. Natural lighting and ventilation were critical for production, and most early industrial buildings included large windows and even skylights for these purposes. Frame buildings were sometimes economically covered in corrugated metal siding and referred to as tin buildings. The general trend in town was the progression from commonplace utilitarian structures with little embellishment to substantial buildings with a uniting theme of materials and some decoration. A good example of a frame industrial building in High Point is difficult to find today, due to vulnerability to fire. One such building remains at 507 West High Street, constructed around 1900 to house O. Arthur Kirkman's mattress company. The long, three-story, timber-frame building stands with its gable end to the Southern Railway tracks. Though the structure is now wrapped in metal siding, the original pine sheathing remains intact underneath.[63]

The Architecture of High Point, North Carolina

Factory of Eagle Furniture Company.

Eagle Furniture Company. *Courtesy of the High Point Museum, High Point, North Carolina.*

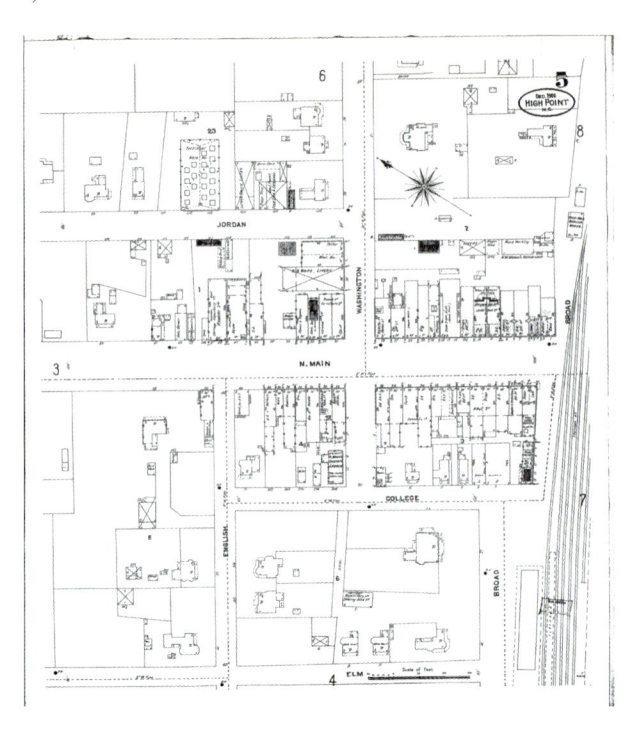

Sanborn Insurance Map, North Side. *Copyright 1906 Sanborn Map Company, The Sanborn Library, LLC. All Rights Reserved. Further reproductions prohibited without written permission from The Sanborn Library, LLC.*

Sanborn Insurance Map, North Side. *Copyright 1906 Sanborn Map Company, The Sanborn Library, LLC. All Rights Reserved. Further reproductions prohibited without written permission from The Sanborn Library, LLC.*

Eagle Furniture Company. *Courtesy of the High Point Museum, High Point, North Carolina.*

The Rise of Industry, 1889–1905

Though industrial buildings made a slow transition from frame to brick construction, commercial space along Main Street was erected entirely of masonry and articulated in nationally popular styles after 1900. Among the earliest office buildings in High Point was the Stanton-Welch Building at 114 North Main Street. Dr. D.A. Stanton and J.J. Welch constructed this Neoclassical Revival–style building around 1901. The three-story building housed the local branch of the U.S. Post Office, furniture agencies and the town opera house. The Chautauqua Club and the Junior Order of American Mechanics both occupied rooms on the third floor. The trend toward grand buildings continued with the ambitious announcement by J. Elwood Cox of a large Neoclassical Revival–style hotel at the corner of South Main and High Streets. The Elwood Hotel was built in phases beginning in 1902, but its impressive façade of three stories at the visual terminus of North Main Street declared High Point's graduation from a village to a town. A second small commercial area of primarily black-owned businesses and churches became the nucleus of High Point's growing and increasingly segregated African American population from the 500 block of East Washington Street eastward.

Residential Architecture

With expansion of the furniture industry, High Point's population had grown to 4,163 by 1900, and the town had spread beyond its initial boundaries. Increased population resulted in new houses erected to the east along Washington Drive and Green Street, to the west along the railroad and English Drive and to the north and south along Main Street. Commercial development was focused around the blocks of Main Street adjacent to the railroad. Industrial development was scattered throughout town, with a higher concentration found south of the railroad.[64]

Workers' housing before 1900 was confined to the region of town south of the railroad tracks. Several tracts were subdivided along East Green Street and South Hamilton Street for single-story frame houses with simple detail. Typically these streets remained unpaved and unguttered. The town also contained several boardinghouses for low-income wage earners. Others resided in spare rooms made available throughout the town on a temporary basis. Two African American neighborhoods grew during this period—the primary focus continuing beyond the 500 block of East Washington Street, the other along Fairview Street, referred to as Southside. Both of these neighborhoods were composed primarily of modest frame houses.

Middle-income housing in High Point from the late nineteenth and early twentieth centuries continued to identify with traditional building forms such as the I-house and one-story triple-A, frequently updated with features of nationally popular styles. Usually executed in frame construction, these houses often combined local vernacular traditions with Queen Anne influences to create an eclectic Victorian style. Although early Victorian styles such as Gothic Revival, Italianate and Second Empire never made much of an impact on local architecture, combinations of elements of late Victorian themes, such as the Queen Anne and the Colonial Revival styles, graced some of High Point's more fashionable houses.

Single-pile houses are located throughout High Point, primarily in subdivisions that were opened before the 1920s, the last decade in which these house types were built in the town. Several examples are located along White Oak and South Elm Streets, as well as in the Cloverdale mill village and Mechanicsville neighborhood. A good representative of the type stands at 1106 Johnson Street. The wood frame Alice N. White House, built circa 1912, is two stories tall with a side-gable roof and a gabled forward wing, giving it an L shape.[65] Another good example stands at 1006 Holton Place in Roland Park. This circa 1910 two-story frame house sits atop a hill looking west and is surrounded by mature oaks. The three-bay façade contains a hipped-roof porch supported by attenuated columns. Decoration is simple, with no sidelights or transom. A hipped roof tops the structure, with chimneys and a one-story ell located to the rear.

Upper-income residents most often chose to reside close to their factories and businesses, building houses along Main

Steele House. *Courtesy of the Briggs Collection.*

Pickett House. *Courtesy of the Briggs Collection.*

Street, the railroad, Washington Drive and English Road. A few large estates existed, notably those of E.D. Steele on East Washington Drive and Dr. D.B. Carrick along North Main Street. These estates encompassed a few acres within the street grid and often contained an assortment of outbuildings, barns and even windmills and water towers. The O. Arthur Kirkman estate at 501 West High Street is the sole remaining example of this chapter in High Point's history.

While examples of Italianate and Romanesque Revival residential architecture were rare and fleeting, the Queen Anne style gained popularity in High Point through "high end" residences constructed when the town was maturing into a manufacturing center. Industrialists built several sprawling frame houses along North and South Main Streets, as well as Washington Drive and English Road. Most of these houses shared the common design characteristics of broad front porches, prominent towers, multiple gables and a dizzying assortment of applied decorative trim that was vaguely reminiscent of British medieval architecture thought to have been popular during the reign of Queen Anne.[66] Contractor Ernest Ansel Snow, who was educated at Cornell University in New York, reportedly designed and built many of High Point's early Queen Anne–style residences that featured towers and elaborate sawn trim in the late 1870s and early 1880s, but no extant houses have been identified as his work.[67] During the 1880s and 1890s, part-time farmer and contractor Isaac Payne of Deep River is said to have built some of the Queen Anne–style residences on West High Street, as well as the Armfield House known as Sapona Side (destroyed) in Deep River, but specific records have not yet been located.[68]

One of High Point's best examples of Queen Anne design is found in the Brown House, constructed for Annettie McBain Brown in 1897.[69] This two-story frame house features a prominent tower capped by a pyramidal roof and cross gables bearing sawn ornament. Clapboard sheathing, complemented by a shingled entablature, graces the walls of the house. A wraparound porch supported by turned posts with exuberant sawn detail and topped by a wooden railing embellishes the façade. Other features, such as multi-colored windows, bay windows and corbelled chimneys, contribute to the elaborate design of the house. The house originally overlooked the Southern Railroad tracks at 401 West High Street and was relocated to its current site nearby at 110 Oak Street in 2004.

The popularity of ornate Victorian houses was fading when Frenchman Ferdinand Ecker constructed his eye-catching frame house at 901 Johnson Street in 1908.[70] It stands two and a half stories tall and is sheathed in clapboards on the first floor and shingles on the second. Numerous dormer windows enliven the cross-gabled roofline; cast-iron cresting crowns the house, matching the wrought-iron railing that tops the broad wraparound porch. The porch is supported by paired Tuscan columns combined with a modillion cornice to insert classical detail into an otherwise Queen Anne façade. The Ecker House demonstrates the waning of Queen Anne excess and the increasing popularity of Colonial Revival features.

As the nineteenth century drew to a close, many of High Point's most prominent citizens returned to the simpler lines of the historic Georgian and Federal styles for architectural inspiration.[71] Popularized by the Centennial Exposition of 1876, Colonial Revival designs were widely embraced in central North Carolina by the turn of the twentieth century. The Colonial Revival brought back to High Point the clean lines, boxy forms and uncomplicated rooflines that the region enjoyed less than fifty years earlier, and in this sense the style was less a revival and more a continuation of traditional building styles and designs that had never completely disappeared.

Elwood Cox House. *Courtesy of the High Point Museum, High Point, North Carolina.*

Perhaps the first Colonial Revival residence erected in High Point was that of civic leader J. Elwood Cox, a one-time gubernatorial candidate and industrialist who built his substantial frame house sometime around 1890. Located on East Green Street, the two-story frame Cox House featured Colonial Revival details that were new to High Point, including Palladian windows, a prominent dormer window and paired columns set upon stone pedestals. The house was demolished around 1955.

In 1900, merchant Tom Kirkman had a house built in the Colonial Revival mode that remains standing at 415 West High Street.[72] The boxy, double-pile frame house sheathed in clapboards features a symmetrical three-bay façade with a full-width front porch. The relatively austere hipped-roof house with a centered front gable is in marked contrast to the irregular form and intricate detail of the Brown House, which was built only three years earlier a few doors down the street.

The Quaker Woods subdivision, platted between 1895 and 1903 at the western end of Church Street, contained several

Ecker House. *Courtesy of the Briggs Collection.*

Lindsay Street, Quaker Woods. *Courtesy of the Briggs Collection.*

good examples of Colonial Revival architecture along Lindsay, as well as Thurston and Howell Streets (today Gatewood and Westwood Avenues, respectively). The Durland House of circa 1905 at the corner of Lindsay and Ferndale (destroyed in 1991), the Harmon House of circa 1905 at 401 North Lindsay and the Siceloff House of circa 1910 at 205 West Parkway (destroyed in 2005) all featured boxy forms and cross-gabled rooflines common to Colonial Revival houses built before 1910. Other common elements were dormer windows, boxed eaves, wide porches and one-over-one windows.

Quaker Woods was the first middle-income subdivision in town, and extended the street grid northwestward, culminating at a semicircular park called the Boulevard.[73] Developed by Homer Wheeler around 1895, the subdivision stood on the former grounds of the North Carolina Friends Yearly Meeting House. Its granite-curbed streets and concrete sidewalks attracted middle- and upper-income families who built large houses in High Point's first exclusively residential district.[74] White Oak subdivision—which included Walnut, White Oak and Cable Streets east of downtown in 1905—also catered to middle-income families who built large residences. Platted by Peoples Realty Company, this neighborhood contained simple Colonial Revival, late Queen Anne and Craftsman styles that were occupied by the city's rising skilled mechanical, clerical and managerial workers.[75] Residences in both neighborhoods took advantage of mass-produced and affordable building materials such as windows, doors, moldings and mantels that were made available through catalogues or local suppliers like Snow Lumber Company.

Schools

Increasingly, in the years leading up to the segregationist Jim Crow era of 1897, laws prohibited the education of blacks and whites together. This resulted in the establishment of several exclusively African American schools. One such school was opened for African American children by Solomon Blair near the present-day intersection of North Centennial Street and Kivett Drive. The two-room schoolhouse was built in 1867 using some funds from President Abraham Lincoln Freedmen's Bureau, and remained in use as a school and part-time church until 1900.[76] The New York Yearly Meeting of the Society of Friends, a network of Quakers from that state, started a school for black children in Asheboro in the 1880s. The school relocated to the Blair schoolhouse in High Point in 1891, and in 1893 moved to a large new structure on land east of town near the newly developed "black" downtown along Washington Street.[77] The institution was named the High Point Normal and Industrial School (later William Penn High School) and was administered by Quaker F.H. Clark until 1897.[78] In that year, black educator Alfred J. Griffin accepted the position of principal and led the school into a long period of growth.[79]

The High Point public graded school was established in 1897 with the approval of a $10,000 bond, in part to finance the purchase of J. Elwood Cox's newly erected house on South Main Street for use as the first graded public school building. Twelve school commissioners were appointed to administer the 350-student system of five grades. Cox had just built the impressive Richardsonian Romanesque residence at the corner of South Main Street and East Green Drive for his family to replace their circa 1890 house just a block east on East Green

High Point Public Graded School. *Courtesy of the High Point Museum, High Point, North Carolina.*

Street. The Romanesque style had been revived by Boston architect Henry Hobson Richardson, who thought the massive medieval architecture incorporating rounded arches, masonry walls and hipped roofs was appropriate for grand residences and civic structures. The Cox residence incorporated all of these characteristics in what would have been the grandest residence in town. However, shortly before the building was completed, the family determined the house did not meet their needs, and Cox made arrangements to sell the structure at a reduced price to the newly formed school board. Not only was High Point's earliest official school residential in appearance; stylistically it was a great departure from the wooden structures that had served as schools in the preceding decades. The school was demolished around 1930.

Religious Buildings

Increasing affluence allowed many of High Point's previously established congregations to expand within the format of the three-stage process described earlier. The final phase involved replacement of earlier frame buildings with masonry edifices of Gothic Revival form that became landmarks within the community. This period of church development in High Point commenced during the last years of the nineteenth century, when many congregations made plans to relocate to prominent sites on Main Street as their original frame mid-century structures aged. Most of their new buildings exhibited the nationally popular Romanesque Revival or Gothic Revival styles. Erected in 1896, the Methodist church on East Washington Street exemplified the period's Gothic taste for ecclesiastical architecture.[80] The sanctuary was housed beneath a cruciform roofline with a prominent forward-facing gable flanked by two towers, the higher of which rose above the tree line to stand visible across the town. The brick building was embellished with tall, Gothic arched windows, but the most elaborate exterior brickwork detail was lavished on the towers. The church was demolished around 1920.

Another third-period church was the First Presbyterian Church, which moved from the small white chapel erected on English Street before the Civil War to a larger Romanesque-style building on South Main Street at East Green Street. Erected in 1896 according to designs by architect C.C. Hook of Charlotte, the handsome brick structure was irregularly massed, with a side-gabled roofline, round-arched windows with stained glass and a tower with an open belfry.[81] The church was demolished around 1930 after the congregation moved to a new building on North Main Street.

Most High Point congregations of the period were divided by ethnicity, and separate sanctuaries for blacks were erected in the Washington Street and Southside neighborhoods. African American exclusive churches were founded and established as the town's black population increased, including First Baptist Church in 1871, St. Mark's Methodist Episcopal Church in 1876 and St. Stephen Metropolitan Church in 1900. These modest sanctuaries were located within established mixed-use African American neighborhoods.

At the turn of the twentieth century, High Point was not yet a half-century old, but it had gained population, industry and civic institutions large enough to rival much older towns in the

First Presbyterian Church. *Courtesy of the Briggs Collection.*

state. In many ways still a large town rather than a city, High Point was attracting attention because of its reputation as a manufacturing center. A representative of the *Charlotte Chronicle* cemented this standing by proclaiming in 1887 that "High Point is the most important manufacturing town on the North Carolina Railroad."[82]

Civic booster J.J. Farriss remarked in 1900,

> *High Point has, perhaps made the most remarkable record in business of any of the smaller cities in the South. Within a comparatively short time it has built up a large manufacturing business which has challenged the admiration of larger markets in all sections of the country. Beginning in a small way, and without the aid of outside capital, it stands forth today the recognized market for furniture and other goods in the South.*[83]

By 1900, High Point had grown to the extent that it was recognized for the first time as having urban status in the U.S. Census reports.[84] North Carolina's furniture industry had found a home in High Point, and the growth of the industry was rapid in the last decade of the nineteenth century. In addition to furnishings, the town was soon to add a second industry to its roster: textiles.[85] Growth in the textile industry would elevate the economic importance of High Point and bring unprecedented wealth and civic growth to the city.

HOSIERY MANUFACTURING AND HIGH POINT'S GROWTH AS A CITY, 1905–1930

The early twentieth century was an exciting time for High Point. Across the town, transportation improved, skyscrapers rose above the central business district, education and living standards improved and population expansion was measured at triple-digit rates.[86] The city earned a reputation as one of the most energetic in the state and was distinguished as an industrial hub. Josephus Daniels, editor of the *Raleigh News and Observer* and former secretary of the navy, wrote about High Point after visiting the city in the 1920s: "Greensboro is a fine county seat and a prosperous city. Winston-Salem boasts tobacco and other factories, but High Point has the basis for building what is destined to be—the largest and most prosperous city in Piedmont North Carolina."[87]

Grand plans for growth were reflected in grand architectural initiatives in the form of new neighborhoods, more churches and schools, a college and a country club. Citizens were quick to keep up with other cities in the region by rubbing elbows with nationally prominent architects and designers such as Earl Sumner Draper, Richard Hobart Upjohn and W.L. Stoddard, complemented by well-trained local designers such as Harry Barton, Charles Hartmann, Northup and O'Brien and Louis Voorhees. High Point's increasing wealth during the early twentieth century is evident in the remarkable collection of Craftsman, Eclectic Revival and Art Deco buildings that chronicle the high expectations of style in the city during that period.

In the early years of the twentieth century, the greatest advantage High Point held over the neighboring communities of Trinity, Archdale and Asheboro was its position on the North Carolina Railroad. In 1894, New York financier J.P. Morgan took over the route and made it part of the Southern Railway system, which connected to a vast network of rail lines across the country.[88] The rail line passing through High Point became a crucial link that connected the Northeastern metropolitan areas of New York, Philadelphia and Washington with Atlanta, New Orleans and other points south. Rail freight service was fundamental to High Point's rapid growth.

Coupled with this superior distribution network was a pool of capital held by successful furniture industry executives who sought additional investments yielding high returns. These entrepreneurial investors tapped into the textile industry, which was growing throughout the South, by taking advantage of existing distribution networks, cheap labor and increasing product demand. With a particular focus on hosiery, the city enjoyed rapid growth in textile manufacturing, and soon its mills exhausted the local labor pool. As mill owners sought to attract new workers to the region, the complexion of High Point became more economically, ethnically and religiously diverse with, for the first time, the development of an extensive class structure.

NEW RAILROAD DEPOTS

No building represents the transformation of High Point from a town to a city more than the Southern Railway Passenger Depot. In 1906, Southern Railway began construction of a new brick passenger depot just south of the railroad on Main Street.[89] The one-story edifice was designed in the Romanesque Revival style, featuring a rusticated ashlar base, round-arched windows and broad overhanging eaves supported by curved braces. The massive hipped roof was shingled with burnt orange–colored French tiles, which contributed an air of solidity and weight to the train station. The depot remained a reference point in the city: the corner of Main and High Streets, known as Depot Square, became a popular meeting spot for the first half of the twentieth century.

Other structures closely related to the railroad were freight depots: one on Broad Street, the second between Depot and Mangum Streets east of downtown. The Broad Street freight depot was a single-story masonry building erected in 1903 with a wide roofline and multiple loading bays. It was converted to a Railway Express Agency in 1925 when Southern Railway opened a larger two-story frame structure between Depot and Mangum Streets in response to rapidly increasing freight shipments from High Point.[90] The second depot had a rectilinear appearance, with two stories covered by a low hipped roof and a central-hipped dormer window. To the rear of the structure, a low shed covered loading areas. This depot shares some details with the Southern Railway Passenger Depot, such as low hipped roofs and wide overhanging eaves supported by brackets.

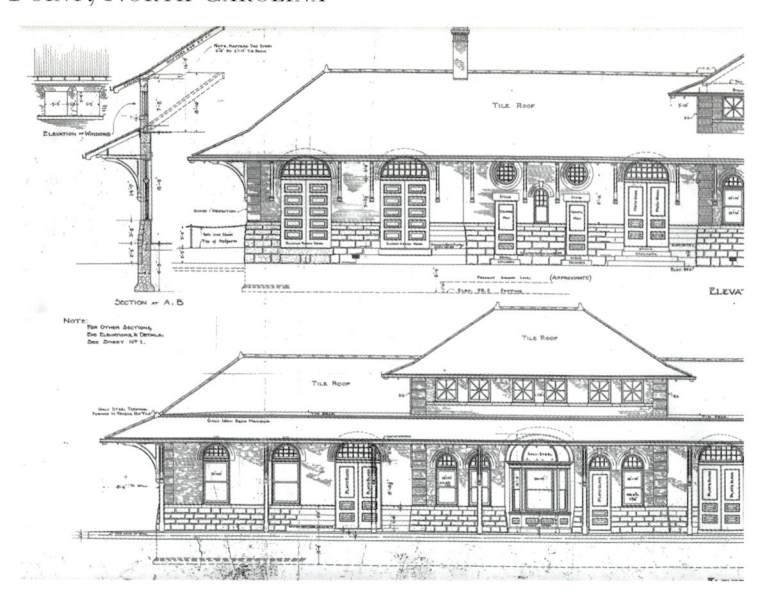

Southern Railway Passenger Station construction drawing. Courtesy of the Briggs Collection.

INDUSTRY AND MANUFACTURING

High Point's furniture industry was enjoying healthy growth and development in 1900. In contrast, there were few textile manufacturers, despite the fact that textiles were a large segment of manufacturing in the South as a whole. During the next two decades, however, fundamental economic changes would tip the city's balance of industry from furniture to textiles. By the middle of the century, hosiery replaced furniture as the largest employer in the city. This important change in the city's economy was the result of several events, notably the Great Depression and its related "run on the banks."

Hosiery Manufacturing and High Point's Growth as a City, 1905–1930

The Furniture Industry

Numerous furniture manufacturers set up shop in High Point in the 1890s and in the first decade of the twentieth century. Tomlinson Chair Manufacturing Company, Lindsay Chair Company, Kearns Furniture and High Point Metallic Bed Company were all founded in 1900. Large companies established in the first decade of the 1900s included Smith Furniture, Welch Furniture and Continental Furniture Company (1901); Dalton Furniture Company (1905); and Marsh Furniture Company (1906). In 1900, the city contained thirty-three furniture companies, but by 1917 civic boosters claimed forty-eight furniture manufacturers and promoted High Point as the furniture center of the world.[91]

The Tomlinson Chair Manufacturing Company complex is representative of furniture plant design, depicting the period that began at the turn of the century as the industry matured away from use of "tin buildings" and toward development of substantial brick plants. Located in the 300 block of West High Street, the first unit of the complex was announced in August 1900. The company purchased several acres of land that had been the Bowman-Field farm and erected a commodious brick industrial building just south of the Southern Railway tracks.[92]

The building's design is simple, rising three stories with large windows to provide natural light to work areas, high ceilings for machinery and an open floor plan with few partitions to allow for a free-flowing work space. In order to meet fireproofing standards, brick was used for the building's walls, but where wood framing was necessary, the "slow-burn" construction method using thick timbers was required by insurance companies. Aside from some decorative corbelling, the design was simple and utilitarian, displaying concern more with function than image. As business for the company grew, additions were made. Expansions to the original building in 1906, 1911 and 1924 created a sprawling campus that dominates the western fringe of downtown. A tall smokestack inscribed with the name TOMLINSON flagged the complex, along with the company's private water tower. The new buildings followed the basic design of earlier phases with slight modifications. By and large, the complex is united under one theme of design: large window openings and red brick.

Tomlinson Chair Manufacturing Company. *Courtesy of the Briggs Collection.*

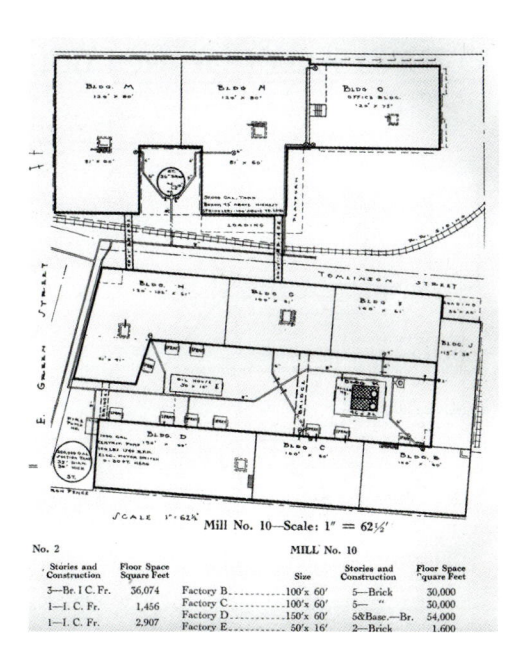

Plans of Tomlinson Chair Manufacturing Company. *Courtesy of the Briggs Collection.*

By the 1920s, Tomlinson had become a leader in furniture manufacturing in High Point and across the South. The company pioneered the design of matched dining room suites and displayed their wares in gallery settings, which was a novel idea at the time. The last sizable addition to their plant was essentially a duplicate of earlier wings but with an elaborate, classically inspired entryway of limestone facing the railroad tracks and leading to the company offices and gallery showrooms. Within a single complex, the Tomlinson plant demonstrates the furniture trade's transition from utilitarian brick industrial buildings to more stylish structures that exhibited classical embellishments on the standard factory form.

With the onset of World War I, it became apparent that the rapid growth of High Point's furniture industry would be slowed and manufacturers would be forced to look to distant markets. Historian J.J. Farriss remembered that

> *immediately upon declaration of war cancellations began coming in and within a matter of a few days all orders were cancelled. For some time business was stagnant as cotton and other agricultural products reached a low ebb in process. Conditions forced our manufacturers to figure on other outlets for their products. Consequently they began trying new fields—New York, Philadelphia and vicinity, New England, Ohio, Michigan and nearby states with results that they found more and better business in the new field.*[93]

As construction of new furniture plants leveled during the 1920s, hosiery mills were opening at a rate of nearly one a year. Though the furniture industry sought market expansion, furniture trade in the city became increasingly service and support oriented. The most important service High Point provided the industry was the Furniture Market. As service and support enterprises expanded in the 1920s, the Great Depression of the 1930s cost High Point nearly half of its furniture manufacturing plants. With this loss, the city increasingly turned to the hosiery industry for job expansion and high profits.[94] As this transition continued into the 1940s, High Point's strongest association with the furniture industry was as a service center after World War II.

Early furniture showroom development in High Point was restricted to underused commercial and industrial buildings that doubled as temporary showroom space. Showrooms were built or maintained by manufacturers in order to display their product lines at semiannual "markets" that were open only to retailers and the press. As High Point's manufactures grew in importance and scale within the industry, interest grew in developing specialized showroom display space locally. When High Point's first furniture showroom opened in 1909, the building it occupied was a utilitarian brick structure located on the east side of the 100 block of South Main Street in a plain, three-story building with a heavy modillion cornice, segmental-arched windows on the upper floors and FURNITURE MANUFACTURERS EXPOSITION written across its top.[95] This building was destroyed around 1930.

In response to increased demand for showroom space, Charles Long, a glass manufacturer, brought the concept of high-grade furniture showroom space to High Point. Long is rumored to have visited the Jamestown Furniture Exposition Building of 1916–17 in Jamestown, New York, and returned with the plans for the future Southern Furniture Exposition Building (SFEB). Architect and contractor William P. Rose of Greensboro refined designs for the ten-story building, which opened in 1921 and at once brought a greater level of recognition and permanence to High Point's fledgling market. Not only did the building rise higher than any other edifice in town, but it was also faced in terra cotta tile, a somewhat novelty material in North Carolina at the time. The classically inspired façade contained all the trademarks of tall buildings of the day, including well-articulated lower floors that served as a base, a "shaft" of regular fenestration on several floors and a "capital" of a heavy entablature that defined the top of the building. The SFEB rose still taller with the addition in the 1940s of four floors that were of simple design by the local firm Voorhees and Everhart.[96]

Meanwhile, the strong association the city held with the furniture trade led to the establishment of numerous furniture suppliers and related services. Suppliers included High Point Excelsior Company, a supplier of "wood wool" or upholstery

Hosiery Manufacturing and High Point's Growth as a City, 1905–1930

The Hosiery Industry

As furniture manufacturing leveled off during the early years of the twentieth century and High Point investors turned their efforts toward the establishment of several large and profitable hosiery mills, the city soon became a center of the nation's hosiery industry. The *Enterprise* wrote in 1935, "The successful rise of the industry here inspired men in other communities to follow suit until today of the approximately 600 hosiery manufacturing plants in the country over one-sixth are located within a radius of 75 miles of High Point—with this city as the largest single producing community in the Southern territory."[97] The real story of High Point's twentieth-century growth was not in furniture manufacturing, as popularly thought; rather, its wealth was from hosiery.

The establishment of the hosiery industry in High Point was due to the efforts of J. Henry Millis and John Hampton Adams, who organized the High Point Hosiery Mill in 1904. Demand for affordable hosiery products was strong, thanks to a national market and an extensive distribution system enabled by Southern Railway. From only three textile mills in 1909, the city was able to boast nineteen by 1922.[98]

The progression of the design of hosiery mills followed patterns similar to those seen in furniture factories. Though the furniture industry transitioned from wooden buildings to factories with load-bearing brick walls around the turn of the century, hosiery mills were largely brick structures that reflected requirements of the insurance industry from their date of construction. As the industry matured, later mills were designed with an eye to aesthetics as well as practicality.

Piedmont Hosiery Mill in the 300 block of English Road exemplifies the earliest phase of mills. The first wing of the sprawling complex was built around 1910 as a three-story brick building exhibiting sturdy pilasters to provide structural support for heavy textile machinery and large segmental-arched windows that allowed generous natural lighting and ventilation. A small, gabled parapet originally occupied the center of the façade. Situated on a city street away from the rail line, the mill

Southern Furniture Exhibition Building. *Courtesy of the Briggs Collection.*

filler, established in 1900. It was followed by High Point Veneer Company and Ecker Glass and Mirror in 1902, Pittsburgh Plate Glass in 1905, Hill Veneer Company in 1907, Raymond Veneer Company in 1910 and Denny Roll and Panel Company in 1913. These companies were often located in simple, unadorned buildings constructed of wood. In some cases, brick was used to improve fire insurance ratings. The loss of manufacturing facilities to fire due to the combustible nature of the products being made within was always a grave risk in the city.

Piedmont Hosiery Mill. *Courtesy of the Briggs Collection.*

required all raw materials and products to be transported on and off site by horse cart.

In 1910, Francis Marion Pickett took advantage of the amenities available to him in the form of electricity, access to the railroad and a large pool of available workers by employing Lockwood, Green & Company of Boston to design an expansive facility on High Point's far western boundary, near present-day Redding Drive.[99] The design brought to High Point standardized cotton mill construction practices shaped by policies dictated by insurance companies. The strict standards for safety and fireproofing procedures gave cotton mills their distinctive appearance. For example, stairwells had to be located outside the main body of the building in order to prevent fire from spreading to higher floors and to enable workers a means of exit. Accordingly, the stair tower at the Pickett Cotton Mills projects from the façade of the main building. Other features include substantial "slow-burn" frame construction that resisted heavy vibrations of machinery and large windows for improved interior lighting.[100]

The Highland Cotton Mill, a yarn manufacturing complex on Mill Avenue south of town, represents the one-story variation of textile mill structures suitable for the spatial needs of spinning yarn. Erected in 1913, the one-story building departs from the early multi-story prototype of weaving mills. Electrical power,

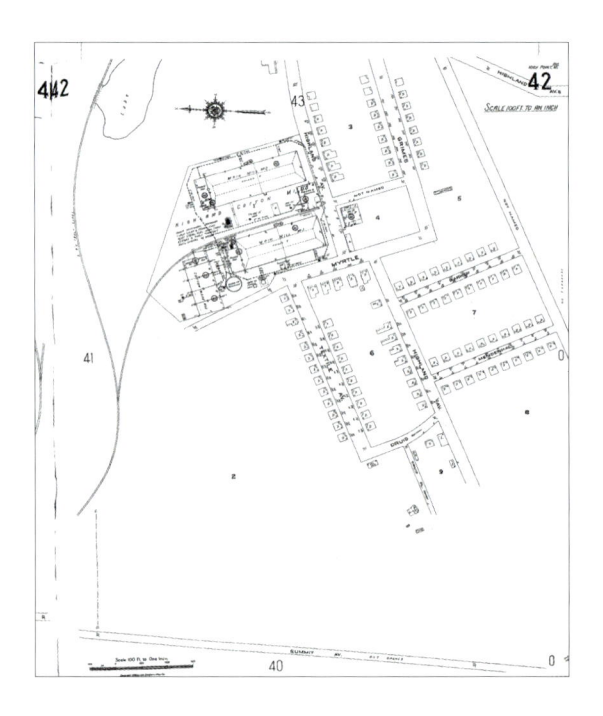

Pickett Cotton Mills. *Courtesy of the Briggs Collection.*

Sanborn Insurance Map, Highland. *Copyright 1917 Sanborn Map Company, The Sanborn Library, LLC. All Rights Reserved. Further reproductions prohibited without written permission from The Sanborn Library, LLC.*

Hosiery Manufacturing and High Point's Growth as a City, 1905–1930

supplied by the city, allowed work space and equipment to be primarily on one level. Electricity also powered lights and machinery and eventually enabled use of air conditioning, which was critical to maintaining humidity levels needed in the manufacturing process of yarn products. As soon as air conditioning was installed in the mid-twentieth century, the large windows of the mill were filled in for energy efficiency throughout the work areas.[101] The company produced cotton knitting yarn, which supplied local hosiery mills that used a specialized knitting process for socks and underwear.

The rapid increase in the number of textile mills resulted in the expansion of all aspects of High Point's structural environment. The city's increased demand for labor exploded to the point that "advertising was broadcast, agents were sent into the mountains and into Davidson, Montgomery, Moore, and Randolph counties telling families of the opportunities for work in High Point."[102] Highland Mills built an exemplary village to attract workers on the south side of town, hailed by sociologists "who noted the planned community and social programs for workers around churches, schools, community center, and sports facilities."[103] Mill villages were nearly self-sufficient communities that centered on a mill as the main employer and patron, around which revolved residential, commercial and religious life. Often insular, mill communities provided schools, recreation and civic opportunities, as well as company-owned stores that extended credit to mill employees.

Opened in 1913, Highland Mills village was among the first planned neighborhoods in the city, containing houses that were necessary to attract workers in an increasingly tight labor market. Laid out in an informal grid plan extending south and west from the mill, the village included church and community buildings close to the mill, with supervisors' houses nearby and workers' housing more distant. Workers' residences were rented from the company and featured simple frame construction, running water and large backyards for vegetable gardens.[104] In Highland, houses were constructed following popular styles of the period. Colonial Revival and Craftsman plans consisted of frame construction and featured shared elements such as front porches and simple room arrangements. Other small mill villages were created around Pickett Cotton Mills and in the Cloverdale neighborhood, though they were not as clearly expressed as Highland. Although Highland Mills village remains largely intact, only elements of the Pickett and Cloverdale communities remain standing today.

Highland Mills village scene. *Courtesy of the National Archives, photo no. 69-RP-262.*

Pickett Mills village scene. *Courtesy of the National Archives, photo no. 69-RP-265.*

In 1930, brothers Milton and Robert Silver established a rayon and silk hosiery mill at 401 South Hamilton Street. This late phase of mill design is a two-story building fronting South Hamilton Street, featuring a handsome Flemish bond brick façade with cast-stone elements that demonstrate a growing sense of pride in the industry. In its central business district location, the mill's decorative façade rivals many commercial buildings in the city.

The Depression took a heavy toll within the furniture industry, but the textile trade fared much better. Many of High Point's most powerful civic leaders were members of the hosiery industry, and their capital was reserved for their own self-improvement. No longer was excess capital used to initiate new business and trades to the extent it once had. Captains of hosiery did not want wage competition, which further dampened desires to expand the city's manufacturing base. The net result of this shift in High Point's industrial complexion was a much different economic climate that no longer enthusiastically embraced growth and diversification of industry. As witnessed by the city's relatively slow growth of 4.5 percent from 1930 to 1940, the once impressive triple-digit growth rate was replaced by an embarrassing period of stagnation.[105]

Not all industry in High Point was related to furniture or hosiery. Though the city's private business club was named the String and Splinter in honor of the city's two major industries, other activity flourished as well. In 1902, Swiss native Emil Stehli established the Stehli Silk Mill in High Point. The company grew steadily and at its peak in the 1930s employed nearly six hundred people. The factory was renowned for its well-landscaped grounds, which included a rose garden, a pergola and winding walkways. The company closed due to a strike in 1942, and most of its plant has since been demolished.[106] High Point Buggy Company manufactured horse-drawn vehicles from 1880 until it converted its product line to furniture in 1923. The buggy works occupied a frame structure covered in corrugated sheet metal off East Green Street that was constructed in phases beginning in 1903. The three-story building with large windows for lighting and ventilation burned in 1951.[107]

Road Improvements

The rise of the automobile necessitated massive road improvements throughout the city beginning in the second decade of the twentieth century. Government bonds issued in 1916 enabled the city to embark on a "get out of the mud" campaign to pave and improve streets.[108] Later that year, Washington Street was one of the first roads in High Point paved with macadam.[109] A primary focus of road improvement was High Point's central business district, where most of the city's commercial growth occurred during the first half of the twentieth century. The heart of the primary business area was and still is several blocks of North and South Main Streets, where the first years of the new century brought new banks, hotels, offices and furniture showrooms. Commercial development soon spread to streetcar neighborhoods that enjoyed easy access, centered on English Street, East Washington Street and East Green Drive.

The Greensboro–High Point Road had been at the center of a long dispute between High Point and the county seat over how to improve transportation between the two towns, the road's condition varying from "prize winning" to "a sea of mud."[110] After proposals to connect the two cities with a splendid new landscaped parkway were cancelled by the arrival of the Great Depression, the existing roadway was widened and paved to become one of the most modern thoroughfares in the state. The expanding highway system soon connected High Point to other cities with graded and surfaced roads, including the Boone-Wilmington Highway to Asheboro and Winston-Salem in 1923 (U.S. 311) and the Central Highway to Thomasville by 1924 (U.S. 70).[111]

Low-rise and High-rise Commercial Buildings

After the turn of the twentieth century, central High Point began to see the construction of multi-story buildings. J.P. Redding announced

Hosiery Manufacturing and High Point's Growth as a City, 1905–1930

Redding Flats. *Courtesy of the Briggs Collection.*

North Carolina Savings Bank and Trust Company Building. *Courtesy of the High Point Museum, High Point, North Carolina.*

plans in 1907 for a four-story structure named the Redding Flats, which contained space for wholesale distributors on the first floor and "nicely fitted flats" on the upper floors in the 100 block of Hayden Place.[112] The following year, high-rise office construction first came to High Point with the North Carolina Savings Bank and Trust Company Building at 126 North Main Street. Rising five stories, the new office building was touted by the *Enterprise* as "one of the most imposing in the State." The Neoclassical Revival–style bank building quickly became a landmark after completion in 1907–08. The building's elegant Beaux Arts façade was designed by Wheeler, Runge and Dickey, Architects, of Charlotte. They incorporated classical elements such as polished granite Ionic columns, arched windows topped by lions' heads and rooftop urns. The office building featured amenities more characteristic of large cities, such as an electric elevator and lights, steam heat and large plate-glass windows.[113] Advertisements at the time bragged that one could see the domain of six counties from its rooftop garden.

After World War I, a distinct period of construction commenced and soon had the pace and vigor of the prewar era. Major construction projects included buildings commissioned by national chains such as J.C. Penney, Sears and Roebuck and Foor and Robinson Hotels. Banks built structures as well, but in most cases were not the sole occupants; instead, they leased office space to smaller service agencies such as insurance agents, doctors and lawyers. Most of High Point's office buildings of the post–World War I period fall into one of two categories: low-rise buildings or high-rise skyscrapers, both of which were built throughout the first half of the twentieth century. These substantial buildings were often steel frame constructions sheathed in brick or stone.

Two exemplary low-rise structures are the 1924 Penny Building at 201 North Main Street and the 1926 J.C. Penney Company at 130 South Main Street.[114] Both two-story buildings feature Neoclassical Revival treatments, including limestone

53

façades with stylized classical pilasters and full entablatures. Another example of a low-rise building of the period is the three-story Jarrell Building at 114 South Main Street, constructed around 1915 in the Neoclassical Revival style for Allen Brothers Department Store. The stylized yellow brick façade features tall pilasters topped by simple Doric capitals, a full entablature and short pediment that contains the name JARRELL. Other examples of low-rise structures during this time period include the Sears Roebuck building at 325 North Main Street and the S.H. Kress & Co. building (destroyed) in the 100 block of South Main Street.

Interest in skyscraper construction in High Point in the first half of the twentieth century was part of a larger trend, as civic pride encouraged banks, hotels and corporations to raise impressive skylines across the state. High Point witnessed the construction of several notable high-rise buildings, including the nine-story Commercial National Bank and the Sheraton Hotel, along with the previously described Southern Furniture Exposition Building.

The Sheraton Hotel at 400 North Main Street, one of a chain of Foor and Robinson Hotels, is a grand illustration of this period. The architecture of the ten-story building favors Renaissance Revival design, with a Spanish tile parapet roof, Ionic pilasters and cast-stone trim around featured doors. Designed by New York architect W.L. Stoddard, it is typical of several other hotels managed by Foor and Robinson.[115] Upon completion in 1921, the $700,000 hotel with 138 rooms was the most impressive in the city and joined the ranks of major hotels in Charlotte, Greensboro, Raleigh and Winston-Salem.[116]

In 1923, R.K. Stewart of High Point built the Neoclassical Revival–style Commercial National Bank at 164 South Main Street, designed by Charles C. Hartmann of Greensboro.[117] The structure's form, alluding to a classical column—a stone base with an arched entry, a shaft of six-story pilasters and a capital-like top—is typical of the Neoclassical style popularly used for office towers of the period. Renaissance details include bracketed architraves at the first-floor windows, an elaborate keystone over the front entry arch and an impressive entablature at the top floor.

Early Neighborhood Centers

As the city grew into one of the largest in North Carolina in the 1920s, numerous neighborhood businesses, factories and residential streets developed away from the historic center. To control growth and regulate land use, a citywide land-use plan entitled "Building Zone Map for the City of High Point" was developed in 1926, with assistance from the pioneering urban planner Earl Sumner Draper of Charlotte. The plan outlined several commercial nodes across the city, with particular focus around major intersections.[118]

The largest of these nodes was the Washington Drive neighborhood, which grew in response to Jim Crow laws that ordered racial segregation throughout the South. A great deal of development in the neighborhood occurred between World War I and the onset of the Great Depression, when R.G. Lassiter, the city's "paving king," employed hundreds of blacks from South Carolina and Georgia. Many brought families who remained

Commercial National Bank. *Courtesy of the Briggs Collection.*

in High Point after the boom days ended, resulting in a rapid increase in High Point's African American population.[119]

The Jim Crow era had a substantial impact on the way High Point developed and grew during the early part of the twentieth century. The laws, named for a white antebellum minstrel show performer who blackened his face, were statutes passed by the legislatures of Southern states that created an ethnic caste system. By 1910, every Southern state had passed laws that mandated the creation of "separate but equal" facilities for blacks and whites in every part of society, including schools, libraries, restaurants and hotels.

High Point historian Ethel Griffin Hughes recalled the frustration and anger of living in such a dark and irrational era:

> *Churches refused black communicants; schools for blacks received whatever was left over from white schools; store clerks waited on black customers, but only if no white customers were waiting; stores installed "black and white only" water fountains; the City-owned theatre admitted blacks in the second balcony only; restaurants refused service to blacks completely. Black people received less pay for equal work and experience; the courts upheld the "white is right" attitude. The whites claimed to have thought that blacks were happy, little realizing that a grin and evidenced stupidity were "skin" saving maneuvers.*[120]

The effect of these laws on High Point included the need to erect duplicate services and institutions across the city for African American citizens, including health facilities, waiting rooms and social clubs. Most of these facilities were inferior to mainstream services, exceptions including William Penn High School, which was donated and financed by New York–based members of the Society of Friends. Opportunities for black entrepreneurs opened, exemplified by Nannie and John Kilby, who managed real estate investments across the city. Others established additional services for the disenfranchised African American population. As a result, neighborhoods such as Southside and East Washington Drive became safe havens in which blacks could socialize, learn and worship.

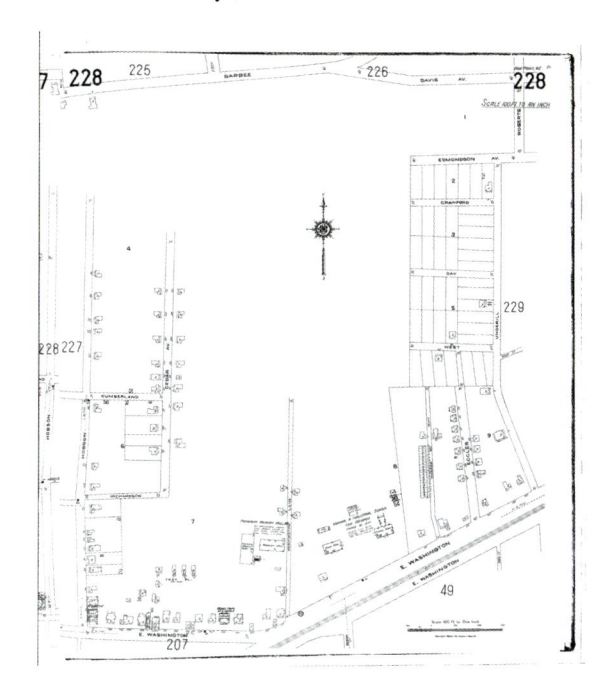

Sanborn Insurance Map, Washington Neighborhood. *Copyright 1917 Sanborn Map Company, The Sanborn Library, LLC. All Rights Reserved. Further reproductions prohibited without written permission from The Sanborn Library, LLC.*

The most substantial buildings in the Washington Drive neighborhood included the First Baptist Church, the Colonial Revival–style William Penn High School and the Kilby Hotel. The three-story Richardsonian Romanesque–style Kilby Hotel, with an elaborate façade featuring round-arched windows and patterned brickwork, was constructed around 1914 at 625 East Washington Drive by Nannie and John Kilby.[121] With its storefronts, dining room and twenty-one guest rooms, the hotel was a center of High Point's African American community and hosted nationally recognized performers. As a black designer, architect and contractor, Fred Lander contributed his talents to a yet unidentified body of work along Washington Drive, including churches and residences. He came to the city in the 1920s to design St. Stephen AME Zion Church and contributed his talents to many projects in High Point and neighboring cities.[122]

West End. *Courtesy of the High Point Museum, High Point, North Carolina.*

Other satellite communities included West End, Fairview and Mechanicsville. Each of these resembled small downtowns, with two-story buildings containing grocers, tailors and general merchandisers on their ground floors, and often apartments above. These commercial districts were further characterized by the placement of their brick buildings close to the street and immediately adjacent to each other, creating continuous street walls along many thoroughfares.

MUNICIPAL PROJECTS

City services expanded quickly through the first decades of the 1900s as the population jumped from 4,163 in 1900 to 9,525 in 1910, 14,302 in 1920 and 36,745 in 1930. Over $20,000,000 worth of building permits were issued in the ten years prior to 1930.[123] The area within the city limits expanded from four square miles to almost ten square miles during the same decade. In 1901, citizens passed a $50,000 bond to build a water and sewer system.[124] It consisted of a series of artesian wells that became contaminated in 1915. A filtering system put in place

North Side Hose Company. *Courtesy of the Briggs Collection.*

by 1919 served High Point until City Lake on the nearby Deep River became the new water supply in 1929.

Municipal offices occupied privately owned commercial structures until circa 1905, when the North Side Hose Company was erected on North Wrenn Street. As a form of efficiency for the growing city, the two-story brick structure housed fire equipment for the North Side firefighting crew, as well as High Point's municipal offices on the second floor. The city's fire department had been organized in 1901 with a volunteer staff of nineteen, and the North Side building served all of High Point north of the railroad tracks.[125] A four-story bell tower that dominated the utilitarian structure featured open arches to allow the ventilation needed for drying fire hoses. A brick cornice, four bays of segmental-arched windows and a double-door opening for the fire truck completed the architectural composition. The city built another Neoclassical Revival fire station a short time later to serve the south side of High Point. Though the North

Hosiery Manufacturing and High Point's Growth as a City, 1905–1930

Fire Station Number 4. *Courtesy of the High Point Museum, High Point, North Carolina.*

1910 U.S. Post Office. *Courtesy of the High Point Museum, High Point, North Carolina.*

Side building remains standing, its counterpart on the south side has been destroyed.

Continued growth of neighborhoods to the north led to construction in 1925 of Fire Station Number 4 at 1329 North Main Street. Built in a Dutch Colonial style that kept with neighboring period Revival-style residences, the brick structure features a gambrel roofline turned to the street. The truck bay filling the narrow street façade was originally mirrored with a matching door in the rear to allow trucks to pass through the building with ease.

Around 1922 the city completed the Municipal Building at the corner of South Wrenn Street and East Commerce Avenue. Likely designed by architect Harry Barton of Greensboro, the imposing two-story Neoclassical Revival–style building sheathed in stone included a theatre as well as offices for the city's growing administrative functions, such as permitting, building inspections and public works. These offices resulted from the city's earlier 1915 adoption of the manager form of government, which divided tasks among separate departments.[126] This location served the city for almost fifty years, until it was sold and destroyed in the late 1960s to make way for expansion of the Southern Furniture Exhibition Building.

The first federal building in High Point, the United States Post Office, was erected in 1910–12.[127] The previous post office had been housed in a private structure north of the railroad on Main Street, but the new building signified a "coming of age" for the city. The monumental building's Italian Renaissance theme featured Indiana limestone sheathing and a central arcade of rounded arches set upon Ionic columns. A heavy modillion cornice underscored the roofline topped by a balustrade. Located at the corner of South Main and Commerce, the grand post office served High Point less than twenty-five years before being destroyed and replaced by a series of plain commercial buildings.

Civic and Social Organizations

Alongside municipal services, civic life in High Point grew during the early years of the new century. Among the earliest civic buildings was the Oddfellows Lodge, constructed in 1907 on East Washington Drive. The three-story brick structure with arched windows housed club activities for the African American fraternal organization, with street-level space for businesses. The building remains a prominent landmark in the East Washington Drive neighborhood.

The number of civic organizations multiplied after World War I. High Point's Chamber of Commerce was established in 1919 in order to advance the city by promoting such projects as the Southern Furniture Exhibition Building, the Sheraton Hotel, the YMCA and the High Point, Thomasville and Denton Railroad.[128] Whimsically, the chamber erected the "World's Largest Bureau" in 1926 to house their agency's offices. The three-drawer replica of a contemporary chest of drawers included details such as drawer pulls and even an implied mirror sporting the name of the city and organization. Constructed in the highly visible Tate Park at North Main and Church Streets, the structure quickly became a pop icon and symbol of the strength of the home furnishings industry in High Point. Upon the destruction of Tate Park for parking around 1952, the bureau was relocated to 508 North Hamilton Street, where it remains in use today as an office.[129]

A civic organization established the first hospital in High Point. In 1904, the Junior Order of American Mechanics opened the hospital in a frame house north of downtown. Initially residential in appearance, through subsequent expansions it eventually became a rambling complex of brick-veneered buildings that provided space for ever-broadening medical practices. The city's second hospital, Guilford General, opened across town on East Washington Drive in 1918.[130] Both hospitals merged in 1944 to form High Point Memorial Hospital.[131]

Schools

Growth of the city's institutions also reflected improvements in primary education. While the rising population increased public school enrollment, educational theory and practice grew more sophisticated. The result was a school building campaign coupled with additional grade levels and improved classes. By 1915, four additional schools for white students had been erected—Elm Street School (1905), Park Street School (1910), Fairview School (1910) and Grimes Street School (1911)—yet school overcrowding and the desire for modern facilities persisted into the 1920s. Fairview School, which had been housed in a wooden building, moved to a new brick structure in 1920. Emma Blair and Ray Street (1920), Leonard Street (1921), Cloverdale (1922), Johnson Street (1926) and Oak Hill (1927) Schools were all born of this period of rapid growth.[132]

Improvements in education extended to the African American community outside the city through a grant from the Julius Rosenwald Fund in 1910 that assisted in the

Florence Elementary School. *Courtesy of the High Point Museum, High Point, North Carolina.*

Hosiery Manufacturing and High Point's Growth as a City, 1905–1930

construction of a school for black students in the rural Florence community just north of High Point. Florence was a Quaker crossroads community established before the Civil War that included many African American residents who valued education. Though education for blacks was provided by the county school system, financial resources were chronically limited. When residents decided to take the initiative to construct a modern school building for black children, they turned to the Rosenwald Fund for assistance. Established by the president of retail giant Sears, Roebuck and Company, the fund assisted school building efforts in African American communities all across the South by providing seed money and building plans. In Florence, the Rosenwald grant was matched by citizens and the county for a two-room frame schoolhouse erected in 1916. Local citizens supplied lumber, labor and other resources as part of an effort to establish "a first-class school." The first Rosenwald-funded schoolhouse was replaced by another in 1927 that contained four classrooms, an auditorium and a kitchen.[133] The brick-veneered structure facing west toward Penny Road was a standard Rosenwald-sponsored design, featuring large banks of windows, a central gable and a classical entryway. The building was destroyed in 1982.

During this period within the city, existing educational opportunities for African Americans were also enhanced. After the Society of Friends of New York donated the High Point Normal and Industrial Institute on East Washington Drive to the public school system in 1923 for use as an accredited school for blacks, the quality of education at the institution continued to improve. The school's main building was heavily remodeled to its present appearance when the name of the school was changed in 1929 to William Penn High School to honor the seventeenth-century Quaker founder of Pennsylvania. The Burford Auditorium facing Washington Drive is a grand brick Georgian Revival design, identified by the arched windows topped with stone trim that grace the sides of the building and by the pilastered portico on the front façade with a small round window within the pediment. Rising above the structure is a tall cupola topped by a copper-sheathed ogee dome.

The citywide building spree culminated in 1927 with the opening of High Point High School for white students. Among the many high-styled school complexes in the state, few surpass High Point's grand 1927 high school. The campus joined the talents of two designers: Greensboro architect Harry Barton and Charlotte landscape architect Earl Sumner Draper. The building blends historic English Gothic design with progressive Art Deco details to produce a new style known as "Neo-Gothic." Design elements such as low, squared towers and Gothic arches are combined with spandrel panels and relief sculpture to create a style unique to the period. The landscape of the prominently sited school ranked among the most impressive in the state, featuring native oaks and hickories along with serpentine walkways and athletic fields.[134] The prominent building was complemented in 1931 by the addition of Ferndale Junior High School just to the east, designed to incorporate details from the high school so that it maintained a campus theme. Both shared athletic facilities on a large tract of land between downtown and Emerywood.

William Penn High School. *Courtesy of the High Point Museum, High Point, North Carolina.*

High Point College. *Courtesy of the High Point Museum, High Point, North Carolina.*

HIGH POINT COLLEGE

Unlike other major cities in North Carolina's Piedmont that had several colleges by the turn of the century, High Point did not acquire an institution of higher learning until the 1920s. The campaign to establish a college in High Point came from the Chamber of Commerce, which solicited funds to attract the attention of the North Carolina Methodist Protestants. The group had sought to found a college for decades, and found a home in High Point with a gift of sixty acres and $100,000 in pledges from leading citizens.[135] High Point College opened in 1924 (changed to High Point University in 1991) with an administration building (Roberts Hall), male and female dormitories (McCulloch Hall and Women's Hall, respectively) and a central heating plant. The architectural design of the High Point College campus was in keeping with traditional initiatives found at many private colleges and universities across the state in the 1920s. Washington, D.C. architect R.E. Mitchell was assisted by High Point architect Herbert Hunter in choosing the English Renaissance style for campus buildings, with the belief that it was "not only the most economical and practical, but best adapted to our environment."[136]

Roberts Hall is the visual centerpiece of the campus, evocative of the 1732–56 Pennsylvania State House in Philadelphia, popularly known as Independence Hall. The two-story brick structure features seventeen bays of oversized windows, and arched dormer windows accentuate the long, gabled roofline of the building. At the center of the main façade is a grand two-story portico and front door topped by an oversized broken pediment. Above the portico rises a tower that sports a circular window (converted to a clock face in 2005), Corinthian columns, a spire and a weathervane featuring the Lamp of Learning. Though McCulloch Hall was demolished in 1994, Women's (McEwen) Hall still stands. The two buildings were nearly identical in appearance, their wide façades marked by Flemish bond brickwork, blind arched windows and central classical entries. Cupolas and gabled dormers decorated the long rooflines that terminate with parapet walls featuring implied engaged chimneys.

RELIGIOUS BUILDINGS

Successes in the textile industry during the 1910s and 1920s enabled citizens to invest lavishly in grand religious buildings executed in fine materials and designed by nationally prominent architectural firms. At the turn of the century, nearly all of the mainstream congregations occupied handsome houses of worship in central High Point, located along main thoroughfares side by side with commercial ventures and, in some cases, factories. The increased wealth of the 1920s enabled congregations to move to the relative solitude of the new suburbs if they so desired, where many churches spread out on leafy campuses that included Sunday school buildings, landscaped areas with playgrounds, picnic shelters and generous on-site parking surrounding a central sanctuary. Another theme of religious change in the city was diversification. Catholicism was introduced in High Point around 1910 with the establishment of the Parish of St. Edward's located at the corner of East Green Drive and Park Street, and the Jewish

B'Nai Israel Synagogue began in 1911 above a storefront near Depot Square. These newcomers heralded changes that would grow more influential later in the city's history.

Among the first congregations to translate the wealth and ambition of the period into a new sanctuary was First Presbyterian Church, when they moved from their South Main Street site in 1928. Minutes of the building committee recommended that the church "employ Mr. Harry Barton of Greensboro, North Carolina, as the local architect to draw up plans and supervise the building of the new Church and Sunday School; and that Mr. Hobart Upjohn of New York City, be employed as consulting architect."[137] The handsome structure that Barton and Upjohn designed remained unrivaled in High Point for nearly twenty years and was among four buildings recognized by the first annual awards of the North Carolina Chapter of the American Institute of Architects in 1929.[138] Sheathed in Tennessee Crab Orchard stone, the T-plan building features a forward-facing gable wing housing the sanctuary, flanked to the rear by a perpendicular wing of Sunday school rooms and offices. A massive Gothic arched window punctuates the façade, and a tall tower at the junction of the wings rises high above the sanctuary's roofline to culminate in four spires in an English Gothic fashion. The church is located on a prominent corner on North Main Street at Parkway, set within a grove of ancient white oaks, black gums and willow oaks.

St. Mary's Episcopal Church also left its late nineteenth-century sanctuary in downtown. Their new church, erected in 1928 at the corner of North Main Street and West Farriss Avenue, was designed through a collaboration of the city's most prolific architects: Eccles B. Everhart, Herbert Hunter and Louis Voorhees. The cruciform plan, Gothic-style structure takes inspiration from English parish churches.[139] The effect is enhanced by use of stone walls, buttresses, tall lancet stained-glass windows and a copper-clad steeple. An education building to the rear of the sanctuary was constructed shortly thereafter and also features Tudor appointments such as half-timbering and herringbone pattern brickwork.

Though begun in the 1920s and curtailed by the economic hardships of the Depression, the tendency of urban congregations to relocate to the suburbs resumed with postwar prosperity. Few congregations could rival the grand edifices erected between the World Wars, which remain among the best-designed and best-crafted architectural monuments in the city.

Residential Subdivisions

As High Point was transformed from an industrial village to a growing city in the early twentieth century, development shifted from traditional land-use patterns that mixed property uses to a system of restricted zones of "compatible" development. Residential zones were particularly restrictive, permitting the occasional exception of religious and educational buildings. With the platting of subdivisions away from the city center and developers' frequent stipulations concerning building specifications, costs and even ethnicity, new neighborhoods grew increasingly homogenous in terms of their residents. By the end of the period, most of High Point's lower-income residents lived in the southern and eastern sections of the city, which were close to blue-collar jobs in the furniture and textile factories. African Americans lived close to William Penn High School or in Southside. Many moderate-income residents occupied subdivisions north and west of the city, adjacent to major institutions such as High Point High School and High Point College. The majority of the city's high-income residents relocated in and around Emerywood, a grand subdivision constructed upon hilly terrain northwest of the city adjacent to the High Point Country Club. Though exceptions to these patterns occurred, they were rare and usually fleeting.

City growth was rapid in the early twentieth century, and citizens were sometimes awed by the pace of development that turned their quiet town into a city. As new workers streamed into the city to fill positions in furniture and textile mills, "a thousand new homes for the wage-earners were built immediately" to accommodate their families.[140] A.M. Briggs recorded a popular sentiment of the day by an unknown High Point poet:

Along the village streets I roam
With weary indecision.
For what was once my dear old home
Is now a subdivision.[141]

Following his success with the Quaker Woods subdivision of 1895, R. Homer Wheeler initiated Johnson Place in 1907. Wheeler positioned High Point's first streetcar suburb near the terminus of the proposed streetcar line on land once owned by the Johnson family.[142] Paved sidewalks, lighting fixtures and water and sewer systems were planned from the initial point of construction. Johnson Place extended the "cream" residential address of Main Street northward and opened additional streets paralleling Main Street to the east, which were settled by middle- and upper-middle-income families who built large houses along shaded streets in popular styles such as Craftsman, Prairie and Colonial Revival.

The success of Johnson Place attracted outside capital from nearby Winston-Salem. In 1912, Roland Park was platted by J.N. Ambler of Winston and marketed by Stephen C. Clark, who later developed nearby Parkway, Sheraton Hill, Montlieu Avenue, Artisan Acres, Wesley Place and Emerywood. The design of Roland Park included a circular "court" and a focus on the existing monumental native oaks and hickories. Its first residences were constructed in the winter and spring of 1913.

The success of Ambler's Roland Park likely prompted Clark to undertake his first development, the Parkway, in 1915.[143] Constructed immediately south of Roland Park, the Parkway consisted of a wide avenue extending from North Main Street west to Palatka Street (now Rotary Drive). The new development featured sidewalks set far from the road and nearly seventy lots. Within a year after the opening of the Parkway, Clark embarked upon yet another, slightly larger, development to the south named Sheraton Hill. While Roland Park took its name from the prestigious Baltimore neighborhood and the Parkway took its name from the broad avenue at its center, Sheraton Hill adopted a theme of furniture styles, using monikers such as "Colonial," "Queen Anne," "Jacobean" and "Adam" for its street names.[144] Like the circular park of nearby Roland Park, Sheraton Hill had as its centerpiece a triangular park created by the diagonal branch of Colonial Drive off Parkway. The park featured a pergola and shelter house overlooking a wading pond. The first house in the Parkway was occupied in July of 1915 and the first residents had moved into Sheraton Hill by 1918. Clark's next project, Montlieu Avenue, developed by his Own-A-Home company, was platted and advertised in May 1924. Sixty-three lots were offered, and sales started briskly that summer.

One of the period's few residential projects undertaken by someone other than Clark was Sherrod Park, which local businessman Archibald Sherrod platted in 1926. Located just north of Montlieu Avenue, its streets feature Craftsman- and Tudor Revival–style houses that visually appear to be a continuation of the Montlieu development. Its centerpiece is a small landscaped area along a brook that bisects the subdivision. A landscape theme of crepe myrtles and pin oaks unified the Sherrod Park neighborhood.[145]

The most prestigious development in High Point began in 1923, just as the town's hosiery industry was reaching maturity. Emerywood represents a fundamental shift of social values in the city as wealthy industrialists and financiers traded their highly visible city center residences for the private and exclusive enclave at the edge of the city. Developer Stephen Clark sought services from renowned landscape architect Earl Sumner Draper to design what he envisioned as the finest development in High Point. The Country Club District of Emerywood, as the neighborhood was first known, reached a level of urban and landscape design identified with the nation's largest cities. Reflective of the "garden city" movement, the development featured curvilinear streets, sidewalks, streetlights and large lots that lowered the traditional density of urban neighborhoods. These ideals were coupled with restrictions on housing size, use, cost, appearance and ownership to create a neighborhood where High Point's growing upper-income residents could escape the crowded streets of the center of town and construct charming, and sometimes palatial, residences in themes of historic European and early American styles. Ever-increasing wealth and a desire to distance residential uses from

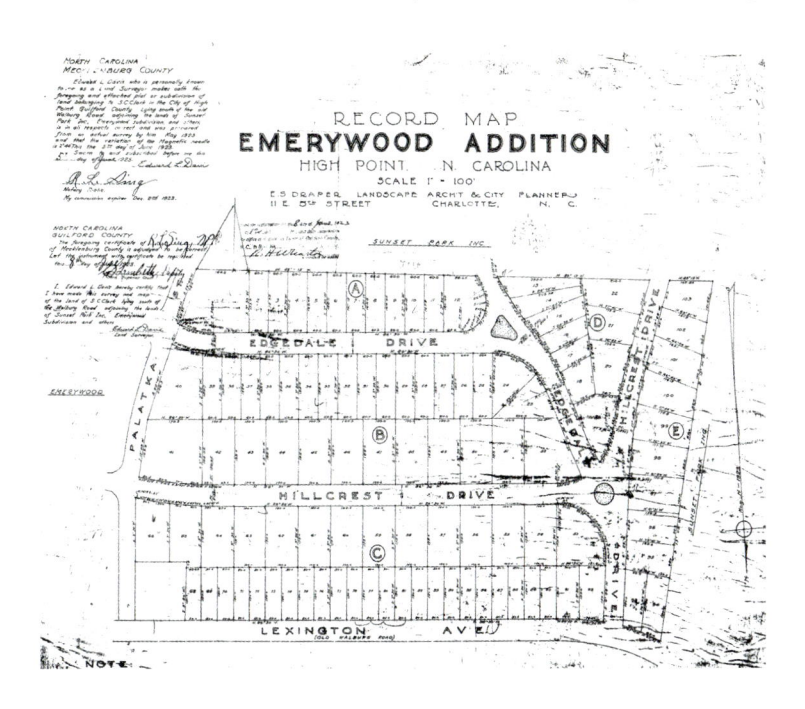

Hosiery Manufacturing and High Point's Growth as a City, 1905–1930

1923 plat of Emerywood. *Courtesy of the Guilford County Register of Deeds.*

commercial and industrial properties fueled demand for the development of Emerywood in the hilly territory northwest of the city. Emerywood West was a later extension of the original subdivision, located west of the High Point Country Club. The greater Emerywood subdivision was united not only by house styles and sizes, but also by streets lined with pin oaks and casually landscaped traffic circles and islands.

Following early leads in Greensboro and Winston-Salem, High Point civic leaders called for the establishment of a country club to further High Point's claim to be a "real city."[146] In 1923, a group of investors founded the High Point Country Club and proceeded to build a clubhouse, nine-hole golf course, swimming pool and tennis courts on land given by developer Stephen Clark. Located at the western edge of the "Country Club District," the new club quickly became a social center for the growing upper- and middle-income residents of the city and sparked a reorientation of social activities away from the city center and into peripheral neighborhoods.

Emerywood was not the only neighborhood to enjoy charming old-world architecture during the late 1920s and 1930s. Pockets of cottage designs appeared in newly established neighborhoods on Greensboro Road, and infill projects were built in traditionally fashionable neighborhoods such as North Main Street. Throughout the 1920s, subdivisions featuring stylish houses following nationally popular trends in design were being announced in every quarter of the city. One such neighborhood was developed as Griffin Park along Underhill Avenue and surrounding streets. In recognition of the neighborhood's stylish residences that were occupied by prominent middle-income African Americans, the street was nicknamed "Black Emerywood." Other notable neighborhoods of the period include Greenway Place, Willoubar Terrace and Forest Park, all located on the east side of town.

Residential Architecture

High Point's early twentieth-century housing represents an important era in the history and development of style and design in the American South and is perhaps the city's most significant contribution to the state's inventory of architectural resources. Eclectic period revival architecture includes an array of styles ranging from classically inspired Neoclassical Revival to historic Colonial Revival and charming European-inspired designs. American homeowners and homebuilders viewed architectural styles as a great mosaic from which themes could be selected. The increasing affluence of High Point's residents enabled them to think broadly when selecting styles, at times with such enthusiasm that unusual modes or lavish details are expressed.

During High Point's explosive growth of the 1920s, professional architects established offices in the city to take advantage of an increasingly sophisticated customer base. These professionals brought with them the knowledge and understanding to design more academic interpretations of Colonial and Medieval styles. Architects such as Louis Voorhees, who studied under architectural historian Fiske Kimball at the

Universities of Michigan and Virginia, and architect Harry Barton of Greensboro were well versed in academically correct architecture. Their designs were executed by skilled craftsmen who were proficient in metalworking, stone masonry, fine woodworking and finishing, plaster rendering, slate installation and numerous other trades. The value of High Point's early twentieth-century housing is heightened through quality of craftsmanship and superiority of building materials.

Colonial Revival Style

Harry Barton's 1916 residence for J.D. Cox, an officer in his family's textile supply company, signaled a growing appreciation of the Colonial Revival style. Barton did not shy away from complex forms, as had the architects and builders of earlier examples in the city. Instead, he used numerous gables and dormers to evoke the image of an ancient rambling Colonial farmhouse, expanded through the centuries. This important two-story frame house features a large Palladian window, a front door flanked by sidelights and an open porch that looks westward across a deep ravine. Located in the western end of Roland Park at 803 Farriss Avenue, the composition occupies a wooded, mid-block site with little regard for the surrounding street grid. In this manner, the Cox House indicates the beginning of the rural aesthetic in High Point that influenced its suburban architecture for the rest of the twentieth century.

Barton's second High Point residence was designed for city school superintendent C.F. Tomlinson in 1921.[147] This Dutch Colonial house at 529 West Parkway Avenue was among the most substantial houses on Parkway. The two-story brick and frame house features details popular during the period, such as a gambrel slab tile roof, a graceful arched entry supported by paired attenuated columns and shutters with cutout designs.

Examples of academic Colonial Revival architecture were built throughout middle- and upper-income neighborhoods across the city, particularly in the 1920s and 1930s in and around Emerywood. For example, the Lucy and J. Vassie

Tomlinson House. *Courtesy of the High Point Public Library, North Carolina Collection, High Point, North Carolina.*

Wilson House, commissioned for a handsome lot at 425 Hillcrest Drive, is evocative of Tudor Place in Georgetown, Washington, D.C., by High Point–based architect Fred B. Klein. Klein incorporated key features of Tudor Place, including the demilune porch, blind arches and hipped roof, and added new features such as a green slab tile hipped-roof, garland relief and a modillion cornice. The Wilson House demonstrates Klein's thorough knowledge of early American architecture, along with his willingness to manipulate features to create a new and unique design.[148]

The Colonial Revival style remained popular through the 1940s and beyond because it was easily adapted to modest homes as well as ranch houses and provided a safe and familiar design alternative to other period or modernist designs. Many later examples are contained in and around subdivisions that saw a great deal of building activity in the 1940s and 1950s. More modest renditions of the Colonial Revival style include the E.L. Briggs house at 920 Fairway Drive, built in 1947. As a reference, the builder of the house used the architectural survey and history *Early Architecture of North Carolina*, which depicts architectural features of eighteenth- and nineteenth-century buildings in the state.[149] Details of the Briggs home include

Hosiery Manufacturing and High Point's Growth as a City, 1905–1930

Wilson House. *Courtesy of the Briggs Collection.*

Briles House. *Courtesy of the Briggs Collection.*

beaded siding, academically proportioned dormer windows and molding copied from the historic examples found in the book.

Neoclassical Revival Style

Among the most favored national styles found in High Point during this period was the Neoclassical Revival style, popularized by the 1893 World's Columbian Exposition's dazzling "White City" of classically composed exhibition halls featuring grand porticoes, cornices and domes. Neoclassical Revival houses often display more modest porticoes with classical columns, tripartite windows and heavy modillion cornices, among other features. One of the first residences constructed in this style was the Briles House at 1103 North Main Street, built in 1907 for the head cashier of the North Carolina Savings Bank and Trust Company. According to family tradition, the Brileses asked an architect from Greensboro (as yet unidentified) to design a house that resembled a grand "Southern Mansion."[150] Their request was answered with an imposing two-story frame house featuring a hipped roof, with a two-story portico supported by paired Ionic columns. The classical language continued with a heavy modillion cornice, tripartite windows and a balcony over the centrally placed front door. The Briles House is the sole survivor of a popular early twentieth-century subgroup of residences in High Point that featured monumental porticoes.

In time, Neoclassical Revival–style houses grew more restrained in their appearance, as reflected by the design of the R.O. Lindsay House of 1912 at 1002 Johnson Street. Built for the manager of Consolidated Hosiery Mill, this two-story frame house features a hipped roof over a simple rectangular block, like the Briles House. The Lindsay House, however, exchanges the grand soaring portico of the earlier period with a broad one-story wraparound front porch supported by paired Doric columns. Three attic dormers display exuberant pediments, and heavy modillions accent the cornice. The inclusion of these elements illustrates a tendency to blend Neoclassical Revival elements with Colonial Revival designs during this period.

Craftsman Style

As a center of furniture design and furniture craftsmanship reflecting international influences, High Point embraced contemporary and exotic designs with enthusiasm. Craftsman and Prairie styles first made their way into High Point shortly after 1910 and quickly became two of the most popular styles of residential architecture in the city. Favored because the style evoked integrity in design and materials, the casual and adaptive Craftsman style was most popular in the form of bungalows and foursquares that were built in all quarters of the city. Widely flexible, the style was as appropriate for a factory worker as it was the factory manager. Craftsman details took the form of exposed rafter tails, deep roof overhangs and wide eaves, stone or pebbledash walls, handcrafted ceramic tiles and stained-glass windows, which collectively conveyed a sense of articulated structure and fine craftsmanship appropriately evocative of the area's furniture industry.

One of the earliest Craftsman-style houses in the city was that of the Dalton family on Johnson Street. Dalton was an up-and-coming attorney when he purchased the site in 1913. The next year, newly married, he and his wife set about constructing their house. The style they chose was foreign to many High Pointers, influenced not by East Coast history but by forward-looking California and the Far East. The two-story frame house has a prominent front gable with wood shingles on the upper floor and clapboards on the ground floor. Diagonal braces support wide overhanging eaves with exposed rafters, and the gable front porch is supported by battered posts set upon granite piers. Many of these details can be found on later houses, although not with the same fine execution seen in the Dalton House.

The Daltons' stylish house caught the eye of High Point businessman O. Arthur Kirkman, who decided to use it as a model for his own house at 501 West High Street.[151] Multiple copies of *The Craftsman* found stored in his attic might also have been a strong influence in the design of this house. The imposing brick structure of 1915 duplicates many of the features of the Dalton House, including the forward-facing main gable and porch roof and diagonal braces that support

Dalton House. *Courtesy of the High Point Public Library, North Carolina Collection, High Point, North Carolina.*

Kirkman House. *Courtesy of the Briggs Collection.*

broad, overhanging eaves with exposed rafters. Kirkman went a bit further in creating a substantial residence by adding heavy brick piers to support the front porch roof, granite sills and lintels at windows, stained-glass windows and pebbledash in the gables.[152] The Kirkman House remains one of the more imposing Craftsman-influenced houses in High Point. Another exemplary Craftsman house is the Perry residence at 1403 Wiltshire Drive, distinguished by trusses beneath the roof eaves, exposed rafters, banded windows, wide brick piers that surround a commodious front porch and stained glass.

The Long residence at 212 Montlieu Avenue and the Orville Williard House at 1000 Greensboro Road were constructed around 1925 as High Point's best examples of "airplane" bungalows, presumably named because the top-floor sunroom, much smaller than the first story, resembled a cockpit and enabled a panoramic view. Their characteristic Craftsman elements include exposed rafter tails, diagonal braces that support wide overhanging eaves and battered porch supports. More typically, bungalows are one or one and a half stories beneath a gable-end or front-gable roof with an engaged or recessed front porch; they usually incorporate Craftsman elements. Craftsman bungalows dominate many inner-city neighborhoods in High Point that were opened during the 1910s and 1920s. The bungalow defines the character of many of the city's earliest historic neighborhoods and statistically may still be the most prevalent house type in many of these middle-income neighborhoods.

PRAIRIE STYLE

The Prairie style was born in the Midwest, popularized by Chicago architect Frank Lloyd Wright, who was influenced by the long horizontal lines of the great American prairie. For many High Pointers, the Prairie style of architecture likely represented the most progressive ideals of the era. A few textbook examples of Prairie-style houses exist in High Point, but most often the style is illustrated by the foursquare, a two-story cubical house type that by the nature of its design has at least eight rooms and thus is usually found in middle- and upper-income neighborhoods, such as Johnson Place, Roland Park, Montlieu Avenue and Emerywood.

The 1911 Dallas Zollicoffer House at 1207 Johnson Street is High Point's best-articulated example of the Prairie style. The well-preserved house with a very low-pitched hip roof displays such characteristic Prairie style details as rough stucco walls, wide boxed eaves, casement windows that are paired close to corners and simple squared columns. Unusual features include a side entry, a front porch accessed only from the interior, solid porch railings and flanking side porches. Two more examples of Prairie-style houses are the 1912 Burnett-McCain House, located at 1008 Johnson Street, and the 1914 Archibald Sherrod House at 1100 North Main Street. Both are large, two-story frame houses, topped with low-pitched hip roofs with gable projections. Prairie details include wooden post-on-stone pier supports, clean boxed eaves and large windows grouped to emphasize horizontality. Distinctive tile elements set within the plaster panels of the masonry porch supports of the Burnett House add to its visual interest. The Sherrod House features an appealing green tile roof. A one-story variation of the Prairie style stands in Roland Park at 303 Otteray Avenue. Constructed around 1920, this frame house displays a low hipped roofline with very wide overhanging eaves that are boxed without adornment. Other Prairie details include slightly tapered, full-height porch posts and horizontally oriented windows.

Though the detailing of foursquare houses often consists exclusively of Prairie elements such as boxed eaves and massive porch supports, often the homes portray a combination of Prairie and Craftsman features, as seen at 614 West Farriss Avenue and 216 Montlieu Avenue. Both houses feature myriad details, such as brick pier and battered porch supports, bracketed cornices and sidelights flanking the front door. These hybrid houses are reminders that architectural history is often not represented by textbook examples of style.

ECLECTIC STYLES

English Tudor, French, Spanish, Italian, Mission and Regency were among the Eclectic styles characterizing High Point's residential architecture in the third decade of the twentieth century. Promoted in journals and magazines, the styles also likely were popularized as a result of increased global travel, which did much to raise Americans' awareness of far-off lands and distant places. Eclectic styles reached their zenith in High Point in the 1920s, primarily along the curving streets of Emerywood. Sherrod Park and Montlieu Avenue also contain several notable examples, and representatives are found in nearly all quarters of the city. These houses represent an exciting chapter in High Point's history and demonstrate its growing sophistication and wealth.

ENGLISH TUDOR

Prominent chimneys, steep rooflines, decorative false half-timbering and use of brick and fachwerk are hallmarks of the English Tudor style of architecture. Popular from 1900 through the 1930s, the style evoked medieval English and Tudor architecture and sought to instill a sense of permanence, age and craftsmanship for primarily middle- and upper-income houses. Among the first examples of the Eclectic styles to appear in High Point was the Randall Terry House at 200 West Farriss Avenue. Constructed around 1912, the two-story brick and frame English Tudor house is one of the earliest in Roland Park. Contributing elements include a cantilevered attic level, a variety of window sizes and heavy flat tiles on the roof. The first floor is sheathed in brick, while the second floor contains false half-timbering. Substantial brick piers support the shed porch roof.

More academic examples of English Tudor style were built in the 1920s, including Harry Barton's design for Tomlynhurst at 403 Hillcrest Drive in Emerywood.[153] Built for the furniture manufacturer S.H. Tomlinson and his wife in 1924, the house features an irregular massing with tall gables and hips. Barton gave the building an authentic appearance by incorporating hewn timberwork, stuccoed fachwerk infill between wall studs and leaded diamond glass windows.

Winston-Salem architect Luther Lashmit, of Northup and O'Brien, designed an English Tudor residence for the Covington family that blended stone and medieval Cotswold features with Renaissance-inspired Norman Revival elements such as limestone trim, label molding and a niche above the main entry.[154] One of the largest houses ever constructed in High Point, the steel-framed, nine-thousand-square-foot residence was erected in Emerywood West between 1928 and 1931 with thirty rooms, including a thirty-six-foot by eighteen-foot living room, a three-story spiral staircase and a wing devoted to support services and staff. Christened "Hillbrook" in reference to the small stream that flows through a steep ravine of lush landscaping orchestrated by Philadelphia designer Thomas Sears, the house occupies a dramatic lot that encompasses the crest of a ridge overlooking Rockford Road.[155] It is approached through large gates and a dramatically curving drive that reveals glimpses of the house through white pine, hemlock and rhododendron. Built for an owner of Harriss and Covington Hosiery Mills, the property represents the tremendous success of High Point's hosiery industry between the two World Wars. It is also a leading example of the elite group of grand estates constructed in North Carolina in that era.

NORMAN REVIVAL

French architecture is represented by the Norman Revival style, exemplified by cylindrical towers, casement windows and white stucco walls. A modest example of Norman Revival architecture can be found in the house built by David McJester as a model for Emerywood Addition No. 4 in 1927. This two-story house at 1107 Greenway Drive incorporates features such as steeply pitched roofs, smooth stucco-covered walls and French-inspired casement windows. A conical entrance tower that overlooks the confluence of forked Greenway Drives is located at the intersection of its L-shaped plan. The most elaborate High Point example of the style is the Slane residence at 1204 Westwood in Emerywood West, known as "Three Musketeers." Designed around 1930 by Luther Lashmit of the Winston-Salem firm Northup and O'Brien Architects, this sprawling house exhibits the tall, sloped rooflines covered in blue slate, conical towers, white stucco walls, French doors and dormer windows typical of Norman Revival style.[156] The nine-bay east façade contains arched windows and a central-entrance pavilion overlooking a level lawn with a circle drive, in contrast to the west façade, which features a full-length terrace that overlooks a steep wooded hillside.

SPANISH STYLE

The Spanish barrel tile roofs and rough stucco-plastered walls typical of Spanish houses can be found throughout High Point, from middle-income neighborhoods around Montlieu Avenue to high-income neighborhoods around Emerywood. Spanish architecture took inspiration from ancient buildings of the western Mediterranean, a region influenced by Moorish, Italian and Spanish cultures. In addition to low-pitched Spanish tile roofs and stuccoed walls, Spanish-style houses often have round arches above doors and principal windows, parapet rooflines, shallow (if any) eaves, patios, decorative ironwork and ceramic tiles embedded in the stucco. A good example of the Spanish style is found at 302 Montlieu Avenue, a hacienda constructed around 1925 with a flat roof and walls of stucco. Additional features include paired windows topped by tiled pent roofs and a wide terrace edged by a low masonry wall. Other somewhat larger examples are found in Roland Park and Emerywood. Constructed around 1925, the two stuccoed houses at 718 West Farriss Avenue and 420 Edgedale Drive are exuberant representatives of their style, exhibiting segmental-arched openings, casement windows and low-pitched roofs; 420 Edgedale Drive retains its original barrel roof tiles. A distinctive arched portal flanks the Farriss Avenue house, and a wrought-iron balcony graces the façade of the Edgedale Drive hacienda.

ITALIAN RENAISSANCE STYLE

High Point contains numerous 1920s expressions of the Italian Renaissance style that stand among the finest in North Carolina. The style can be articulated in a variety of forms, ranging from large urban palazzos to country villas. Palazzos incorporate classical elements such as bracketed window cornices and eaves, medallions and carved stone relief. Villas, in contrast, reflect simpler rural antecedents and lack the degree of detail seen in high-style examples. Nonetheless, features such as arched windows with keystones, balconies and barrel tile roofs provide a Mediterranean flavor to these houses.

High Point is known for two palatial examples of the palazzo style. Around 1920, hosiery magnate J.H. Adams commissioned an as yet unidentified architect for an Italian Renaissance–style residence at 1108 North Main Street.[157] The mansion's cubical three-story form is appropriate to its urban setting, exhibiting a green-tiled deck-hipped roof, stucco walls and a three-bay arcade. Classical motifs such as columns, medallions and heavy brackets under the eaves give this house an air of grandeur rivaled in High Point only by Pennybyrn, the home of real estate and auction tycoon George Penny, designed by Greensboro

Armentrout House, 420 Edgedale Drive. *Courtesy of the High Point Museum, High Point, North Carolina.*

J.H. Adams House. *Courtesy of the High Point Public Library, North Carolina Collection, High Point, North Carolina.*

architect Raleigh James Hughes around 1926.[158] Set back from Greensboro Road at Penny Road behind a sweeping lawn near the Jamestown city limits, this palazzo has a beige brick exterior with substantial cast-stone trim framing arched windows and doors. Its hipped roof is supported by a modillion cornice of stone, and details include relief carved into balconies under the second-floor windows and in blind arches of the first floor.

Several houses in Emerywood feature Italian villa design elements, such as symmetrical façades, low-pitched hipped roofs with bracketed eaves and round-arched windows. One of the most impressive Italian country villas is the Gurney H. Kearns House at 308 Hillcrest Drive. This two-story brick house was constructed around 1925, with a symmetrical façade dominated by the front door featuring an elliptical fanlight and sidelights, surrounded by an arched porch supported by Tuscan columns, all topped by a hipped Spanish tile roof.

Other notable Italian country villas were built for the Murray family in 1925 and the Edwards family around 1935. Located in the Parkway subdivision, the Murray House is a simple two-story, stucco-covered house with a low hip roof, broad overhanging eaves, a symmetrical façade and a substantial entablature above the front door. The two-story Edwards House is located at the entrance to Emerywood and features distinctive arched windows over the arched front door, keystones over the first-floor windows and a barrel tile roof. The second floor is plastered with stucco, with rustic brick coping around windows and corners.

MISSION STYLE

Mission-style houses are rare in High Point, but a few good examples stand in Roland Park and on Wiltshire Avenue. The style shares architectural features with Mediterranean-inspired styles such as Italian Renaissance and Spanish, but it is distinguished from them by design elements common to the architecture of the American Southwest's Spanish missions, such as low-pitched, hipped roofs and ogee-shaped parapets centered above symmetrical façades. The two-story brick house at 108 Brantley Circle in Roland Park, constructed around 1913, is a particularly good example of the Mission style. In addition to the ogee parapet, it displays arched windows, applied molded medallions on the second-floor walls, a front terrace and a main entrance surrounded by classical columns and topped by a rail. Less than a block away, a one-story variation of the Mission style built around 1925 at 111 West Farriss Avenue features stuccoed walls.

EXOTIC STYLES

A cluster of Pueblo Revival–style houses, at 800 and 802 Willoubar Terrace and 707 and 710 Woodrow Avenue, contain elements that mix influences from Spanish Colonial buildings and Native American pueblos in the American Southwest, such as castellated parapet rooflines, masonry walls of brick and rough stucco and squared or arched door and window openings. The house at 800 Willoubar Terrace stands only one story in height but displays the full array of Pueblo Revival features. These unique houses represent an unusual chapter in North Carolina's diverse Eclectic period of architectural history.

Perhaps the most exotic of High Point's archive of Eclectic styles of the period are two houses constructed side by side by friends, the Harper and Welch Houses designed by Glendale,

California architect Clarence D. Tedford.[159] The Terry and Peggy Harper House follows an Arabian theme, with a turban-domed front porch supported by spiral colonettes, barrel tile roof, rounded blind arches above the second-story windows and rounded keyhole entry. The J.C. and Wilna Welch House features decorative tiles, a barrel tile roof and a horseshoe-shaped plan that encloses a peaceful courtyard and sumptuous gardens. The two stuccoed houses were originally painted pink, a color that attracted additional attention to their prominent placement along the main highway to Greensboro.

Multifamily Housing

Multifamily dwellings appeared early in High Point in the form of over-store apartments. Essays by native High Pointers about the turn of the twentieth century make numerous references to over-store residential units, which were not solely reserved for storeowners but were also for rent to the general population. The 1906 Redding Flats, a four-story building on Hayden Place that is now heavily altered, is reported to have contained residential units.[160] The first apartment buildings in the city made their appearance during the 1920s, serving as infill housing in established neighborhoods. The A.E. Taplin Apartment Building of 1923 in the Parkway development is among the earliest. This three-story stuccoed building at 408 Parkway features Italian Renaissance details, including a tile roof and balconies. An architecturally related structure built around 1926 at 1615 English Road in the West End neighborhood, also three stories and masonry, resembles the apartment blocks seen in urban areas in Northern cities, with recessed light wells rising on each side to complement similar indentations on future neighboring buildings and to allow for light and air to reach side windows.[161] The Mediterranean style was applied to the Hardee Apartments (Jarrell Apartments) at 1102 North Main Street, a stuccoed building containing two floors divided bilaterally to create four separate units. Each unit features a front porch and is accessed via a central hallway.[162]

Recreation

Recreational opportunities in High Point grew slowly, initially consisting of landscaped settings for specific uses such as strolling and picnicking. By 1915, the city had developed two parks, one known as Wheeler Park, the other Marklye's Grove.[163] A landscaped park created in 1912 in the middle of Brantley Circle was not so much practical as it was aesthetic. Nearby, the Triangle Park at the entrance to Sheraton Hill was a prototypical neighborhood park of the period, featuring a pergola and shelter house overlooking a wading pond.

As High Point grew and continued to industrialize in the 1910s, city promoters and the *High Point Enterprise* began to call for parks "with facilities for swimming and play." Brantley Circle and Triangle Park were both set aside by developers in order to appeal to young families with the opportunity for safe and specialized playground space, but the city of High Point offered little in the way of public space until Tate Park was developed at the corner of North Main and Church in 1915. The park housed a bandstand, rose gardens and the offices of the Chamber of Commerce (World's Largest Bureau) until it was sold to First Baptist Church in 1952 and paved over for parking.[164]

The 1926 "Building Zone Map for the City of High Point" called for city-owned park space, primarily along streams and floodplains unsuited for development.[165] These plans remained unexecuted by the time the financial collapse of the Great Depression halted public works around 1930. Plans for park space were resurrected when the Blair family gave the city seventy-three acres of land along Richland Creek in the southern periphery of the city. The new Blair Park was dedicated in 1931 as the "initial unit of the city's proposed system of parks," and within a few years featured a playground, municipal golf course and clubhouse, constructed by convict labor with the use of Federal Works Progress Administration funds. Popular High Point architectural firm Workman, Everhart and Voorhees likely designed the park's clubhouse, which was destroyed in 1990.

High Point Enterprise Building. Courtesy of the High Point Museum, High Point, North Carolina, High Point Enterprise *Collection.*

CEMETERIES

Three notable High Point cemeteries date to the first decades of the twentieth century. Greenhill Cemetery began in 1910 when the City Council purchased six acres of land at the corner of Meredith Street and Leonard Avenue to serve as a municipal burial ground for High Point's African American community.[166] Prior to that time, black citizens were interred in a reserved section of Oakwood Cemetery. As the section filled, city leaders purchased Greenhill for expansion. Markers and monuments, some composed of milk quartz and brick, are organized in grid form typical of the period. Landscaping at Greenhill Cemetery, like Oakwood, includes feature plantings and trees. Real estate developer Stephen C. Clark opened Oakwood Memorial Cemetery next to city-owned Oakwood Cemetery in 1935 to meet the rising demand of white residents.[167] The cemetery continued established traditions of markers in a variety of shapes and sizes, mausoleums and classically inspired sculpture within a park-like setting of mature hardwoods and winding roads. In contrast, Floral Garden Park Cemetery, begun the same year west of the city on Rotary Drive, differs from the earlier cemeteries by utilizing markers of uniform grade-level profile that feature little in the way of individualization. Landscaping also is controlled, with feature trees and plantings arranged in discreet areas within a uniting theme typical of the "Memorial Park" movement. This movement advocated uniformity of markers set flush with the ground, punctuated with grand sculpture and gardens, in contrast to the individualized memorials and personalized landscaping of Victorian and Eclectic cemeteries. Developed by an investor from Hagerstown, Maryland, the Floral Garden Park grew quickly to become one of the largest in the city.[168]

The success of the hosiery industry in the 1920s brought great wealth to the city and drastically altered the appearance of High Point's architectural environment. In order to safeguard this highly profitable income stream, the industry's leaders discouraged recruitment of new industries that could be viewed as a threat to wage stability. The resulting reduction of local capital for investment in alternative industry would change the complexion of High Point, converting it from an "open door" city of entrepreneurs to one focused on concerns of established industry. By the 1960s, the rapid growth so characteristic of the city early in the century would be replaced by near stagnation.

MODERN PERIOD AND CIVIL RIGHTS ERA, 1930–1975

High Point had grown into one of the largest cities in North Carolina by the 1930s and 1940s. At the time of the Great Depression, the city's population had grown to 36,000, nearly doubling its size from only ten years earlier. The furniture and hosiery industries were at their height, and commercial interests grew to accommodate demands of an increasingly affluent population. Rapid growth gave the city a heightened profile, sometimes known as the "manufacturing center of the South" and other times as "Little Chicago," due to its notoriously high crime rate. By 1950, High Point opened a central planning department that regulated land use and enforced building codes.[169] During these years of postwar recuperation, the city's increasingly diverse ethnic and religious population maintained a central focus on manufacturing. *High Point Enterprise* staff writer Forrest Cates described the city in 1958 as

> *a city of noise, ambition and neighborliness. It is an early-riser and a hard-worker. It is becoming increasingly more even-tempered and progressive. Once in the city, the morning traveler begins to feel the city's pulse. It is the beat of machinery, for High Point is first a city of industry, and its inhabitants are a population of skilled and semi-skilled factory workers.*[170]

In 1960, High Point stood in sixth place among the largest cities in the state, its population having soared to 62,000 through aggressive annexation of surrounding areas.[171] During the 1960s, the city grew by only 1.9 percent, to 63,259. This period is characterized as one of consolidation of established industries, such as furniture and hosiery; development of new industries related to furniture and hosiery, such as chemicals, yachts and commercial photography; and investment in civic institutions that provided increased opportunity in education, healthcare and recreation. In recognition of this spirit of improvement and cooperation in solving critical local issues, the city was designated an All-American City by the National Civic League in 1963, the fourth such citation in North Carolina.[172]

With increased wealth came large-scale social and civic projects, like public housing projects and the placement below grade of the railroad tracks through the center of the downtown. The city also enjoyed the creative energy of designers and architects drawn by the region's prosperity. Local architects such as Robert Conner, Tyson Ferree, William Freeman, Clayton Mays and Leon Schute designed a body of contemporary work that complemented the commissions of regional and national architects Fred Babcock, William Henley Deitrick, Edward Loewenstein, Odell and Associates and Edward Durrell Stone. Examples of their work remain as hallmarks of their times, reflecting new approaches to architectural theory, the growing professionalism of the field and the globalization of building design.

Commercial Architecture

The financial depression that followed the stock market crash of 1929 stifled downtown development until the late 1930s, when construction resumed at a reduced pace. Two notable Art Deco office buildings remain standing to exemplify the period, both designed by High Point architect Tyson Ferree.[173] The *High Point Enterprise* Building, erected at 309 North Main Street in 1935 as the home of the city's newspaper, is among High Point's best examples of the style. Originally a two-story building with a stepped gable parapet, it presents a façade sheathed in limestone and stylized pilasters suggestive of a classical portico. The addition of a third floor around 1950 entailed a reinterpretation of the stepped gable parapet roofline. Other features, such as a stylized cornice, front door surround with flanking, arched sidelights and a stylized entablature, continue the Art Deco theme. The two-story Professional Building erected in the late 1930s at the corner of South Main Street and Green Drive combines brick with classically inspired sandstone trim. Soaring stylized pilasters coupled with a high crown of stepped forms centered over the entryways give the building a decidedly vertical emphasis.

Horizontal in form with emphasis on rounded corners and fluid details, the Streamline Moderne style of architecture grew out of the Art Deco movement, with inspiration from sleek steamships of the period. One of High Point's best examples of the style is the Modern Upholstery Company at 1101 Greensboro Road, an unusually high-style example of a suburban commercial building featuring rounded corners with glass brick inserts, a yellow brick façade and a distinctive curved wall at the entryway. Built in 1955, this building took advantage of its location along the well-traveled Greensboro–High Point Road to attract attention and convey a progressive image to passersby.[174]

After World War II, office construction in downtown High Point slowed as development shifted to suburban or rural areas of the city. Shopping patterns also changed as retail development began to relocate away from downtown north and south along Main Street. Commercial strip development gradually replaced

College Village Shopping Center. *Courtesy of the High Point Museum, High Point, North Carolina,* High Point Enterprise *Collection.*

Modern Period and Civil Rights Era, 1930–1975

the streetscapes of formerly upper- and middle-income housing along main thoroughfares, offering access to automobile-bound shoppers. College Village Shopping Center began a new chapter in High Point's retail history when it opened in the city's northern suburbs in 1959. Located at the intersection of East Lexington and North Centennial Avenues, the twenty-store, 133,000-square-foot center developed by Curtis Smithdeal drew shoppers from downtown with tenants such as mass-merchandisers W.T. Grant and F.W. Woolworth's, grocers Winn-Dixie and Kroger, druggist Eckerd, Smith Dry Cleaners, women's clothier the Diana Shop and the College Village Barber Shop. Shoppers enjoyed canopy-covered walkways, mercury vapor lights, air conditioning and the promise that none of the one thousand parking spaces were more than 360 feet from stores.[175] In 1960, Southgate Shopping Center followed the lead established by College Village. Smithdeal developed a 100,000-square-foot center at South Main Street and West Fairfield Road that contained a Big Bear food market.[176]

Heeding German architect Mies van der Rohe's proclamation that "less is more," many designers sought to simplify the appearance of buildings by reducing or eliminating applied ornamentation and expressing structural systems. From Mies's own designs, as well as those of Le Corbusier and Walter Gropius, came several new, internationally recognized styles, including Modern, New Formalism and Brutalism. High Point contains numerous examples of each style: the minimalist Modern style that reduces a structure to its basic parts, New Formalist designs that express rhythm in stylized colonnades and heavy Brutalist compositions that manipulate masses of poured concrete.[177]

In 1950, a 160,000-square-foot addition on the south side of the Southern Furniture Exposition Building (SFEB) nearly doubled the size of the complex. The total absence of windows in the utilitarian brick structure reduced construction costs. Other showroom buildings erected in the postwar period, including the nine-story National Furniture Mart around 1955, were similarly utilitarian, often illustrating Modern influences with utilitarian brick façades, few or no windows and architectural variety introduced primarily through the color of the brick. For example,

Bivens and Caldwell Building. *Courtesy of the High Point Museum, High Point, North Carolina,* High Point Enterprise *Collection.*

the brick for the 1952 SFEB addition is white, while the National Furniture Mart brick is orange. The trend of strictly practical showroom façades was broken in 1967 with the construction of a 375,000-square-foot addition to the SFEB known as the Green Drive Wing.[178] Designed by Freeman and Associates, the eleven-story Brutalist-style structure featured monolithic slabs of beige and brown brick in varying heights that lend an abstracted massing to the building. Bleached concrete panels and dark corrugated metal composed the Commerce Wing of 1974. The eleven-story, 800,000-square-foot building was designed by Six Associates of Asheville, also in the Brutalist style.[179]

Two notable office buildings stand on North Main Street in what had been considered countryside at the close of World War II. The Bivens and Caldwell Building at 1923 North Main Street was designed around 1957 by local firm Mays and Parks, Associates.[180] Clayton Mays and Robert Parks, both graduates of Clemson University, settled in the city the preceding year, and their design for the early computer manufacturer was one of their first major commissions. The Modernist building, sited on a prominent corner lot in a growing neighborhood of strip development, represented a new approach to architectural design in the city by giving external expression to its interior spaces through articulation of walls and structural elements using Solite masonry blocks and an innovative lighting system integrated with the ceiling joists and narrow windows.[181] Just a block away, the Bennett Advertising Building at 1813 North Main Street contributed to the growing dialogue of Modernist designs along High Point's main streets. Composed of boxed forms and banded windows by Robert Conner around 1960, the two-story building is approached on the north side by a covered drive, over which the second floor extends.[182]

Robert Conner attended Duke University and worked for the architecture firm Voorhees and Everhart from 1948 until he opened his own practice in High Point in 1956. He designed a sleek Modernist building for the Scottish Bank in 1962.[183] Rising four stories over Hayden Place, the bank is constructed of a pale concrete, with walls on the east and west interrupted by bands of windows. The main entry, aligned to take advantage of clear sightlines toward Main Street, is in a recessed two-story glazed curtain wall accentuated by bold green aggregate trim and complemented by an expanse of small green and red tiles arranged in a textile plaid pattern. A broad plain of concrete stamped with a diagonal shingle pattern extends from the entry to the northeast corner of the building.

A small but well-detailed office for the *Greensboro Daily News* at 715 North Main Street is attributed to the Greensboro architect Ed Loewenstein, who came to North Carolina in 1946 after graduating from the Massachusetts Institute of Technology.[184] The 1962 building's dark façade of rough-face stone tiles acts as a background to cut-away metal awnings and sculptural metal screens over the windows. A spire bearing an abstract relief projects beyond the parapet roofline. Colored tiles embellish the upper storefronts, and polished granite lines a small garden in front of the building. With its landscaping that offers an unexpected break in the concrete of the central business district, the building stands in contrast to its context of street-hugging storefronts built of traditional brick and stone. This small office building represents the innovative approach to architectural design celebrated in the postwar period by using new materials, structural practices and spatial arrangements.

Growing interest in downtown investment in the 1960s and 1970s led to development of two large office buildings. The four-story Wachovia Building was designed by noted Charlotte firm Odell and Associates around 1965.[185] The bank replaced the Dr. J.J. Cox Building with a notable example of New Formalist architecture, featuring a façade of strong vertical columns, a clearly articulated base, a flat roofline and buff aggregate materials. A few years later, One Plaza Center became the largest office building constructed in downtown High Point in the second half of the twentieth century. J.N. Pease and Associates of Charlotte designed the Brutalist office tower of white concrete punctuated by deep-set windows. Constructed in 1971–72 at the former site of the Elwood Hotel (at the foot of North Main Street) and rising eight floors above a below-grade plaza, the tower set a progressive tone for development of downtown High Point and redefined the appearance of the center city.

The Industrial Landscape

As experienced in earlier decades, industrial designs tended to be more utilitarian than those for commercial buildings. Though commercial buildings often beckoned some level of detail and ornamentation in order to provide scale and interest, no such frivolities were deemed necessary for industrial buildings. With the efficiency of a single-level construction and the use of small electric motors and affordable electricity, new industrial

Scottish Bank. *Courtesy of the High Point Museum, High Point, North Carolina.*

Modern Period and Civil Rights Era, 1930–1975

buildings became sprawling, climate-controlled environments with artificial lighting. As new mills were constructed with few if any windows, earlier mills were often modified by filling in their window openings with brick or cinder block and sometimes glass block, altering the mill architecture of the city.

A common model for industrial buildings of this period was a plain shell structure that housed machinery and processing equipment behind a small front office block displaying modest design elements, as exemplified by the Amos Hosiery Finishing Plant, built on Russell Street around 1963. The large white brick building adorned with evenly spaced vertical seams houses the manufacturing facility, while the smaller front office block features an entry sheathed in large masonry blocks and windows set within a glazed curtain wall. When 3M Corporation decided around 1960 to supply the region's furniture manufacturers with adhesives and finishing supplies from High Point, the company constructed a handsome office and warehouse building at 2401 Fraley Road in south High Point. The one-story warehouse is very plain, but the front office windows with cement surrounds and aggregate panels in between provide visual interest. Other features include rough-cut stone planters at the foundation and metal awnings. The site was heavily landscaped to complement the corporate setting of the surrounding post–World War II industrial park.

Civic Projects

In contrast to commercial development, civic projects received a boost in the 1930s as federal economic recovery programs disbursed money into local economies. Thanks to the Works Progress Administration, a new federal post office of Art Deco design executed in Indiana limestone was erected in 1932 on South Main Street on the site of the recently vacated High Point High School. Designed by the local firm Workman, Voorhees and Everhart with stylized reliefs of eagles, fluted columns and garlanded friezes, it replaced the 1912 post office that was considered unsuitable for expansion.

In keeping with its aim of projecting itself as a large and growing city, High Point sought to establish its own county apart from Guilford County and its seat, Greensboro. These efforts failed in one way or another throughout the first half of the twentieth century. However, in 1938 High Point succeeded in efforts to land a convenient county office with the completion of the Guilford County Office and Court Building on South Main Street. The

3M Corporation. *Courtesy of the High Point Museum, High Point, North Carolina.*

1932 U.S. Post Office. *Courtesy of the High Point Museum, High Point, North Carolina.*

Guilford County Office and Court Building. *Courtesy of the High Point Museum, High Point, North Carolina.*

courthouse is notable as the 101st courthouse in North Carolina and one of the country's few courthouses outside a county seat.[186] The construction of the second courthouse quelled High Point secessionists, since county business no longer required a long trek to downtown Greensboro, which was seventeen miles away. The building is one of the city's finest examples of Art Deco style, designed by High Point architects Louis F. Voorhees and Eccles B. Everhart with brick and sandstone sheathing and large figures representing furniture, textiles and agriculture in bold relief mounted on the classically inspired central pavilion.[187] Shortly after a new county building was erected around 1960, the 1938 building was converted to offices.

By the 1930s, problems caused by the at-grade placement of the railroad through downtown had grown intolerable. Numerous accidents were reported, and the city was effectively split in half whenever a long train stopped on its way through town. City Council directed Pittsburgh engineering firm Morris Knowles Inc. to investigate a solution to the problem.[188] The firm delivered four suggestions: 1) lowering the roadways to pass beneath the tracks; 2) elevating the tracks; 3) lowering the tracks below grade and building street bridges across them; and 4) relocation of the railway out of downtown.

The city chose the third option, and federal, state, city and private railway funds were combined to finance the massive project. Beginning in 1937 and completed ten years later, the entire project cost $1,458,714 and the lives of three workmen.[189] The concrete-walled cut, crossed by seven bridges, altered the appearance of High Point while facilitating vehicular travel by eliminating the dangerous grade crossings that bisected the city. The unifying theme of the project was the use of Streamline Moderne motifs, such as stylized fluted pilasters countered by strong horizontal courses scored into the cast concrete, which created visual interest on the retaining walls below grade level. The bridges originally featured a matching Streamline Moderne theme, with concrete abutments linked by heavy cast-iron railings. All of these have been replaced with higher bridges to accommodate new railway requirements; only the Kivett Drive Bridge remains. The Main Street Bridge replacement in 1995 replicates the original detailing.

After a lull during the 1940s and 1950s when few municipal projects were started, Robert Conner designed an innovative structure for the Washington Drive Branch of the High Point Public Library around 1960.[190] The inward-oriented structure presents pink Roman brick walls to the public streets surrounding the site. Rising one story, the walls are broken only by a ribbon of short windows placed high on the façades. Above the window band are turquoise-colored panels that rise to the roofline. The main entryway permits access from Fourth Street to a covered courtyard, richly landscaped and surrounded by generous windows. The building shelters its occupants from the noise of the surrounding city streets, yet opens into a controlled courtyard full of light and vegetation.

Civic architecture reached a pinnacle in the late 1960s with the construction of the new Municipal Building, designed by New York–based Edward Durrell Stone with local support from High Point's Leon A. Schute.[191] Stone earned an international

Modern Period and Civil Rights Era, 1930–1975

Washington Drive Branch High Point Library. *Courtesy of the High Point Museum, High Point, North Carolina.*

Masonic Lodge. *Courtesy of the High Point Museum, High Point, North Carolina.*

reputation for designing civic structures such as the 1962–63 North Carolina State Legislature Building in Raleigh, known for the dramatic integration of foliage—in this case rooftop gardens—that also characterizes his High Point design.[192]

The High Point Municipal Building consists of three horizontal planes sheathed in white marble, each six-foot-thick slab separated by bands of inset windows. In front of these bands of windows and at the periphery of each marble slab are hanging planters containing shrubs. The entire complex is topped by a pyramid sheathed in copper panels set in a parquet pattern. Interior spaces include a large lobby of white marble walls illuminated by skylights and a dramatic council chamber open to the pyramidal roof. The Municipal Building stands as one of the purest examples of New Formalism in the state, and its abstracted forms place it among the most impressive civic structures in the region.

Civic life expanded as many organizations established permanent and well-designed clubhouses. The Masonic Lodge, for example, constructed a sleek Modernist clubhouse at 453 South Main Street around 1960. The building was designed by William F. Freeman, Associates, a prolific architectural and engineering firm headquartered in the city that specialized in large-scale commercial and institutional projects throughout North Carolina and abroad. Freeman was a graduate of the School of Design at North Carolina State College. The two-story building's second floor is the main public level of the lodge, cantilevered above the first and featuring a masonry wall topped by a high band of windows screened from Main Street by an arcade of simple metal columns.[193] From this floor, "floating" stairs descend to street level, expanding and contracting to various widths as they fall. The first floor features glazed surfaces and little ornament. Two Ionic columns salvaged from a previous clubhouse and positioned to flank the foot of the front steps contrast with the building's minimalist austerity.

At nearly the same time, the YWCA moved into a new building at 112 Gatewood Avenue. Designed by High Point architect

High Point YWCA. *Courtesy of the High Point Museum, High Point, North Carolina.*

Leon Schute, who secured many institutional projects in the city, the building gives the appearance of being a one-story slab floating just above the site, with its western end cantilevered over an automobile access point and driveway.[194] The south façade of the flat-roofed structure is veiled by a cast-concrete screen, a device popularized by Edward Durrell Stone. Behind the screen are turquoise-colored spandrels topped by large plate-glass windows that permit filtered light inside the building. The New Formalist design established a new tone for Modern architecture in the city by incorporating unorthodox building techniques, forms and materials in its design.

New Public Schools and College Buildings

After Ferndale Junior High School and Brentwood School were opened in 1930 and 1931, respectively, little additional school construction took place until the 1950s. The Brentwood School, erected in 1931, is typical of its day with its Art Deco cast-concrete entrance surround and message inscribed above the door: Happy is the Man that Findeth Wisdom. An unusual chapter in the construction of public school facilities is illustrated with the Rock Gymnasium in the Allen Jay community. Made possible through a local appeal to President Franklin Delano Roosevelt, the facility was constructed in 1938 with a large amount of donated materials, including the rock used to erect its load-bearing walls.

By the time construction resumed twenty years later, schools tended to be plain and rarely taller than one story. Like industrial buildings, they were seen as having highly organized and functional spaces, with efficiencies gained by keeping all facilities on as few levels as possible. Another example of increasingly functional school buildings was the two-story Charles F. Tomlinson School on Chestnut Drive. Designed by William Henley Deitrick of Raleigh in 1950, the school included smooth-pressed brick walls, floor-to-ceiling windows and a low, flat roofline with a broad overhang.[195] Deitrick's

Tomlinson School. *Courtesy of the High Point Museum, High Point, North Carolina.*

Montlieu Avenue Elementary School. *Courtesy of the High Point Museum, High Point, North Carolina.*

High Point commissions also include the William Penn High School Auditorium of 1954 and Montlieu Avenue Elementary School of 1956.

At fledgling High Point College, nearly all of the financial gain that had been won during the 1920s was swept away in the Depression, forcing the Board of Trustees to declare

Modern Period and Civil Rights Era, 1930–1975

bankruptcy in 1934. The school persevered, however, establishing fund drives in the 1930s to erect two additional buildings, a gymnasium and a library. Both projects were financed through gifts from prominent High Point families. The Harrison Hall was dedicated in 1933 as a temporary and architecturally simple brick structure used as a gymnasium (destroyed 2005). In contrast, Wrenn Hall, built in 1937 as the college's library, maintained the Georgian appearance of the campus. The masonry building features an elaborate elliptical transom window and a broken ogee pediment above the main entry, a full entablature with a modillion cornice and parapetted end gables with chimneys. By 1944, all capital debt had been retired through numerous fundraising activities, and the school again stood on solid ground. Enrollment surged, and the school won accreditation by the Southern Association of Colleges and Schools in 1951.

With its financial problems in the past, the college looked forward to new building programs. Post–World War II building projects departed drastically from historical antecedents by looking to progressive Modernist styles for inspiration. Two significant examples of the Modern period stand on the campus, both designed by architect Leon Schute. Haworth Hall of Science of 1967 and the McPherson Campus Center of 1972 share certain characteristics, including common bond brick walls accented by concrete pilasters flanked by narrow windows.[196] The rooflines of both buildings are accentuated by a wide band of concrete, and main entry points are signified by heavy concrete lintels. Both buildings meld New Formalist designs with Brutalist architecture within the context of the campus's traditional red brick and white trim vocabulary, yet take a broad interpretation of size, scale and form. Such experiments in contemporary architecture were popular in the 1960s and 1970s, but more recent building projects on campus have embraced neo-traditional design. In 1991, the college became a university.

Religious Institutions

Religious institutions continued the pace of expansion set in the early twentieth century by rapid population growth and diversification of faiths. The general pattern of expanding to larger and more substantial sanctuaries in the suburbs that began in the 1920s among established Christian denominations continued with recovery from the Depression. Congregations

First Baptist Church. *Courtesy of the High Point Museum, High Point, North Carolina.*

were often anxious to follow their members out of the inner city to areas with undeveloped acreage that permitted multiple buildings in park-like settings and the ever important on-site parking spaces. This trend continued into the 1960s, by which point several notable and impressive landmarks had been erected in High Point's expanding reaches.

One institution that contradicted this trend, however, was the First Baptist Church on North Main Street, which remained downtown and erected a Colonial Revival brick church designed by Roanoke architects Eubank and Caldwell in 1941. The traditional sanctuary features a classically inspired portico topped with a high steeple. Other classical details include limestone quoins, arched windows with keystones and a broken ogee pediment above the main entry. For the First Baptist Church, the issue of downtown parking was resolved with the paving of adjacent Tate Park in 1952.

Catholics participated in the city's postwar suburban development when they built their first High Point church, Immaculate Heart of Mary Church, on Montlieu Avenue in 1947. The sanctuary takes on a simplified Neo-Gothic appearance, its brick façade accentuated by tall, squared windows and a low-pitched slate roof. Detail is concentrated in the two-and-a-half-story tower with a pointed arch entry, tall windows trimmed in sandstone and a metal spire. The church grounds now house a private school by the same name and include playing fields, mature trees and parking.

In 1953, High Point Friends Meeting (formerly Central Friends) became the first city congregation to relocate from the noise and congestion of Main Street to a secluded suburban location on Quaker Lane. Architect Howard Olive of Voorhees and Everhart designed a staid and traditional Georgian Revival meetinghouse on a peaceful knoll just west of center city. Graced by a Tuscan portico and clear glass windows topped by flat arches, the simple structure and generously landscaped campus of High Point Friends Meeting provided a touchstone to the past in an increasingly modern city.[197]

When the Wesley Memorial Methodist congregation relocated from the 300 block of North Main Street to the suburbs in 1958, they constructed a sprawling complex that fused Modern and Gothic design to create a Neo-Gothic–style campus. Harold E. Wagoner, a nationally recognized church architect from Philadelphia, designed the sanctuary, chapel, offices and classrooms with assistance from Charles C. Hartmann of Greensboro. Central to the design of the expansive campus was the large sanctuary with a soaring nave, stained-glass windows by Henry Willet of Philadelphia and the tallest spire in the city.[198] The Chestnut Street complex of stone structures and lush landscaping is the last of High Point's great religious properties to demonstrate hand craftsmanship, historical precedence and monumentality.

B'Nai Israel Synagogue relocated from North Hamilton Street to a new location in the northwest suburbs off Westchester Drive around 1965. This unique Modern-style building at 1207 Kensington Drive in Emerywood Forest was designed by High Point architect Robert Conner and at once established a sense of permanence as well as progressiveness for the congregation.[199] The complex includes a large sanctuary complemented by an extended educational building to the north. The sanctuary rises to a height of two stories and is topped by a dramatically undulating roof. The concave, stuccoed façade wall bears a menorah and the name of the congregation in Hebrew.

Residential Architecture

Residential development in High Point in the mid-twentieth century followed standards set in place by Emerywood in the 1920s, primarily in the form of curvilinear streets, large lots, retention of native vegetation and adherence to strict zoning. New development could be found in all quadrants of the city, most often segregated along economic and ethnic lines and filled with housing that began to reflect unified building codes enforced through inspections.

Architectural styles chosen by High Pointers for their houses reflected the increasing housing options and variety of design available to most Americans of the period. The availability

Modern Period and Civil Rights Era, 1930–1975

of diverse plans and styles is illustrated in popular media, including the *High Point Enterprise*, which published renderings of contemporary houses each Sunday. Functional trends included inclusion of a garage to house automobiles within the family home; increasing interest in strengthening indoor-outdoor relationships by using elements such as patios and picture windows; and a greater interest in ergonomics, exemplified in single-story and split-level plans, open living spaces and low-maintenance decoration. Gradually, styles departed from the historical influences of early America and Europe, and designers began to embrace styles that incorporated simple lines, natural materials and respect for natural setting. Many in High Point's design community led this shift by erecting houses in cutting-edge styles that became prototypes for others in the city.

Regency Style

The Regency style was a brief but elegant update of the Colonial Revival style. A popular choice for residential design during the 1930s and 1940s, the style features low-pitched roofs or flat rooflines, symmetrical façades and attenuated porch columns evocative of the late eighteenth-century architecture of English designer Robert Adam. High Point has a handful of Regency-style houses scattered across the city in middle- and upper-income neighborhoods. Among the best examples is a two-story brick house at 1007 Ferndale Boulevard, built by general contractor Roy Shelton. The house takes the form of a cube with a central front door sheltered by an awning of formed metal supported by metal posts, and a low-hipped roofline partially hidden by a parapet wall. Another good example is located at 1121 North Rotary Drive—another cubical brick house with a symmetrical façade centered on a main entry with details such as a brick frieze embellished with a Greek Key design and double-hung windows with wooden under-panels and shutters.

Increasingly, residences eschewed the historical connotations of pre–World War II period revivals in favor of minimalist designs that looked forward instead of backward. Regency and Ranch styles were the first residential modes to presage this trend, culminating with the highly simplified and Modern designs of the 1960s and 1970s. This trend crossed social lines as the finest homes in Emerywood often shared common treatments with middle-income and worker housing. By the mid-twentieth century, some high-income clients sought to illustrate status through progressive minimalist designs that harmonized with nature, in contrast to the celebration of grandeur seen in period revival styles a generation earlier.

Minimal Traditional Style

As both Frank Lloyd Wright's horizontal designs and Art Deco's streamlined features permeated America's architectural tastes, interest in the historical detail of Eclectic Revival houses began to diminish. Popular housing styles turned away from the period cottages of the 1920s and 1930s and looked toward the progressive designs of Ranch houses. Minimal Traditional houses may be viewed as the transition between Eclectic houses and the era of the Ranch house in their simpler forms and minimal detailing. The stifling effect of the Great Depression was deep but quick, reaching bottom in High Point in 1933. Residential construction resumed by 1935, when new neighborhoods opened across the city, many full of Minimal Traditional houses, which were most popular from the 1930s to the 1950s. Parcels left undeveloped in Emerywood were purchased and developed in the 1930s with Minimal Traditional houses, including several on Rotary Drive, Ferndale Avenue, Arbordale Drive and East Farriss Avenue. These houses most often are one story and usually feature a forward-facing gable, frequently complemented by a prominent chimneystack. Detail tends to be restrained, often limited to an arched doorway or front porch stoop. Examples of Minimal Traditional houses are found across High Point, as exemplified by 1300 Greenway Drive (circa 1935), 701 West Farriss Avenue (circa 1945) and 507 Sunset Drive (circa 1960). These one- and one-and-a-half-story brick and frame houses feature such details as large picture windows, front-facing chimneys and half-width front porches.

Ranch houses. *Courtesy of the High Point Museum, High Point, North Carolina.*

Ranch Houses

High Point's earliest Ranch houses were constructed in the 1930s, and the style remained popular in the city well into the 1980s. Ranch houses are a single story, but often have two levels of living space by incorporating a full finished basement that is frequently above ground on the rear, due to the slope of the lot. Early instances of the form adapted a Colonial motif, such as the house at 1106 Forest Hill Drive. Constructed in the 1930s, it is adorned with a broken pediment over the front door, a heavy modillion cornice and segmental arches between the side porch posts, with the Ranch form present in the long, unbroken roofline of the one-story house.

In the 1950s and 1960s, the Ranch house returned to its low, horizontal roots in the American Plains, as exemplified by the one-story brick house standing at 510 Emerywood Drive with wide overhanging eaves, very low-pitched hipped roofs and alternating expanses of masonry and glass walls. Landscape is well integrated into the site and foundation plantings maximize privacy.

International and Modern Styles

Initially promoted by a small group of European and American architects, International-style buildings began to appear in North Carolina in the 1930s.[200] Most examples of the style were architect-designed, though many were also inspired by plans advertised in shelter magazines. The style is not common in High Point, but a small number of residents commissioned examples worthy of mention. Like their commercial counterparts, International-style houses are characterized by flat roofs, unornamented walls of brick or stucco and windows—usually metal casements—that are often shifted toward the corners of the building. W.K. Whitsell, an industrial arts teacher at High Point Central High School, directed his class in building an International-style house at 1101 Council Street. Constructed in 1950, the two-story concrete house is notable for the absence of a pitched roof.[201] Walls are sheathed in stucco and feature windows at the exterior corners. The house has always been a bit of an

Frank Dalton House. *Courtesy of the High Point Museum, High Point, North Carolina, High Point Enterprise Collection.*

oddity in High Point, but recently appreciation has grown for its unusual design.

Several architect-designed houses built in High Point during the 1950s exhibit flat or canted rooflines, use of stained or natural siding, broad expanses of glazing and a strong orientation to exterior spaces like courtyards, patios or decks. Many of these houses are clustered near High Point University and scattered throughout Emerywood as infill. The former group, including residences standing at 1001, 1003 and 1007 West College Drive, are notable in having been erected by building contractor Everette Hill in the early 1950s.[202]

The local firm Mays and Parks, Associates, attained a reputation in High Point for progressive and modern designs. Among their first commissions were residences for Judge Byron Hayworth at 902 Fairway Drive and Sloan Gibson at 601 Emerywood Drive, both in 1958.[203] The two houses were designed from the inside out in response to their sites and took into consideration views, sun exposure and challenging topography. Unlike the surrounding period cottages of a generation earlier, both houses are distinctly individual, responding to the uniqueness of their sites without historical references. The Hayworth House consists of two low-pitched gabled units joined by a glazed courtyard; the Gibson House responds to its topography with a long, single story that is stepped downward to the north to follow the contour of the land. Formal spaces are situated toward the upper portion of the house; private spaces are to the rear, made more private by orienting windows toward a secluded courtyard. Pink salmon brick was the choice of the owner, while metallic robin's egg blue panels were the choice of designer Robert Parks. Broad overhanging eaves shade windows with an eye toward energy efficiency in the South's temperate climate.

Around 1963, women's fashion retailer Ruth Ellis commissioned an eye-catching one-story house at 605 Hillcrest Drive from Mays and Parks.[204] Upon completion, the house was featured in a national shelter magazine.[205] The architecture of the house is highly progressive, with a blend of exposed wooden beams and wide eaves inspired by Asian architecture, intimate exterior spaces partially enclosed by framing members and a textured brick wall. The public interior spaces flow between each other and are oriented toward exterior views carefully chosen for privacy. Parking in the front of the property uses circulation patterns integrated into the landscape design. As a result, the house stands in sharp contrast to the traditional houses that characterize the neighborhood.

Some of High Point's most notable progressive residential architecture of the 1950s includes houses that architects designed for themselves. Robert Conner's 1956 house for his family at 1405 Emerywood Drive blends with its forested environment through its western red cedar sheathing and low roofline. On the interior, windows enjoy broad vistas into the woods, and walls are built of historic bricks salvaged from a demolished downtown building.[206] In contrast, William F. Freeman's residence at 1403 Rockspring Road is juxtaposed against its deeply wooded site as a cubical form with a flat roofline and walls of alternating panels of Philippine mahogany, masonry piers and glass.

Two distinctive architect-designed houses represent High Point's Modernist residential architecture of the 1960s and early 1970s. Freeman's striking 1964 residence for veneer broker Mont L. Sechrest exhibits expanses of glass and masonry piers that punctuate the roofline at differing heights. Two wings, one for the owners and the other for guests, are linked by common living and dining spaces. Decorative veneers that adorn interior spaces reflect the occupation of the owner. The entire ensemble overlooks a quiet courtyard with a swimming pool and exotic desert landscaping of stones and cacti.[207]

As the home furnishings industry made High Point increasingly influential in the world of design, architects from outside North Carolina sometimes received commissions in the city. Salt Lake City architect Fred Babcock was tapped to design a residence for contemporary furniture designer Thayer Coggin and his wife Dot in 1972.[208] The low, horizontal building includes high-banded windows toward the street that contrast with vast glazed windows to the rear, overlooking the Emerywood golf course. Babcock's design blends with the rolling terrain and revival architecture of Emerywood through muted brick tones, lush landscaping and a copper roof.

Multifamily Development

In the 1930s, High Point began to enjoy greater options in multifamily housing. Expanding upon early models constructed by J.P. Redding and A.E. Taplin, modern apartment buildings in the city offered ever-increasing density, amenities and open space with apartment blocks such as the circa 1933 ECKER APARTMENTS on North Main, distinguished by its classic Art Deco motifs in cast cement at the main doorways. The 1935 ROWELLA, one block south on North Main Street, contains Art Deco appointments and a central courtyard that is landscaped with grass and feature shrubs.[209] In contrast, the WILLIAM AND MARY APARTMENTS at 620–628 North Hamilton Street (circa 1938) were more utilitarian in their appearance, said to have been built with recycled materials. These brick apartments are composed of five freestanding units, each connected to the next by an archway.

OAKWOOD COURT at 117 Oakwood Street, along with ROWELLA, WILLIAM AND MARY and the MADISON AND MONROE (destroyed), were all constructed by Rowland and Ella Gantt, a husband and wife team who developed and managed several properties across the city.[210] All were designed on an urban model that assumed high-density projects would be constructed adjacent to their sites. Apartment buildings were inward-looking arrangements, such as the courtyard-focused ROWELLA, or addressed the street, as exemplified by the WILLIAM AND MARY APARTMENTS. Many of the apartments had wooden garages, few of which remain today.

EMERYWOOD COURT on North Main Street was completed in 1939 adjacent to Emerywood. When constructed, the ten-unit complex held the best reputation in town, and attracted high-income clients. The complex is modeled on the garden apartment prototype initiated by housing reformers in New York in the 1920s, and features three-story brick apartment buildings with metal casement windows encircling a quiet central courtyard.[211] Aligned close to Main Street, this project provided a well-planned, urban prototype for High Pointers. The buildings display classical motifs around main doorways, a balustrade relief on the parapet and brick quoins at their corners.

In contrast to the urban model of EMERYWOOD COURT, HILLCREST MANOR was built in 1949 north of Lexington Avenue in the form of two-story garden apartments.[212] Developer Curtis Smithdeal took inspiration from the "garden city" movement and the ideal of informal landscaping established with Emerywood. He commissioned a design incorporating masonry units with traditional side-gabled roofs arranged casually within a suburban landscape that includes scattered parking areas, broad lawns and mature trees and landscaping. HILLCREST MANOR superceded EMERYWOOD COURT as High Point's most desirable apartment complex when it opened.

Built in 1961, the WEST LOCKE APARTMENTS continued the garden-style theme but discarded traditional design in favor of a contemporary composition.[213] Located at 511 Westwood Avenue, the regular rectangular structures show the influence of International style or Modern architecture in their masonry exteriors and flat roofs. Parking is allocated beneath the buildings and veiled by a decorative masonry screen. Standing in stark contrast to their traditional residential neighbors on the edge of downtown, these strikingly modern apartments represent global ideals in design making their way to the local level in High Point.

High Point's Housing Authority was established in 1940, the first in Guilford County. The department borrowed funds from the United States Housing Administration to clear areas that qualified under federal guidelines as slums and redevelop neighborhoods of modern apartments in their place. The local authority was loaned $1,770,000 by the federal government, and the project moved forward in accordance with segregation laws of the time, with two "separate but equal" projects on the basis of need. On the east side of the city a site was selected near William Penn High School for black citizens. This complex of 200 apartments was named for Reverend Daniel Brooks, a popular Methodist minister best remembered for negotiating the sale of land that later became William Penn High School. The prominent local architect Tyson Ferree patterned the design for DANIEL BROOKS HOMES on mid-nineteenth-century English worker housing, with brick walls, steeply pitched roofs and numerous chimneys (since removed). The second project was larger—a 250-unit complex located between Asheboro, Park and East Russell Streets. Reserved for white citizens, the site was named for Clara Ione Cox, minister of Springfield Friends Meeting and champion of social issues in High Point. Voorhees and Everhart designed CLARA COX HOMES in the Colonial Revival style and arranged the units along a gently curving road network, with ample parking and landscaped lawns that contrasted with the traditional grid street plan of eastern High Point.[214] By mid-century, the garden city movement expressed decades earlier in Emerywood was brought to these older districts in order to decrease the urban and industrial density of the city.

RECREATION

Before the dedication of Blair Park in 1931, active recreational spaces in High Point consisted of private lawns and the golf course at the country club in fashionable Emerywood.[215] In the years after the establishment of Blair Park, recreational space grew quickly. In 1934, City Lake Park near Jamestown was developed around the city's new water source. Federal funds helped to construct the park, which included picnic areas, a zoo and the largest outdoor swimming pool in North Carolina at the time. Adjacent to the pool, an extensive bathhouse with a gymnasium on the second story was constructed in a Modern style with streamlined details and clean lines. To the east of the pool, an amphitheater had a seating capacity of 2,500 people. Ball fields, a playground and a rose arbor promised to make the park "the playground of the Piedmont…to attract thousands of picnickers here from distant points."[216] In the early 1940s, with encouragement from Jamestown patron and County Commissioner William Ragsdale, two early nineteenth-century buildings on the park grounds that were associated with early Jamestown were restored and opened as museums.

In order to complement the proliferation of parks restricted for use by High Point's white citizens, the city established Washington Terrace in 1935 for use by black citizens. The twenty-seven-acre park defines the eastern end of the Washington Street neighborhood and provides a pastoral and scenic setting for recreational activities. The park originally contained a playground, as well as a swimming pool, wading pool, bathhouse, viewing terrace and many athletic facilities.[217] The pool was the first African American facility of its size in North Carolina, but Washington Terrace did not meet the caliber of City Lake Park in terms of amenities.

To serve the growing neighborhoods of northeastern High Point, including Montlieu Avenue, Sherrod Park and Johnson Street, additional recreational space was developed by the 1950s as Armstrong Park along the banks of a stream that parallels East Parkway and East Farris Avenues. The site provided a natural setting for recreation and beauty adjacent to Kirkman Park Elementary School. Neighborhoods on the south side of the city benefited from the completion of Goldston Park in 1951, containing a softball field, basketball court, horseshoe courts, picnic tables, a barbeque pit and a playground.

City Lake Park facility. *Courtesy of the High Point Museum, High Point, North Carolina.*

Turn of the Twenty-first Century

High Point is fortunate to have had early leaders who valued its architectural past. Beginning in the 1920s, proponents of historic preservation have worked toward recognizing and preserving the region's earliest architecture. Ranging from Quaker meetinghouses to gold processing mills, eighteenth-century residences to early furniture factories, conservation-oriented citizens, developers and historians have used a broad variety of tools to raise awareness of historic sites.

High Point has a small but important collection of nineteenth-century historic sites and a wealth of twentieth-century historic resources. The city contains some of North Carolina's most comprehensive collections of twentieth-century residential architecture, including Craftsman bungalows, Eclectic-style estates, period cottages and International-style designs. These buildings document the diverse complexion of the city and provide High Point with its own unique sense of place. Many of these buildings were designed by architects recognized on the regional, national and even international level. The Neo-Gothic, Art Deco and New Formalist designs for churches, municipal buildings and educational facilities are testimony to the city's progressive image that patrons and designers wished to convey to visitors and future generations.

High Point has never shied away from good design, and at times has been quite daring in embracing contemporary styles that are unusual in this generally conservative state. Through the presence of the International Home Furnishings Market, the city has benefited from progressive international designers who address a visiting audience of stylish and informed furnishing-industry patrons more than the native population; yet High Pointers traditionally are quick to embrace new and foreign designs as their own.

Through publications, exhibits at the High Point Historical Museum and downtown revitalization efforts, citizens of High Point are rekindling interest in their historic sites. At the same time, new challenges will test residents, including attitudes about mid- and late twentieth-century architecture, adaptive use of historic places and the promotion of good contemporary design. Residents, scholars, designers and visitors will gain greater insight about the people of this city and its history by looking around them and learning about the significance embodied in the architectural environment of High Point.

PART II.
INVENTORY OF HISTORIC PROPERTIES

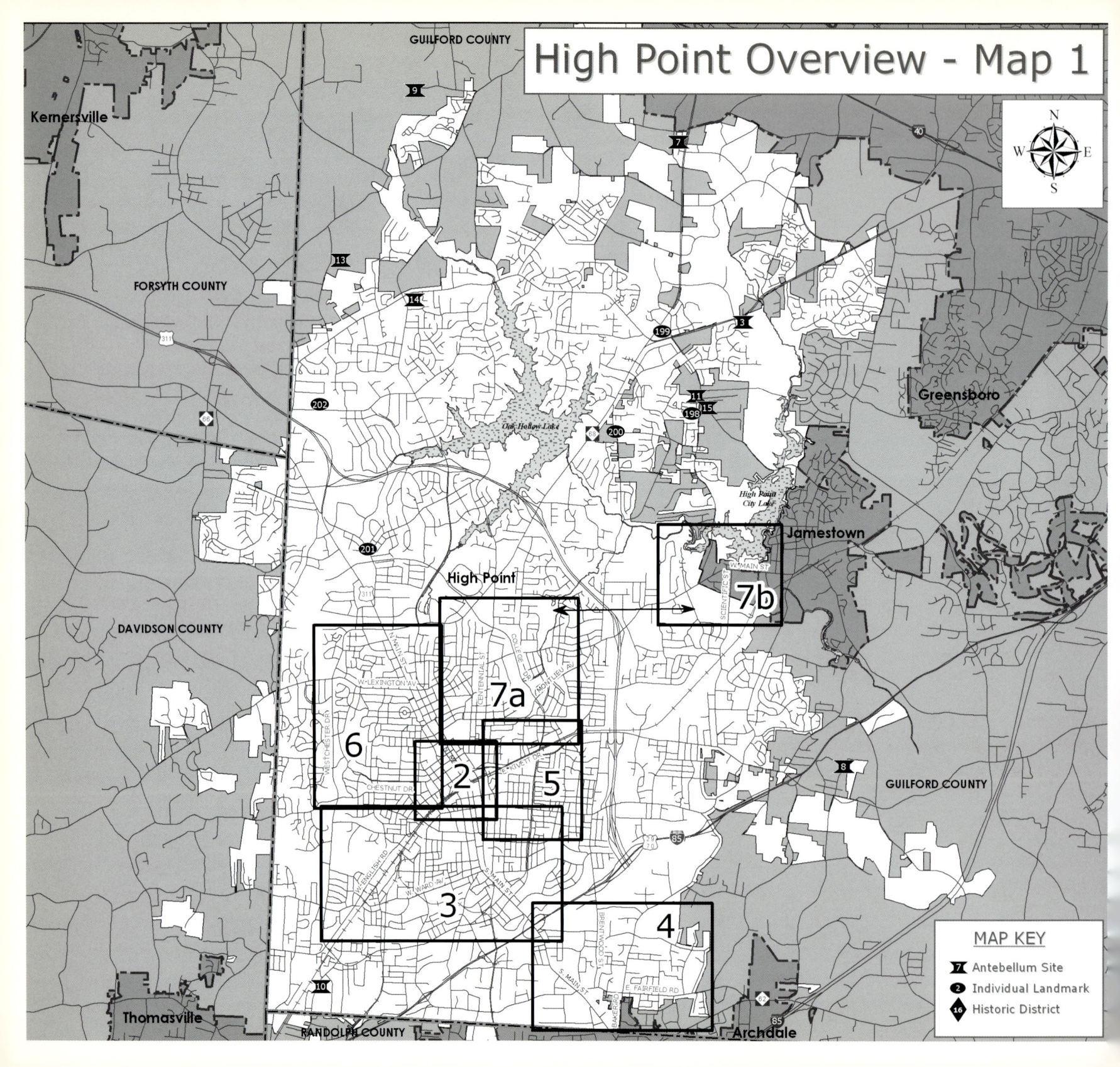

High Point Overview - Map 1

MAP KEY
- 7 Antebellum Site
- 2 Individual Landmark
- 16 Historic District

INTRODUCTION

High Point enjoys hundreds of historic buildings that document and chronicle the history of the city from early settlement to the present day. Though the city occasionally is perceived as not having much history, investigation reveals the opposite is true. Buildings scattered across High Point's landscape contribute to a better understanding of how people before us worked, socialized, worshipped and celebrated. Their achievements and their tribulations can be read from High Point's man-made environment like a great tapestry, and untold associations are revealed through architecture, design and style.

This section is a selection of a number of buildings recorded as part of a comprehensive survey of historic sites. Some sites are better documented than others, as many of High Point's earliest places have deep histories that extend over two hundred years. In contrast, there may be little known about exemplary buildings from the mid-twentieth century, but these lapses in information might encourage future research.

Selecting the structures and sites to be included in this inventory was quite difficult. Limits on the scale of this publication meant that numerous extant residences, offices, schools and neighborhoods, as well as destroyed buildings, could not be presented in the following pages. The sites included were chosen as representatives of architectural styles, types or forms. Through detailed description of exemplary buildings, the reader may glean information applicable to comparable sites of interest that are not portrayed in this book.

Buildings are often named for their primary occupants, and details of the achievements of these people at or near the time of construction of the structure are provided when possible. A full account of life achievements of each occupant would extend this book to an unwieldy size, so context has been limited to provide insights on the conception and early use of these places.

Nearly all sites remain in private ownership; the vast majority serves as homes and working businesses. Though all historic buildings contribute to the special sense of community enjoyed universally, enthusiasts should respect the privacy of their owners, as well as all laws regarding trespassing. Some locations have been withheld to discourage vandalism.

The evaluation of the significance of place is an ongoing process, subject to the values of the community, the surveyor and popular culture. Assessment frequently is not definitive; hopefully the information herein will motivate readers to undertake additional investigation of historic properties in High Point for future survey publications.

The inventory of sites includes a selection of antebellum buildings that predate the establishment of High Point in 1859. Sites and structures built after the establishment of High Point are organized geographically by quadrant, then by neighborhood and then by street and number. Each site number corresponds with a numeral found on quadrant maps of the city. Sometimes neighborhoods appear as numbered entries while other numerals represent individual sites.

All images found in this section are courtesy of the Office of Archives and History, North Carolina Department of Cultural Resources.

GL signifies local landmark designation through the Guilford County Historic Preservation Commission.
HD indicates historic district designation by the City of High Point.
NR denotes a site listed on the National Register of Historic Places.
SL specifies sites listed on the National Register Study List and possibly eligible for the National Register, pending further study.
EA marks properties that enjoy protection by a preservation easement.

SITES BUILT PRIOR TO THE CIVIL WAR, 1750–1861

Numerous hamlets were located in southwestern Guilford County before High Point was established in 1859, many of them associated with members of the Society of Friends. Communities such as Jamestown, Westminster (near Deep River Friends Meeting), Browntown (northeastern Davidson County), Bloomington (near Springfield Friends Meeting) and Pennfield (in Davidson County) created a network that supported a primarily agrarian economy. Elements of that landscape that remain today are rare and fleeting, but provide insights into how inhabitants of what later became High Point lived. Remaining farmhouses, places of worship and occasional commercial and educational buildings speak to the isolation of the Piedmont before transportation into the region was improved. Dramatic changes occurred after the Plank Road and the railroad transected the area in the 1850s, demonstrated by a general improvement in building construction and style.

1. HALEY HOUSE
1859 East Lexington Avenue
GL 1982, NR 1971

The Haley House is the earliest surviving documented structure on its original foundation in Guilford County. In spite of its importance as an example of early Piedmont architecture, relatively little is known of its builders, Phebe Wall and John Haley. Phebe Wall's family moved to North Carolina from Concord Meeting, Pennsylvania. The Walls were Quakers, and Phebe continued her involvement with the Society of Friends, being a charter member of Deep River Monthly Meeting when it was founded in 1778. John Haley's background before marrying Phebe remains unknown.

The Haleys completed their two-story Flemish bond brick house in 1786, a date commemorated by a stone medallion placed in the west gable of the house. The south-facing building was constructed along the lines of the Quaker plan, a floor plan traditionally used by members of the Society of Friends. The form was characterized by a large all-purpose room with two smaller twin chambers located to one side. Guilford County contains one of the best collections of Quaker-plan homes in the nation.

John Haley had a distinguished career, serving as county road commissioner, sheriff and a blacksmith before his death sometime between 1809 and 1813. The house was sold to James Wheeler in 1818 and later to Jonathan Welch in 1838. During this period, a wood-frame wing (no longer extant) may have been added to the west of the house.

Welch turned the house into an "ordinary," a term Southerners used for taverns. Its prominent location alongside the Petersburg to Salisbury stagecoach road (now Lexington Avenue) made it a natural choice for such an establishment. Though the ordinary closed around the time of the Civil War, the house remained in the Welch family for 110 years. The house was sold in 1943 to the Donald W. Conrad Agency, which extensively renovated it. By the mid-1960s, developers threatened to demolish the Haley House in order to construct an apartment complex.

Mary Lib Joyce and John Bivins grew alarmed at the thought of losing High Point's earliest property. In November 1966, the City of High Point purchased the building and the High Point Historical Society was established to restore the building and erect the High Point Historical Museum on its grounds. Based on remaining physical evidence, the house was returned to the appearance it had at the time of John Haley's death. The site was inscribed on the National Register in 1971, and restoration was largely completed by the mid-1970s. At that time, the medallion in the gable was incorporated into the design of the city's official seal.

2. Hoggatt House
1859 East Lexington Avenue

A 2006 scientific study of the Hoggatt House indicates that the trees used to erect the main section of the log house were felled between 1799 and 1801. Though Hoggatt family elders moved to the area around the present-day intersection of Phillips Avenue and Rotary Drive around 1752, the house was likely constructed by their son Joseph in 1801. A one-room log addition was constructed adjacent to the house by Mahlon Hoggatt in 1824 and exhibits many features similar to the main section. The site remained in the Hoggatt family for 110 years. It was removed to its current site in 1973 for use as part of High Point Museum and Historical Park. The house suffered from a fire in December 2004, but was restored and reopened a year later.

Sites Built Prior to the Civil War, 1750–1861

Constructed originally as a single-room residence, the Hoggatt House features a stone foundation, a loft and a wood shingle roof. Other details include a large cooking fireplace, small window openings and hand-manufactured hardware, such as hinges and nails. This one-room structure was expanded by a second pen, or room, in 1824. Roughly dimensioned logs are laid horizontally and joined at each corner using a V-notch technique. Corner joinery represents a familiar and often used fastening technique in the Piedmont that traces its roots to southeastern Pennsylvania. Logs were "chinked" using a combination of wood shims, slabs of tree bark and native clay, sometimes mixed with grass and twigs.

3. Deep River Cabin
5209 Wendover Avenue/Deep River Park

This single-story log and frame house is located within Deep River Park and is thought to have been constructed as early as 1800. The south-facing building is a well-preserved example of a saddlebag plan, so named for two equal-size rooms flanking a central chimney stack. The easternmost room is likely the oldest, featuring V-notched logs chinked with wood slats and clay, few windows, a loft and a segmental-arched mantelpiece around a large cooking fireplace.

Though the origins of the house are not known, its first owner is thought to be Levin Stack, a maker of Jamestown Rifles, whose shop was located just north of the residence. The chain of title is unclear until 1871, when George Borum bought the property from the trustees of William Collins. The surrounding property was part of the extensive hunting preserve of Clarence Mackey, who had a lodge on Guilford-Jamestown Road in the 1910s.

4. Jamestown Indulged Meeting House
602 West Main Street, Jamestown/City Lake Park
NR 1973

Located within High Point's City Lake Park, the meetinghouse is among the oldest religious buildings in the Piedmont and is reputed to be the oldest Quaker meetinghouse in the state. It was likely constructed in the 1820s as a convenient place of worship when weather or high water prevented neighborhood Friends from attending Deep River Friends Meeting, several miles to the north. The building was constructed of brick in traditional meetinghouse form. Exterior details were unusually proficient for the period, surpassing standards for most residences in the county at the time. These elements include segmental-arched windows, board and batten doors, Flemish bond brickwork and a handsome corbelled cornice. The interior is simple, with plaster walls, wide plank flooring and exposed ceiling joists.

Historian Martha Robbins Tilden recalled the meetinghouse's use after the Civil War as a school funded by Northern financier George Peabody. The nearby cemetery is said to contain graves of some early Quakers, as well as members of a later primitive Baptist church. Restored by the city in 1934 for use as a museum, the building stands as one of the first preservation projects in the city.

5. Mendenhall Store
602 West Main Street, Jamestown/City Lake Park
NR 1973

Centered in the midst of the early village of Jamestown was the Mendenhall Store. Built by Richard Mendenhall in 1824, the two-story brick building resembles structures typical of the Philadelphia region more than anything in North Carolina. Such similarity may be for good reason, since Mendenhall spent time in Chester County, Pennsylvania, as an adolescent. There he likely cultivated an eye for Pennsylvania architecture and designed his store accordingly. His circa 1811 residence across the street is operated as the Mendenhall Plantation by the Historic Jamestown Society.

Architecturally, the store is remarkable for its quality of construction and high level of design. The Flemish bond brick walls are elevated above the ground by a stone foundation that encloses a full cellar, rare for Piedmont buildings. The façade of the store includes twelve-light sash windows topped by jack arches. A corbelled cornice tops the façade, complemented by parapet gables that rise above the roof and culminate in tall chimneys.

It is possible that Mendenhall envisioned other stores with side gables and two or three stories along both sides of Main Street (then called Federal Street), much like a period Pennsylvania town, sporting large windows, elaborate brickwork and stoops. He likely used brick not simply because it was a superior building material, but also because it was considered fireproof in urban settings.

Little is known of the store's history. Mendenhall was a tanner, and it is assumed that he ran his tanning business from the store building. His home was (and still is) across the street from the store, and the two buildings demonstrate the two most important facets of Mendenhall's life: home and work. This oldest commercial building in High Point was restored in 1934 by the city for use as a museum and now serves as commercial space.

Sites Built Prior to the Civil War, 1750–1861

6. Andrew Lindsay House
location withheld

Milton D. Forsyth's detailed 1992 report on this site documents it as the first residence of William Buis (Bewes), a Dutch or German Palatine settler of the early 1750s. Buis operated an ordinary (or tavern) at the site that was later sold to Robert Lindsay. During Lindsay's ownership, the house served as the original meeting place of the Guilford County Court from 1771 through 1774. Lindsay improved the site and developed the surrounding two-thousand-acre plantation before his death in 1801. His son Andrew Lindsay inherited the core of the plantation and added to the acreage again before his death in 1844.

The house that remains standing just upstream from the Deep River is a remnant of the once rambling plantation house that contained the Great Hall, used for the first county court. The hall no longer exists, having been destroyed in 1926. The remaining two-story portion of the house likely dates from the improvement by Andrew Lindsay and his wife Elizabeth Dick in the 1820s. Investigation completed on the house by Winston-Salem architects Charles Phillips and Joseph Oppermann revealed construction techniques typical of the 1820s, including Federal-style moldings, plaster walls and early machine-cut nails.

The Lindsay House is quite important as the most tangible reminder of High Point's largest plantation. Few similar early complexes remain in Guilford and surrounding counties. The site once included mature English boxwoods, a grove of mulberry trees with a silk mill, a formal garden, slave quarters and burial grounds for slaves and family members. Of this complex, the only remaining evidence above ground is the house and cemeteries. Surviving period detail is lavish and exemplary of a fine early nineteenth-century plantation house, including narrow beaded siding, cornice, brick nogging within the timber frame walls, plaster finish, chair rail and evidence of an enclosed corner staircase. A portion of a six-panel door survives, grained to resemble mahogany.

7. Jonathan Harris House
3921 Sedgebrook Street
SL 1976

Jonathan Harris was born in 1806 in the Deep River community, possibly a third-generation member of Deep River Friends. In 1835, he married Louisa Stuart and purchased two tracts of fertile bottomland to compose a farm of 178 acres. Likely the Harris House was constructed at this time. Harris is best remembered for being charged with treason for distributing the antislavery publication *Compendium of the Impending Crisis of the South*. He was eventually found not guilty and later was elected to serve in the North Carolina House of Representatives from 1870 to 1872.

The two-story, three-bay log structure is oriented to the south and perpendicular to the public road and is arranged along the configuration of the Quaker plan. Original molded clapboards cover the log structure, and flush sheathing exists under the porch roofs. An extraordinary detail is the diagonal diaper pattern found in the brick of the main chimney, which is more common in the mid-Atlantic states and occurs infrequently in the Carolina Piedmont.

Interior trim in the Harris House is far more substantial than other Guilford County houses of the time. Details include high-paneled mantels and chair rails with Grecian ovolo, with square profiles popular in the second quarter of the nineteenth century. Interior walls are constructed of vertical planks, and the remaining corner fireplaces allude to the original floor plan. Later owner Stephen Davis was also a prominent Quaker farmer and likely added an eastern one-story frame wing of simple detail. The Harris House represents an important prototype of Quaker architecture in the American South. In 2006, the house was carefully dismantled for reconstruction on Deep River Road.

8. McCulloch Gold Mill
6328 Kivett Loop
GL 1986, NR 1979, EA

At the height of the Carolina gold rush in 1832, Cornish engineer Charles McCulloch partnered with Elizer Kersey to erect this granite structure in order to extract gold quarried from local mines and embedded within "milk quartz." The structure was modeled closely on tin engine houses found in the Cornwall section of southwestern England and features a prominent Gothic arch, thought to be among the oldest surviving such elements in the United States. The chimney was used to ventilate the gold ore smelting process, which processed recovered gold into bars that were easy to transport. Aside from the gold mill, other elements—such as a complex system of dikes, races, ore dumps and roads—surround the complex, as well as a moat and drawbridge that ensured protection of gold inventories from roaming bands of criminals. Processed gold was collected and stored at this fortified site before being transported to Charlotte for minting.

By the time of the Civil War, the Carolina gold rush was nearing an end and the mill fell into disuse. By the mid-twentieth century, the site was a romantic ruin and acquired the name "Castle McCulloch." A late twentieth-century project reconstructed collapsed walls of the ruin and uncovered many of the unique landscape features. The site remains today as an uncommon early American industrial site and a reminder of an important chapter in North Carolina's history.

9. BEESON HOUSE
8744 Bame Road
GL 1996, NR 1980

Although the early history of this house remains a mystery, the Beeson House is one of the Piedmont's most impressive and well-preserved early Quaker residences. Phebe Stroud and Isaac Beeson purchased this 484-acre parcel straddling the west prong of the Deep River in 1757 and sited a house on a rise overlooking the rich bottomlands. Oral history and bricks found on the property dated to 1787 indicate that the Beesons might have been able to improve or construct a house of more substance adjacent to their home in eighteenth century. The current Beeson House, however, reflects the period of ownership of Polly Bell and Richard Beeson in the 1830s, as indicated by construction technology and contemporary design of the period. The south-facing façade is three bays wide and two stories tall, with a front door slightly left of center. Later alterations to the façade include the addition of a two-story portico; various frame additions extend to the rear. Federal details include flat lintels of brick above nine-over-nine pane sashes on the first floor and six-over-six sashes on the second. Family tradition states that the bricks from the house were fired in a temporary clamp located in the area of the riverbank a few hundred yards northwest of the house.

The Quaker-plan house sports a large hall with boxed stairs, twin parlors with corner fireplaces and plaster load-bearing walls. Finish throughout the first floor follows a wide range of styles, including Georgian mantels in the twin chambers and Federal chair rails containing Grecian ovolos and beads throughout. This interior decoration stands among the most exuberant known of the period in the county, including early paint schemes that enliven the trim with contrasting colors and textures. The consistency of detail throughout the house demonstrates that the builder was aware of greater national architectural fashion and actively sought to incorporate these concepts into the language of the Beeson House.

10. JOHNSON HOUSE
627 Old Thomasville Road

The Johnson House is thought to have been constructed for Criscilla Jane Burton and Henry Lytle Johnson in 1842, shortly after their marriage. The house, though much altered, stands as a tangible reminder of early log buildings that were once common in southwestern Guilford County, with only one room and a garret beneath the rafters. The house portrays the modest living accommodations common to most area residents before the Civil War. The hardwood logs are hand hewn into a roughly square dimension and joined by a simple V-notch. A dry laid fieldstone foundation and early stone chimney with a brick flue likely date from the nineteenth century. By 1900, the house featured an additional log room to the east and a free-standing kitchen nearby. Interior details of the house include exposed ceiling joists, flush wall sheathing and evidence of a now-removed boxed corner stair to the right of the fireplace. Small windows likely would have been added sometime after initial construction. Later owners Nannie Lambeth and Grady Jacob Kinley and their sons preserved the structure in 1966 for use as the clubhouse for Lakewood par 3 golf course. At that time, the roof was lowered in height and pitch, the east wing was removed and a board and batten door was reconstructed using the deteriorated original as a pattern.

11. CHESTNUT HILL
1753 Penny Road
GL 1996, SL 2001

Named for the large chestnut tree in its yard that was planted by R. Joy Briggs around 1900, this residence is typical of Piedmont architecture in its pleasing jumble of additions that reflect the casual approach to building design in the region during most of the eighteenth and nineteenth centuries. Sarah Scott, who came to the area from Perquimans County, North Carolina, in 1843, purchased the nucleus of the frame house from gunsmith Jehu Lamb. Her house was a simple two-level hall and parlor–plan structure, with impressive detailing such as a Federal mantel, applied chair rail and molding on the fireplace end wall and exposed beam ceilings. In 1852, the house was expanded for use by the Florence Female Academy across Penny Road. Winslow Davis built the large Italianate-inspired addition to the building that was a dormitory for scores of girls attending the academy.

Sites Built Prior to the Civil War, 1750–1861

After the Civil War forced the closure of the school in 1861, the house passed through numerous owners before being purchased by Israel Kerner of Kernersville. Kerner, and later his brother Theodore, used the property as a changing station for horses on their way from Kernersville to Fayetteville. Henry Ledbetter, best known for manufacturing Jamestown Rifles, purchased the house in 1878 and directed his three grandsons in construction of an addition containing a kitchen flanked by broad porches.

All three periods of construction are represented at the site and portray a variety of building technologies, including Federal-era six-panel doors, antebellum-era tempera paint, early door hardware and bead board from the 1870s. Chestnut Hill was carefully restored in 1997 and was recognized as a local landmark at that time.

12. MARSHALL-JAY HOUSE
606 East Springfield Road
SL 1977

Tradition dates the Marshall-Jay House to 1790, but the house was more likely constructed around 1848 as the home of Quakers Zelinda and David Marshall. David Marshall was hired from New Garden Boarding School as a teacher at the nearby Springfield School. The two-story house is a good example of Quaker architecture, its rooms arranged in the Quaker plan with a large all-purpose room on one side, balanced by two small bedchambers on the other side. The Marshalls' stay in Springfield was fairly brief, as the couple moved to Kansas in the years just before the Civil War. The house went through several owners during the economic hardships of the war but eventually became the home of the Jay family.

Allen Jay was a minister of the Society of Friends from Indiana who moved to war-ravaged North Carolina, where he was employed by the Baltimore Association to Advise and Assist Southern Friends (see Model Farm). He and his wife Martha helped to redefine Quakerism in the state and assisted in setting up schools and advancing progressive farming techniques. Their mission completed, the Baltimore Association closed the farm around 1891 and the Jays relocated to Providence, Rhode Island.

The Marshall-Jay House went through numerous owners before the King family donated the house to Springfield Friends Meeting in 1946. Springfield Friends undertook the restoration of the house, aided by pioneering North Carolina preservationist Ruth Coltrane Cannon of Concord. Cannon, president of the North Carolina Society for the Preservation of Antiquities, was inspired to assist Springfield through contacts she made in her involvement in the restoration of Old Salem and the Governor's Palace in New Bern. The house remains an important site for Quakers as an office for the American Friends Service Committee.

13. Welborn-Payne House
428 Dilworth Road

14. Elihu Mendenhall House
1106 Skeet Club Road
GL 1993, SL 1977

Likely built in the 1840s, the two-story hall and parlor–plan frame house is thought to have been constructed by members of the Welborn family before acquisition by Isaac Payne in 1877. Oriented to the south and perpendicular to the public road, the residence illustrates traditional antebellum architectural details of the central Piedmont, including a side-gable roof with brick end chimneys, boxed eaves and returns, flush sheathing beneath the full-width front porch and a dry-laid fieldstone foundation. Four-over-four windows, rolled asphalt siding and bead board sheathing used on the porch likely indicate early twentieth-century modifications. Unusual diagonal lattice porch supports were added in the 1960s. Nearby, scattered outbuildings date from the late nineteenth to the twentieth century. Payne was a carpenter who built houses (as yet unidentified) on West High Street and in the Deep River community. He was also a farmer who raised tobacco, corn and wheat.

The oldest portion of the Mendenhall House is likely the one-story rear wing oriented westward to face the Cape Fear Road, now Johnson Street. This wing contained a hall and parlor–plan and a massive central chimney. Though no records exist, it is likely that this two-room house was constructed by Quakers Miriam Hockett and James Mendenhall on land given to Mendenhall by his father Elijah around 1793. Elijah was a son of James Mendenhall, after whom nearby Jamestown was named.

James and Miriam's twelfth child was Elihu Emery Mendenhall, born in 1817. After attending New Garden Boarding School, Elihu married Anna Hill of Back Creek Meeting in neighboring Randolph County in 1841. In 1845, the house passed to them, and prior to the Civil War they had the large two-story portion of the house constructed. Sited amidst a sweeping lawn, the timber frame house stands prominently overlooking Skeet Club Drive near its intersection with Johnson Street. The house takes many features from the then-popular Greek Revival style of architecture, including a double-leaf front door flanked by sidelights and transom, a temple-form front porch, six-over-six windows and post-and-lintel mantels. The family took liberties in embellishing their otherwise simple house with flourishes made popular by New York architect A.J. Davis, who designed Blandwood in nearby Greensboro. The romantic elements include wide eaves with exposed rafters and lattice porch supports with scalloped brackets. The demure overtures toward Italianate architecture are the earliest examples of the Romantic period in the city.

After his first wife Anna Mendenhall's unexpected death on December 23, 1856, Elihu joined the Board of Trustees of the Florence Female Academy, located in the village of Florence four miles east of the house (see entry #15). His second marriage was to Abigail Hill in 1859, and the couple was well regarded in Deep River for their hospitality as well as their convictions. For several winters after the Civil War, Abigail taught the children of freed slaves in her yard, and more than once Elihu was warned that he would be hanged for his Union principles.

Three years after Abigail Mendenhall's death in 1916, her son Elihu Clarkson (Clark) Mendenhall sold the farm to Floyd and Edna Venable. The Venables moved into the house on Christmas Day and converted the homeplace into Northview Dairy Farm. A barn was constructed on site from elements of the nearby Bennett's Mill. The operation was later purchased by the Blair family and produced milk and cream for several customers in High Point, including the Sheraton Hotel, through the name Blairwood Dairy.

15. FLORENCE FEMALE ACADEMY
1703 Penny Road
SL 2001

Among several schools for young women was the Florence Female Academy in northeastern High Point. Zora Klain, an early scholar in women's studies, wrote in 1924, "Two Quaker women, Margaret Davis and Penelope Gardner, from 1850 to 1865, conducted an elementary boarding school at Florence, NC, at first primarily for girls, but later boys were enrolled."

The main building of the academy was constructed around 1853 at the intersection of today's Penny Road and East Fork Road, in the center of what was then the bustling community of Florence. High Point did not yet exist, and Florence rivaled nearby Jamestown in activity until the North Carolina Railroad shifted commerce to Jamestown in 1856.

The two-story brick building was impressive for this section of the county, featuring large windows for natural light and wide, overhanging eaves in the Italianate style, which worked well to shelter the building during heavy summer showers. The first floor was used for classrooms and administration; the second floor was dormitory space. The school was so successful that only a few years after opening, the owners purchased an old house across the road from the school and converted it into a dormitory (see entry #11). Both the main building and the dormitory remain standing after 150 years, a rare surviving pair in the Carolina Piedmont.

Little is known of the Florence Female School's teachers and students. A flyer dated October 1857 announced that Abigail Hill had become the principal teacher. She had just graduated from Westtown School near Philadelphia, where she was a student on a teaching fellowship. The flyer also announced tuition to be five dollars and that "care will be extended for the comfort and orderly deportment of the students." Upon Hill's marriage to Elihu Mendenhall in 1859, the school served both girls and boys briefly before it closed permanently before the end of the Civil War. Later, the house was renovated for use as a private residence.

16. THE OAKS
location withheld
EA

The Oaks was named for a stand of ancient oak trees that stood in the front yard of the house built for Orianna Wilson and Nereus Mendenhall. Nereus Mendenhall was born in the Richard Mendenhall Plantation house in Jamestown and attended Haverford College and Jefferson Medical College in Philadelphia. Upon his return to Guilford County, he practiced medicine for six years before taking a position as a surveyor for the North Carolina Railroad. Nereus increasingly grew interested in teaching and eventually took on administrative and teaching roles at nearby schools, including New Garden Friends School near Greensboro. He served as clerk of the North Carolina yearly meeting from 1860 to 1871 and was elected to the state legislature for the 1874–75 term, during which time he worked as a member of the building committee to establish a state hospital for the insane in Morganton. In his retirement, he enjoyed a trip to Mexico and Central America in 1886.

Distinctive details include brick gable end chimneys, wide overhanging eaves and flush siding under the porch and in each gable. Porch supports are slightly tapered posts. The interior of the house is arranged along the lines of a modified Quaker plan, with a central hallway containing stairs to the second floor. Flush wood sheathing, a simple mantel and double-panel doors characterize the interior. Expansion of Mendenhall at Piedmont Center office park in the late 1990s threatened the Oaks with demolition. The house was relocated to a site off Penny Road in 1998 and remains privately owned.

Sites Built Prior to the Civil War, 1750–1861

17. THIRD SPRINGFIELD MEETING HOUSE,
555 East Springfield Road
SL 1977

Springfield was one of many Quaker settlements of the late eighteenth century. By 1773, a small gathering of Quakers, or Society of Friends, worshiped together in a log structure overlooking a field scattered with numerous springs. The group became a fledgling meeting by 1780 under guidance from Deep River Friends Meeting several miles to the north, and the cemetery was established at that time to receive Mary Hoggatt (see entry #2).

Friends purchased land for a meetinghouse to replace the log structure in 1786, and a larger meetinghouse replaced the first in 1805. The second building was replaced by a third in 1858, which served the congregation for almost seventy years. Constructed of brick, the side-gabled Third Meeting House features two front entrances, one for each sex, in a tradition that reflects early Quaker principles of equality. The symmetrical six-bay façade also contains large six-over-six windows flanking each entrance with handsome flat lintels and sills of the Greek Revival style. The building was embellished by Romantic period details, including wide overhanging eaves with exposed rafters, introduced to the region by New York architect A.J. Davis.

The creation of the Springfield Memorial Association in 1906 led to interest in preserving the Third Meeting House when it was supplemented by a new structure in 1927. John J. Blair led arrangements to restore the old meetinghouse to its original state for use as a Museum of Old Domestic Life. The establishment of the historical museum in the meetinghouse is likely High Point's earliest illustration of historic preservation and stands among the earliest examples in the South.

Downtown - Map 2

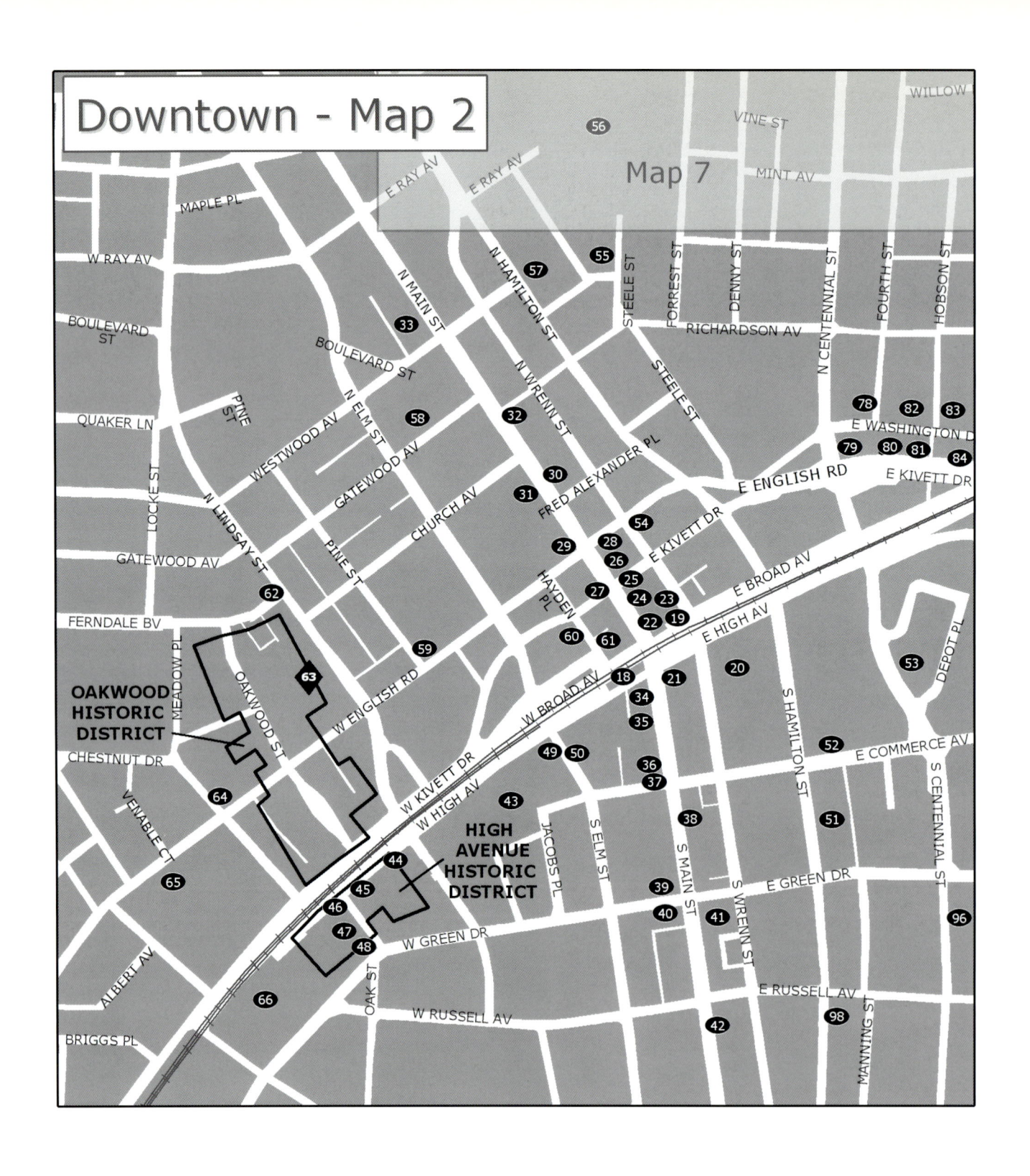

DOWNTOWN HIGH POINT

Depot Square

High Point was founded in 1859 at this crossing of the Fayetteville and Western Plank Road with the North Carolina Railroad. Encompassing a large open space in the heart of the city, Depot Square has been the historic heart of the city since incorporation. The prominence of this site was verified in 1906, when the Southern Railway Company chose it for the new passenger railway depot.

During the Great Depression, the appearance of Depot Square was radically altered when the grade-level railroad tracks were placed below street level in an excavated cut. This change reduced grade-level intersections within the center city but also acted as a divide between northern and southern downtown. Below-grade railways are common in denser cities where grade level is opened to development. The rail cut through central High Point, nicknamed by some the "F.D.R. Canal," is perhaps the most distinctive element of downtown. The walls of the railway cut are notable in having fine Art Deco–inspired embellishments such as fluted pilasters and chevron patterns scored into concrete.

Aside from early and mid-twentieth-century architecture, Depot Square has seen some recent additions of notable modern design. One Plaza Center of 1972 stands eight floors above street level and remains the largest office building in downtown High Point. Historically, political rallies and community Christmas trees utilized the square. In 2004, two statues were located in the square: one, a commemorative World War I sculpture dating from 1923, was relocated from Hayden Place; the other, a contemporary work of sculptor David Dowdy, is entitled *Plank Road Foreman*.

18. SOUTHERN RAILWAY PASSENGER DEPOT
100 WEST HIGH STREET
SL 1975

The Southern Railway Passenger Depot is one of the most recognized landmarks in High Point and one of the best examples of Richardsonian Romanesque architecture in North Carolina. It has anchored the southeastern corner of Depot Square since 1906 and gives the square its name.

Design of the depot is attributed to the office of the chief engineer of M.W. & S. of the Southern Railway. An article in the *High Point Enterprise* on April 18, 1906, stated:

The new passenger depot which is now underway here will be one of the most complete structures, costing under $40,000. The building will be erected of Mt. Airy granite up to the window sills and finished in red brick with granite trimmings. Near the center of the building there will be a bulged room for operator and ticket agent. The other rooms in the building will be white and colored waiting rooms, ladies dressing room, baggage and express rooms and large boiler rooms. So far the work has progressed very slowly on account of the wet weather, but the contractors informed us this morning that much better time would be made on the work in the future. The foundation has been put down, and much of the stone has been dressed ready to be placed.

Additional details of the one-story building include a hipped roof topped by orange tile, round-arched windows and arched braces supporting the wide overhanging eaves.

The building has been used as a passenger depot continuously since constructed, though from 1975 to 2003 the waiting room was located on the platform under the wide eaves. In 2003, the building was restored to its original appearance, including a polychromatic paint scheme. It was rededicated as a rail passenger facility and received a Merit Award by the Federal Highway Administration in 2004.

19. WACHOVIA LOAN AND TRUST COMPANY
100 North Main Street

20. SHOWPLACE
211 East Commerce Avenue

Defining the northern edge of Depot Square, this building is the oldest on the square, having been constructed around 1903 for Wachovia Bank and Trust as its fourth branch and the first in High Point. At the time it was constructed, Chalmers Glenn, son of Governor Robert Glenn, was cashier.

Archival photos show that this brick building was first designed in the Beaux Arts style. The original façade featured arched windows, modillion cornices and a roof topped with a balustrade. The first floor was marked with large plate-glass windows that overlooked the bustle of Depot Square and the rail line. The building holds an important place as the visual terminus to South Main Street, looking north into the central business district. After Wachovia relocated to the North Carolina Savings Bank and Trust Company Building farther north in the 100 block of North Main Street in the 1920s, it was used by numerous establishments before it was remodeled around 1960 to its current appearance, with horizontal windows and a modern brick façade. The building was associated with Central Savings Bank until 1995. The bank installed a prominent corner-mounted clock on the façade that is today preserved at the High Point Museum.

Anchoring the southeastern corner, Showplace is the newest and perhaps most important building on Depot Square. Designed in a dynamic style by San Diego architects Hyndman and Hyndman in 2000, Showplace serves as High Point's primary convention center and holds regular events and exhibitions. The building also serves as a central venue for the biannual furniture market, which uses the site and surrounding grounds as a hub.

Showplace stands as an excellent example of Deconstructivism, an approach to building design that attempts to view architecture as unrelated, disharmonious abstract forms. Showplace takes an organic interpretation of the style, with a gently curving façade of glass punctuated by free-flying buttresses. The entire structure is united by a rolling roofline topped by an upward rising blade that extends the full depth of the building. A serrated roofline tops each side elevation, and a mammoth interior atrium visually unites interior spaces.

21. One Plaza Center
101 South Main Street

This eight-story office building constructed in 1971–72 as a component of the city's urban renewal program stands as the only major office building constructed in downtown High Point during the second half of the twentieth century. The building forms the visual terminus of North Main Street and creates the southern boundary of Depot Square.

The Charlotte architectural firm J.N. Pease and Associates designed the office tower. The firm was run by Colonel Pease and his son Norman, who was heavily influenced by the Modern designs of European architects Walter Gropius and Mies van der Rohe, both associated with the German architecture and trade school Bauhaus. Pease and Associates' design for One Plaza Center is a simple rectangular form that features a bold grid pattern of contrasting white walls and dark recessed windows on the north- and south-facing walls. The east and west walls are solid. The building is capped by an inset platform, on which has been placed the name of the main tenant. To the north of the building is a sunken plaza, a trademark of the designers. The massive concrete form and punched windows of the façade distinguish the building as a good example of Brutalist architecture. In 2000, a glass pyramid was erected in the plaza adjacent to High Street, beneath which is located a restaurant.

North Main Street

Extending from Depot Square northward, North Main Street contains notable buildings that represent nearly all major periods of High Point history, ranging from the late nineteenth to the late twentieth century. Main Street originated as a segment of a Native American trading path that connected the mountains in the west to the Atlantic Ocean to the east and has been known by many names, including the Cape Fear Road, Great Fayetteville and Western Plank Road, Salem Street, Main Street and finally U.S. 311.

22. Zeke Farabee's Store
104 North Main Street

This two-story brick building is likely the oldest commercial building in downtown High Point, perhaps dating to the 1850s. Maps drawn in 1885 by the Sanborn Insurance Company show this building, one of the few brick buildings in town at that time, as a general store. The simple three-bay masonry façade features decorative brickwork, a heavy cornice and flat arches over each window. According to early resident S.L. Motsinger, the establishment at this location was known as Farabee's Store and "sold about everything from wooden shoe-pegs to grindstones." The building's twentieth-century history is connected to Mann Drugs, which grew under the direction of D.A. Dowdy into a chain of twenty-five stores. By the mid-1970s, the chain had stores as far away as Sanford, Aberdeen, Boone, Lenoir and Laurinburg. The façade was covered with siding in 2002.

23. 106–110 North Main Street

Likely constructed around 1899, this Neoclassical Revival commercial building is among the earliest on Main Street. Sanborn Insurance maps from the late nineteenth century show that 106 and 110 North Main Street were built as one "block."

Early photographs reinforce evidence from maps in depicting twin units, both with three bays of windows with flat arches in the upper stories, a heavy entablature atop a patterned brick façade and traditional storefronts at ground level. Today the southern half of the building (106) is exposed, while the northern half (110) is covered by a false front.

24. North Carolina Savings Bank and Trust Company Building

126 North Main Street
SL 1977

High Point's contribution to North Carolina's early history of skyscraper construction is found in the North Carolina Savings Bank and Trust Company Building. Born from a rivalry for the city's tallest building, the tower was announced soon after the four-story building called the Redding Flats was erected in 1906. North Carolina Savings Bank and Trust Company commissioned the impressive five-story office tower that opened in 1908. The building instantly became a civic landmark, touted as "one of the most imposing [buildings] in the State." The $60,000 structure featured modern amenities common to office buildings in large cities, such as an electric elevator and lights, steam heat and large plate-glass windows. Its fire- and burglar-proof vaults were said to be the largest of their kind between Richmond and Atlanta.

The architects, Wheeler, Runge and Dickey of Charlotte, won accolades for the building's classical and progressive façade. Neoclassical Revival features included polished granite columns with Ionic capitals flanking the entrance, rooftop urns, balustrades and soaring arched windows with keystones depicting lions' heads. Perhaps the most intriguing feature was the legendary roof garden, known as a scenic refuge from the hustle of the growing city and for the view it offered across six counties. High Pointers proudly displayed the image of the tower in promotional material and postcards years after it was built. The structure remained the tallest in the city until the ten-story Southern Furniture Exposition Building was erected in 1920.

During the 1960s, the building was modified in order to create a street-level storefront. Some original detail around the main entry remains intact and visible after considerable renovation in 2005.

25. HARRIS BUILDING
144 North Main Street

Prominently sited at the corner of North Main Street and Kivett Drive (formerly Washington Street), this Neoclassical Revival building was constructed by the Harris family around 1900. The two-story brick building features classical elements from the 1920s, such as a heavy modillion cornice. The four-bay Main Street façade of paired windows and traditional storefronts remains highly visible and represents a dwindling number of traditional downtown buildings in the city.

26. Wachovia Bank and Trust
200 North Main Street

Standing three floors above the street, this building was among a handful of major downtown construction projects in the 1960s and one of a small number of modernist buildings in High Point designed by a regionally recognized architectural firm. Completed in 1964 according to plans by noted Charlotte firm Odell and Associates, the bank is a good example of New Formalist architecture. Characteristics of the style include a façade featuring strong vertical components that mimic a classical colonnade, a clearly articulated base and a flat roofline that appears to float above the building. The building maintains the street wall, though demolition of adjacent buildings has isolated the bank from its urban context. The structure was altered in the late 1990s when the exterior aggregate sheathing was replaced with smooth tile.

27. Penny Building
201 North Main Street
SL 2001

The Penny Building, erected in 1924 by the Penny brothers (see entry #197), was most notably owned and occupied by optometrist Dr. Max Rones. The three-story building incorporated fine classically inspired details of the period, designed by a yet-unidentified architect. The first story comprises storefronts separated by stone pilasters and a round-arched door and windows framed in stone. Brick sheathes the upper two stories, featuring paired windows, decorative brick spandrels and stone sills and a boldly molded cornice. These Neoclassical Revival details were popular just before the Art Deco influence swept over the Main Streets of America during the Depression. The 1920s were prosperous in High Point, and the quality of the Penny Building stands representative of that period.

28. H.R. Welborn & Co. Tobacco Manufacturers/Beeson Hardware
214 North Main Street

One of only two brick structures identified by High Point historian S.L. Motsinger on North Main Street in the 1880s, this building dates to the earliest settlement of the city. The four-story building located at 214 North Main Street holds associations with tobacco manufacturing in High Point. It was constructed around 1884 for use as the H.R. Welborn & Co. tobacco manufacturing company, one of two High Point firms of the 1880s that specialized in plug and twist tobacco. The entire manufacturing process took place in the building, with rolling on the first floor, storage on the second and picking and stemming the leaves on the third and forth floors, respectively. The business changed hands in quick succession. By 1885, Welborn sold the establishment to Gordon, Pegram & Company. Gordon lived in the Five Points neighborhood in High Point, and Pegram was from Winston. Pegram took up residency in the building, which kept fire insurance rates low by having the site manned at all hours.

In 1888, Gordon and Pegram sold the business to J.H. Jenkins & Co., but the new owners closed the company only two years later. In contrast, the next owners, Beeson Hardware, were housed in the building for almost one hundred years before relocating east of downtown. The present three-bay façade, built in the 1920s by Beeson Hardware, remains largely intact. Interestingly, in the process of renovating the building for use as residential units in 2004, residue of tobacco leaves and molasses was discovered on the surface of the fourth floor, confirming the building's initial use.

29. *High Point Enterprise* Building
309 North Main Street
SL 2001

Architect Tyson Ferree designed the *High Point Enterprise* Building in 1935. The three-story building is an excellent example of Art Deco style that looked optimistically to the future. The façade features stylized pilasters topped by capitals of simple geometric forms, suggestive of a classical portico. Other features include a symmetrical five-bay façade, a stylized cornice and a notable surround at the front door that includes arched sidelights and a stylized entablature. The entire façade is sheathed in hand-carved limestone, possibly imported from Indiana. Many of the front windows feature beveled glass in metal frames. Originally two stories, the building gained a third floor after World War II. Though more recent, this addition respectfully continued the

Art Deco vocabulary of the 1935 façade, to the extent that it is almost indistinguishable from the original. For High Point, the art of the written word was housed in a forward-looking modern structure that exemplified the international designs of a new age in architecture.

After the newspaper vacated the building in the 1970s, the building became the Holt McPherson Center, home of city arts organizations. Named for a popular editor and longtime employee of the *Enterprise*, the arts center provided gallery, work and office space to several arts organizations in the city for nearly twenty-five years before being sold for furniture showroom space in 2000.

30. SHERATON HOTEL
400 North Main Street
SL 2001

The Carolinas had a plethora of grand hotels that were constructed during the Roaring Twenties in large cities to serve business, convention, travel and social needs. High Point's grand hotel was the Sheraton, opened in November 1921. It towered ten stories over the city and cost $700,000 to construct. This was a full-service facility, with 130 well-appointed rooms with wall-to-wall carpet and private bathrooms, a luxurious dining room called the Sheraton Grill, a beauty and barber shop and a lobby featuring plush chairs, a balcony, chandeliers and a molded plaster ceiling.

The designer was William Lee Stoddard, a New York City–based architect who was recognized as one of the leading hotel architects in the United States. Stoddard designed such edifices as the O. Henry Hotel in Greensboro; the Hotel Charlotte in Charlotte; the Penn-Harris in Harrisburg, Pennsylvania; the Tutwiler in Birmingham, Alabama; and the Winecoff and the Georgian Terrace in Atlanta, Georgia. Contractor J.L. Crouse of Greensboro erected the beige brick building, which features Renaissance-inspired details such as segmental arches and an elaborate cornice at its base, and a Spanish tile pent roof supported by Tuscan pilasters and terra cotta ornamentation at its top.

The Sheraton was part of the Foor and Robinson chain of hotels, a company that played a key role in the development of Southern cities. More than just a place for businessmen and travelers to stay, these hotels were the location of social events, including weddings and meetings. In High Point, the Sheraton was the place for executives to dine for lunch and dinner, a function eventually replaced by the private String and Splinter Club founded here. The hotel reportedly was the site of one of the early organizational meetings of the National Association for Stock Car Auto Racing, and the North Carolina Coal Institute was organized here in 1946. John F. Kennedy spoke to a gathering in the hotel during his 1960 presidential campaign. The vast hotel lobby was known as a hive of activity, with guests arriving by taxicab from the train station and deals being hammered out over cigars.

By the 1960s and 1970s, most of these grand hotels were showing wear. Newer "motor hotels," or "mo-tels," replaced the function of the old places, with added benefits such as open parking lots and swimming pools. In High Point, the New South and the Townhouse were notable examples of lodging geared to the automobile-traveling public. The Sheraton was converted into housing for elders around 1980. Other hotels, such as the O. Henry, the Washington Duke in Durham, the Robert E. Lee in Winston-Salem and the Charlotte, were destroyed.

31. First Baptist Church
405 North Main Street

Established in Jamestown in 1825, the First Baptist congregation relocated to High Point in 1860 and remained the town's only Baptist congregation until 1898. Their current building stands on a parcel that has been in church ownership since relocation. The sanctuary, designed in the Colonial Revival style by Roanoke architects Eubank and Caldwell, was completed in 1941. Erected by R.K. Stewart and Sons, the gable-front structure features a high steeple atop a classically inspired portico. Other classical details include limestone quoins, arched windows with keystones and a broken ogee pediment above the main entry. Rear wings include the Sunday school annex, which is older than the sanctuary.

32. First Methodist Church
512 North Main Street

The First United Methodist Church was founded in 1895 as the First Methodist Protestant Church. The current sanctuary was built in 1924–25 in the Colonial Revival style. Inspired by early Georgian architecture, the five-bay façade features Flemish bond brickwork, fanlights over three bays of double-leaf entryways, twelve-over-twelve windows and a three-bay portico of Corinthian columns. The steeple of the church rises above the façade, atop a pedestal featuring a round window. The church, along with First Baptist Church nearly across the street, is one of downtown High Point's last remaining religious institutions housed in grand and classically inspired structures.

Downtown High Point

33. *Greensboro Daily News*
715 North Main Street

This small but detailed office for the *Greensboro Daily News* is attributed to architect Ed Loewenstein of Greensboro. The dark, sculptural façade features rough-faced stone tiles that act as a background to angled metal awnings and sculptural metal screens. A spire projects beyond the parapet roofline and features an abstracted relief. Colored tiles embellish the storefronts above the doorway, and polished granite walls line a small planter in front of the building. The landscaping is an unexpected break in the concrete of the central business district and stands in contrast to its context of street-hugging storefronts built of traditional brick and stone.

South Main Street

Like North Main Street, Main Street south of the North Carolina Railroad tracks has had various designations over the years: the Old Cape Fear Road, the Great Fayetteville and Western Plank Road, Fayetteville Street, Main Street and U.S. 311. Extending south from Depot Square, the street is distinguished with several notable buildings, such as the Southern Furniture Exhibition Center, the Commercial National Bank tower and a number of Art Deco buildings.

34. Jarrell Building I
114 South Main Street

Constructed around 1915 by the Jarrell family, this Neoclassical Revival building originally housed the Allen Brothers Department Store. The stylized three-story, yellow brick façade features tall pilasters topped by simple Doric capitals that define the four-bay upper façade. Between the pilasters are tripartite windows topped by tall round-arched tripartite transoms with muntins in an intricate geometric grid. The first floor is evenly divided among two storefronts. A full entablature and stepped and gabled parapet bearing the family name JARRELL crown the façade.

35. JARRELL BUILDING II
130 South Main Street

This two-story Neoclassical Revival building was among the first in High Point to be constructed of steel girders with concrete floors and ceilings. First occupied by the J.C. Penney Company in 1926, the building has a graceful four-bay façade that appears to be faced in limestone with stylized classical ornamentation, including five pilasters that define the bays, a full entablature and three-part windows. The first floor contains a traditional shop front that has been heavily remodeled in recent years. The parapet of the building features the inscription JARRELL, the name of the early High Point family who built the structure.

36. JOE COX BUILDING
156 South Main Street

Joe Cox, a member of a prominent High Point family, constructed this Neoclassical Revival–style building around 1925, at nearly the same time as Elwood Cox's Commercial National Bank next door. The façade is composed of full-height paneled pilasters topped with stylized Corinthian capitals and seated upon pedestals. A full entablature with dentil cornice and a paneled parapet bearing classical urns adorn the roofline of the building. The façade was restored around 1990.

37. COMMERCIAL NATIONAL BANK
164 South Main Street
SL 2001

The Commercial National Bank is the premier office building constructed in the city during the first half of the twentieth century, and the first major office building in High Point after the 1907 North Carolina Savings Bank and Trust building on North Main Street. The building was designed by Charles C. Hartmann of Greensboro and constructed in 1922–24 by R.K. Stewart of High Point. Bank President J. Elwood Cox heralded the newly opened bank building as "the finest in North Carolina." The opening day crowd numbered 2,500, and all were given souvenirs—desk knives for men and notebooks for women. The building's stone base, arched entry and monumental pilasters are all typical of the Neoclassical Revival style, popular for office towers of the period. Italian Renaissance details include fasciae over the windows on the first floor supported by brackets, an elaborate keystone over the front entry arch and an impressive entablature at the top floor. The vast lobby was reconfigured around 1960 by the North Carolina National Bank to designs by architect William Freeman.

38. SOUTHERN FURNITURE EXPOSITION BUILDING
209 South Main Street
SL 1977

The first ten stories of the Southern Furniture Exposition Building were constructed between 1919 and 1921. The idea of having a large exhibition building for the purpose of displaying furniture is credited to furniture manufacturer Charles F. Long, who dedicated himself to securing the capital and support necessary to erect the structure. The concept for a central block of showrooms was allegedly copied from the Jamestown Furniture Exposition Building of 1916–17 in Jamestown, New York. Long, the project manager and the building's first manager, was charged with the duty of visiting Jamestown in order to obtain direction for the proposed High Point building. He returned with a full set of blueprints, which were slightly altered by the architect and builder William P. Rose of Goldsboro, Greensboro and Raleigh before being turned into reality. At the time, Rose had just completed the 1918 Guilford County Courthouse in Greensboro.

Charter members of the building's board of trustees included many of High Point's leading businessmen of the day, but the list of stockholders was remarkably diverse. In some cases, local tradesmen were given shares of stock as compensation for their work on building the tower, while industry leaders across the South purchased shares and thereby helped keep the showroom solvent and operating. The building quickly came to be seen as a point of pride for the city.

Upon completion, the $1 million building dominated downtown High Point, dwarfing nearby homes and businesses. Though the back and sides of the structure were left simply finished in brick, the Main Street façade was sheathed in glazed tile and adorned with classical elements such as pilasters, cornices and a broad entablature on the ninth floor. Instead of stone, which had to be laboriously cut, all of these features were executed in terra cotta, clay that could be inexpensively formed into shapes and then glazed to give it a durable, polished surface. The furniture building's outer skin was relatively rare to North Carolina, but was already common in the fast growing cities of the Midwest, especially Chicago.

The Southern Furniture Market grew to the point that additional space was needed by the end of the 1930s. Building administrators looked to city architects Voorhees and Everhart to build upward for more space. They added four floors in 1940 to create High Point's tallest building. Though this addition continues the design of the original to some degree, its architects streamlined the windows and used white glazed brick for the front façade instead of terra cotta tile. Additions in 1949 and 1955 expanded the structure southward. By that time, windows were seen as unnecessary to the building's function, resulting in this wing's simple expanses of red brick.

By 1967, the High Point architectural firm William F. Freeman and Associates endeavored to return some of the style the complex once had. The firm designed an eleven-story wing toward Green Street that incorporated vertical masses of brick in shades of buff and tan. The uppermost floor crowned the building with a band of windows housing the quarters of the Top of the Mart restaurant and ballroom facilities. In 1974, the largest addition to date was completed on Commerce Street. Designed by Six Associates of Asheville, this massive structure exhibits a façade of corrugated black metal set off by massive poured concrete pilasters. The designer of this wing was able to cut costs by utilizing a thrifty sheathing for the building, a formula repeated for the additions of the Design Center (1982) as well as the Hamilton wing (1987).

39. GUILFORD COUNTY COURTHOUSE
258 South Main Street
GL 1983, NR 1988

The former Guilford County Courthouse has a history relevant to High Point, Guilford County and North Carolina. The courthouse was born from a movement just after the turn of the twentieth century to form the state's newest county from parts of Guilford, Randolph and Davidson Counties. During this period of rapid growth in High Point, the city felt slighted that it did not have the autonomy and status associated with being a county seat. In addition, the road connecting High Point to Greensboro, the county seat, was so notoriously poor that it took a full day to negotiate a round trip between the two cities.

In 1911, politicians attempted to win approval for the creation of Piedmont County. The proposed county would take in most of southwestern Guilford County, Archdale and Trinity in Randolph County and areas of Davidson County around Thomasville and Wallburg. High Point was proposed as the new county seat. The proposal was defeated soundly in the statehouse, but High Point's desire for autonomy was not. Increased rivalry between Greensboro and High Point peaked a second time with resubmission in 1913 to create Aycock County, following the same lines as those proposed for Piedmont County. Yet again, the effort was defeated. In this context, High Point Commissioner Joe F. Hoffman Jr. convinced county government officials to place a branch courthouse in High Point. As a result, the county became unique in North Carolina by having dual seats of government with the construction of the state's 101st courthouse.

Local architects Voorhees and Everhart were selected to design the building. The firm chose the Art Deco style, an expression well executed by them a few years before for the nearby United States Post Office (see entry #41). The building's stylized details include three figures, each portraying one of three major industries of the city: furniture, textiles and agriculture. Other features include sandstone trim around windows and entryways, Flemish bond brickwork, tall windows featuring metal muntins and a canopy over the front door bearing GUILFORD COUNTY in metallic lettering. High Point contractor R.K. Stewart and Sons constructed the building with the help of consulting engineer William F. Freeman. It was dedicated on January 27, 1938.

County offices vacated the structure in 1980 after a fire, and three years later the legal firm Wyatt Early Harris Wheeler and Hauser restored the building for use as their offices. The building remains important to the community as a tangible reminder of the important role it played in the development of High Point and the county, as well as for its exemplary Art Deco design.

40. PROFESSIONAL BUILDING
300 South Main Street

This Art Deco building was designed around 1938 by High Point architect Tyson Ferree, who also maintained an office here. Located on a prominent corner, the structure was the largest office building erected in the city during the 1930s. Featuring Art Deco motifs at its prominent corner entrance façade, the building stands in close proximity to other Art Deco landmarks: the old post office and the old courthouse. Art Deco appointments include a chevron design of fiddlehead ferns over the front door and a stylized modillion cornice, all executed in cast cement. Streamlined banks of windows defined by wide pilasters mark the long façades facing the streets. A.E. Taplin was the general contractor for the project, later known as the Phillips Building for its primary tenant, Phillips-Davis, a fabric-converting firm.

41. UNITED STATES POST OFFICE
100 East Green Street
SL 2001

The former United States Post Office stands as one of the city's finest examples of Art Deco design. Construction began in 1932, and the building was dedicated by the Honorable James A. Farley, postmaster general, on the Fourth of July, 1933. Local architects Workman, Voorhees and Everhart designed the two-story masonry building, sited prominently at the corner of East Green and South Main Streets. The contractor was Spence Brothers of Saginaw, Michigan, who completed the $450,000 project with assistance from supervising engineer R.A. McGary.

Along with the Guilford County Courthouse, the post office represents the best example of Art Deco design in the city and is among the few buildings in town to combine human and animal forms in its design. The exterior of the post office is sheathed in limestone, rendering it one of the most conspicuously substantial structures in town. Relief on the exterior elevations includes fluting, swags and frets, all highly stylized in simple geometric forms. The highlights of carved ornamentation are handsome American eagles that guard each entryway to the building. Other notable features include masonry block screens and bronze spandrel panels between first- and second-floor windows. The interior of the post office was exceptional, with abstracted classical details expressed in marble veneer walls, heavy steel doors and windows and specially designed furnishings. Though much of the interior has been lost, the building remains one of the most important and well-built landmarks in the city.

42. Masonic Lodge
453 South Main Street

The Masonic Lodge, constructed around 1960, contains two floors, the upper providing the main entrance. Its innovative façade is cantilevered above the first floor and features an arcade of simple metal columns screening a masonry wall topped by a high band of windows. From this floor, "floating" stairs descend to street level, expanding and contracting to various widths as they fall. The recessed first floor features glazed surfaces and little ornamentation. The glass, brick and metal façade contrasts with the two classical, freestanding Corinthian columns flanking the front steps. The entire design was created by High Point architect William Freeman. Victorian-inspired brackets have been added to the metal columns in recent years.

West High Street Neighborhood
NR 2007

High Street extends west from Depot Square, paralleling the North Carolina Railroad tracks. The street illustrates early industrialists' penchants for erecting impressive residences along major thoroughfares, including railroad tracks, as a point of civic pride. As a result, High Street features some of High Point's most impressive houses as well as important landmarks. Originating as a service road for the railroad, High Street at one time continued to Thomasville. This access was ended in the early twentieth century as numerous factories and loading docks were built south of the tracks and the route to Thomasville was shifted north to English Street. Today, portions of High Street survive well preserved as the city's third National Register historic district.

43. Tomlinson Furniture Company (Market Square)
305 West High Street
GL 1989, NR 1983

Members of the Tomlinson family, natives of nearby Archdale, announced construction of the Tomlinson Manufacturing Company in August 1900. Partnering with Durham industrialist Julian S. Carr, directors of the plant purchased several acres of land from the old E.H.C. Field homeplace on West Green Street and erected an expansive brick industrial building just south of the Southern Railway tracks. The formula for the building's design was simple: lots of windows flooded work areas with natural light, high ceilings accommodated machinery and an open floor plan with few dividers provided an open work space. The building was constructed of brick for its obvious fireproof qualities, but where wood framing was necessary, thick timbers were used for their "slow burn" quality, which lowered insurance premiums. Overall, the industrial building was straightforward and utilitarian in design, a structure more concerned with function than image.

As business for what became Tomlinson Chair Manufacturing Company grew, expansions were made to the original building in 1906, 1911 and 1924 that created a sprawling structure dominating the western fringe of downtown. A tall smokestack inscribed with the name TOMLINSON and a private water tower dominated the complex. Additions followed the basic design of the first, with slight modifications including window and ceiling clearance. A rail spur, loading yards, lumberyards and a drying kiln enhanced the complex.

By the 1920s, Tomlinson was a leader in furniture manufacturing in the South. The company pioneered the manufacturing of matched dining room suites and displayed their wares in gallery settings, which was a novel idea at the time. By 1940, the company employed 648 skilled men, 65 unskilled men and 36 skilled women in its four mills. The largest plant, the main facility on High Street, contained 446,495 square feet of space in ten buildings. Value of production stood at $5,000,000.

By the 1970s, Tomlinson closed and a consortium of citizens banded together to convert the historic landmark into a furniture design center. The venture met with great success, and the first phase of the Market Square Design Center opened in 1982, with subsequent expansions opening as additional portions of the complex were suitably restored. In 1988, plans were announced for a sixteen-story postmodern tower designed by Odell and Associates of Charlotte adjacent to the old plant.

44. MELROSE HOUSE
407 West High Street
GL 1998

Constructed for Henry W. Fraser around 1915, this commodious early Colonial Revival house is a rare surviving example of grand residences that stood at the edge of the central business and industrial district early in the twentieth century. An oversized dormer bearing a Palladian window dominates the hipped roof of the two-story frame house. Other notable details include a modillion cornice, large double-hung windows, Ionic porch supports and a handsome granite foundation. Interior appointments include eleven-foot-tall ceilings, quarter-sawn oak wainscoting, oak mantels and pocket doors and a stained-glass window, installed in 1923 to commemorate the death of Fraser's wife, Alma. Fraser co-founded Alma Desk in 1895 and Myrtle Desk in 1899. Myrtle Desk was named for Fraser's only daughter,

Ida Myrtle Fraser. The two manufacturing plants are located a short walk down High Street, in keeping with the desire of early industrialists to reside close to their investments. The George F. Wilson family, who purchased the house in 1926, operated the High Point Motor Company.

45. Tom Kirkman House
415 West High Street

Newspaper accounts throughout the summer of 1900 chronicled the construction of the Tom Kirkman House, a boxy frame, two-story residence constructed upon a slight rise overlooking High Street and the Southern Railroad tracks. In contrast to the exuberant Queen Anne–style Brown House built nearby just a few years earlier (see entry #48), the Kirkman House took design cues from the early American–inspired Colonial Revival architecture. Highlights of the interior include an elaborate stairway embellished with sawn ornament, spacious rooms and hallways, double-hung windows and oak floors. Kirkman operated a successful dry goods store on Main Street.

46. O. Arthur Kirkman Estate
501 West High Street
GL 1987, NR 1988, EA

The Kirkman Estate is a rare surviving example of an urban estate, developed during a period when industrialists were attracted to the idea of collecting their investments and holdings in close proximity to their homes. Though not common in High Point, the Kirkman Estate contained the family's residence, office, transit depot, factory and warehouse close to the heart of the city, yet within the context of ancient oaks and lush landscaping.

Born in 1875, O. Arthur Kirkman became one of High Point's most successful industrialists and renaissance men. In 1898, Kirkman purchased the land that was to become his midtown estate: a recently closed private school that had been in operation on the western edge of the city since 1879 (see entry #47). Kirkman and his wife, Lulu Blanche Hammer, converted the schoolhouse into their home and commenced assembling a collection of business interests and investments.

The O. Arthur Kirkman Manufacturing Company was one of the first businesses on the site, established on the western boundary of the estate in 1899. The company manufactured cots, bedsprings, mattresses and pillows in a large wooden structure that still faces the present-day railroad. The factory is a large timber frame structure indicative of High Point's earliest industrial buildings. With utilitarian features such as a gabled roof, the building resembled a large barn sheathed in wood planks and covered in corrugated metal.

With their growing wealth, the Kirkmans turned their thoughts toward building a new home, grand in scale. Their sentimentality ran deep with the converted schoolhouse they both had attended as children. Instead of demolishing the school, they moved the building to the rear of the property and away from the railroad tracks, where the structure continued its usefulness as a rental property. The historic school still stands today, adapted as commercial space at 106 Oak Street.

Influenced by the design of the Carter Dalton House on Johnson Street (see entry #116), the Kirkmans embraced the popular Craftsman style of architecture for the new house they built in 1915. The two-story brick edifice features such period details as exposed rafter tails and triangular knee braces supporting wide overhanging eaves, complemented by patterned brickwork and gables of textured stucco, or "pebbledash." A substantial Spanish tile roof originally decorated the house and added to the richness of textures that lent a handcrafted feel to the building.

The interior of the Kirkman home exceeded all known domestic interiors in High Point of the period. Quarter-sawn oak-trimmed doors and windows and stained glass worked together to deliver a warm interior of rich colors and tones. The plan of the house is arranged around a T-shaped hallway, open at the intersection of the "T" to a stained-glass skylight two stories above. A grand staircase culminates at a large stained-glass window that admits golden afternoon light past a happy elk, symbolic of Kirkman's ties with the Elks Club.

With his new home in place, Kirkman continued to build his business investments. In 1917, he initiated the Interurban Motor Line, the first motorized bus/taxi service between Greensboro and High Point, and constructed a "depot" for this service in his side yard. Kirkman also organized, founded and managed the High Point, Thomasville and Denton Railroad after 1918. Many of his business dealings were administered from a one-story brick office building constructed in a grove of ancient oaks in his side yard. The Kirkmans maintained their urban estate until their deaths, at which time their son, O. Arthur Kirkman Jr., and his wife Katherine maintained their residence at the home until their deaths in 1985.

47. LYNCH'S SELECT SCHOOL FOR BOYS
106 Oak Street
GL 1989, NR 1989, EA

This one-story frame structure was constructed in 1879 as one of three buildings that comprised the campus of Lynch's Select School for Boys. The campus anchored the western edge of the village, just south of the railroad tracks. Other buildings (no longer standing) included two barracks of approximately fifteen rooms each. The sole remaining structure of the campus is the main building, containing an auditorium, a study hall and two recitation rooms. The building was utilized by other schools until 1898, when it was converted into a residence for Lulu and O.

Arthur Kirkman. The Kirkmans added porches and subdivided rooms to accommodate their needs. Around 1913, they moved the structure south from its original location overlooking the railroad tracks to make way for a grand new residence (see entry #46). The schoolhouse retains many original features, including early windows, window and door surrounds and siding.

48. Annettie McBain Brown House
110 Oak Street

Among High Point's most notable examples of Queen Anne design, the Brown House originally stood overlooking the Southern Railroad tracks at 401 West High Street before relocation to this site in 2004. The two-story frame house was constructed for Annettie McBain Brown in 1897. It features a prominent tower capped by a pyramidal roof and a cross-gabled roofline. Clapboard sheathing, complemented by a shingled entablature, covers the walls of the house. The wraparound porch is supported by turned posts and exuberant sawn detail, topped by a wooden railing. Additional applied ornament that embellishes the façade illustrates the availability of mass-produced ornament during the period. Other features, such as multiple-pane windows, bay windows and corbelled chimneys, contribute to the elaborate Queen Anne design. In 1984, the house was adapted for use as an office and showroom by Altizer-Cole Fabric Company. It was threatened with destruction in 2005 before being relocated to its present location and sensitively restored for use as offices.

Downtown South

The streets off South Main Street throughout downtown are primarily industrial and commercial today, though these areas remained popular mixed-use neighborhoods well into the twentieth century. Residential components were squeezed out due to standardized zoning, building codes and land values; however, elements of the area's early commercial and industrial heritage remain. Reinvestment in the area has resulted in some notable additions to the neighborhood within the past thirty years, most associated with the expansion of the furniture market.

49. HIGH POINT MARBLE AND TILE BUILDING
110 South Elm Street

This unusually decorated two-story building held the offices of the High Point Marble and Tile Company, whose name was once emblazoned at the top of the façade in mosaic tiles. Other tile embellishments of the circa 1925 building remain intact, including pilasters displaying intricate themes of urns, pendants and panels, all executed in colorful mosaic tiles. The building was renovated in the late 1970s, resulting in the loss of early storefronts and the tile sign and insertion of a metal exterior stair to provide access to the second floor.

50. NATUZZI AMERICAS BUILDING
130 West Commerce Street

Along with Showplace, the Natuzzi Americas Building represents one of High Point's most celebrated examples of Deconstructivist architecture. Erected in 1998 by designs of Italian architect Mario Bellini, the building portrays an abstracted bow of a ship sheathed in nine hundred Italian-made bronze panels. The west wall of the building is composed of glass, with projecting glass fins that add interest, color and dimension. The glass wall has the effect of a cross section of the ship that represents the transatlantic relationship of Italian-owned Natuzzi and its High Point showroom. Bellini's work also includes an addition to the Louvre in Paris, the National Opera Theater in Tokyo and the National Gallery of Victoria in Melbourne, Australia. This is his only major work to date in the United States.

51. HIGH POINT CITY HALL
211 South Hamilton Street

High Point City Hall opened in May 1975 after a long period of construction woes. The land was acquired by the city around 1963 through a federal program that cleared large portions of central High Point, mainly east of downtown, in the name of "urban renewal." The construction of a new city hall was necessitated by expansion of the Southern Furniture Exhibition Building's Commerce Wing onto the site of the old city hall.

For the new city hall, internationally renowned architect Edward Durrell Stone was chosen, in coordination with prominent High Point architect Leon Schute. Stone practiced in the International style and earned a high profile for his first major work, the Museum of Modern Art in New York City (1937–39). Later in his career, Stone's numerous projects included the North Carolina State Legislative Building in Raleigh (1963), the John F. Kennedy Center for the Performing Arts in Washington, D.C. (1971), and the eighty-two-story Amoco Building in Chicago (1973).

Stone's buildings share common characteristics. His projects are often isolated within open plazas or landscaped settings. His trademark floor plans provide large multi-functional central spaces encircled by smaller rooms of more definite purpose. At a time when most Modern architects incorporated simple materials and minimal decoration into their designs, Stone used luxurious materials such as marble and decorative details to set his buildings apart. High Point City Hall features all of these common characteristics. Located within a landscaped plaza with a broad base and pyramidal roof of copper, its basic form recalls the North Carolina Legislative Building of ten years earlier. High Point City Council Chamber, with a high vaulted ceiling, is located dramatically beneath the pyramid. The building is also sheathed in marble, a trademark of Stone's designs. The floor plan is arranged around the central atrium and council chamber, with the offices of various city departments ringing the exterior walls to take advantage of peripheral windows. Stone's High Point building is also unique in certain respects. With height, planes of marble and ribbon windows have increasingly deep setbacks. Also, vegetation grows from planters outside the ribbon windows, providing the building with a "hanging gardens" motif. The structure is among the most futuristic municipal buildings in the state and distinguishes High Point with a progressive identity.

52. J. Elwood Cox Manufacturing Company/ Hall Printing

305 East Commerce Avenue

One of the first industrialists in High Point was Captain W.H. Snow, who founded Snow Lumber Company in 1880. One of the smaller companies that formed from Snow's holdings was a spoke, handle, shuttleblock and bobbinhead manufacturing company run by Snow's son-in-law, J. Elwood Cox. In time, Cox sold the division of his company that dealt with spokes and handles and concentrated on shuttleblocks and bobbinheads. He renamed the business J. Elwood Cox Manufacturing Company.

Around this time, roughly 1900, Cox erected this three-story utilitarian brick building, featuring large windows to allow natural light for task work and a heavy, slow-burn wood frame. In later years, the textile industry's demand for shuttleblocks and bobbinheads began to wane, and less space in the sprawling brick building was needed for their production. Barber-Hall Printing, owned by Arthur Barber and W.B. (Will) Hall, moved into space on the second floor of the building in the 1920s. Eventually the firm took over use of the entire building and developed a method of color printing that was sought by High Point's furniture industry for advertising. Hall Printing remained in the building until 2002, when it was converted to furniture showrooms. A three-story atrium was cut into the corner of the building to create a new entrance for the showroom.

53. Southern Railway Freight Depot

121 South Centennial Street

Although the main office looks very much like a house, this frame building was constructed around 1925 as part of the main freight depot for Southern Railway in High Point. Manufacturers' freight was unloaded from trucks parked at bays on the eastern side of the building and placed into boxcars located on tracks along the west side. The simple freight shed is attached to the residential-looking office building to the south that features a pyramidal roof, central-hipped dormer and wide overhanging eaves supported by diagonal braces. The building is covered with German siding and sits atop a brick foundation. Modifications were made in 2003, when the building was converted to a dinner theater, though many original features were retained.

Downtown High Point

Downtown North

The diverse side streets off North Main Street were the core of the village of High Point at the turn of the twentieth century. Glimpses remain of village life, including the town hall, the burial grounds, residential neighborhoods and factories. Rapid growth of the city in the mid-twentieth century eradicated much of the Victorian-era village, supplanted with civic and commercial buildings of notable design. The neighborhood remains one of the most diverse in the city today, including additions of health care and furniture showrooms to nineteenth-century uses.

54. North Side Hose Company Number 1/ City Hall

One of the first adaptive use projects in High Point was initiated in 1979 by Jake and Mazie Froelich. The couple purchased the circa 1905 North Side Hose Company Number 1, a firehouse that also housed city offices and a jail. Designer Pat Plaxico was invited to orchestrate the innovative restoration. Though the tall hose-drying tower had long been removed, retention of handmade brick walls, segmental arched windows, original ceilings, heart pine flooring and even the firemen's lockers on the second floor preserved the original charm of the building.

55. Steele Street Neighborhood

One of High Point's few remaining historic downtown residential communities, this neighborhood is located along the southern and western edge of Oakwood Cemetery and serves as the northern edge of the downtown street grid. This neighborhood—centered on Steele Street, Monroe Place and Oakland Place—contains numerous one- and two-story brick and frame residences and boardinghouses inhabited by middle- and low-income workers. Good examples of Colonial Revival–, Craftsman- and Prairie-style residential architecture can be found on generous suburban lots throughout the neighborhood. A notable brick foursquare stands at 402 Steele Street, and a rectilinear apartment building is located at 501 Oakland Place. Though several residences have been destroyed, the core of this neighborhood remains relatively intact.

56. Oakwood Cemetery/ Oakwood Memorial Park

Northern terminus of Oakwood Street
SL 2001

Since 1859, Oakwood Cemetery has been the city's premier burial ground and a showcase of funerary art. The grid-plan municipal cemetery is situated upon a ridge just north of downtown. Its primary access is from Steele Street. The oldest portions of the thirteen-acre cemetery include Civil War–era graves for soldiers who died at the Barbee Hotel when it was used as a temporary military hospital. In honor of this distinction, the Junior Order of Mechanics erected a Confederate Monument in 1899. The eastern portions of the cemetery were reserved for African American citizens, including Reverend Daniel Brooks, Willis Hinton and John Robinson. As the city grew more prosperous, its funerary art became more elaborate. Notable monuments include the Greek Revival Wrenn arcade, the Roman-inspired Creelman crypt and the Kirkman plot that features a full-size sculpture of an angel. Other plots are sometimes organized around a central stone bearing the family's name, surrounded by smaller stones. Numerous obelisks, urns and plaques give Oakwood Cemetery a strongly romantic feel, illustrative of its Victorian past. The landscape of the cemetery is rich with feature plantings and trees, some quite rare and aged, situated with care among the stones. Oakwood Cemetery blends without pause into its private and curvilinear neighbor Oakwood Memorial Park, developed by Stephen Clark in 1935 to serve the growing demand for burial space. The memorial park features mausoleums and family plots simplified from their Victorian neighbors, inscribed with the names of some of High Point's most recognized citizens.

57. World's Largest Bureau

508 North Hamilton Street

Chamber of Commerce officials conceived the idea to construct the "World's Largest Bureau" in 1926 to serve dual goals: to provide office space for the chamber and to raise High Point's profile as a center of furniture manufacturing. Located in Tate Park at the corner of North Main Street and Church Avenue, the one-story frame building gave the illusion of a four-drawer bureau through applied molding and paint. It was topped by a metal structure that resembled a mirror bearing the phrase HIGH POINT NC—THE INDUSTRIAL CITY—BUREAU OF INFORMATION. The interior was initially not partitioned and featured panels of selected woods popular in the furniture industry.

After World War II, the Chamber of Commerce outgrew the small building and sold the structure in 1951. The bureau was moved from Tate Park to a new site on North Hamilton Street, where it served as the headquarters of the North Carolina Jaycees until 1969, when the organization allowed the local chapter to use the space. The appearance of the building has been altered many times throughout its existence in order to mimic popular home furnishings design. Originally painted white with applied decorative floral designs, the façade was streamlined in the 1950s and embellished only with gold trim. By 1996, the structure was again reworked, this time with wood graining, faux brass pulls and two socks spilling from a half-opened drawer to symbolize High Point's position in the hosiery industry. The building is an important example of early automobile roadside culture, along with Thomasville's chair and Winston-Salem's Shell service station.

58. Young Women's Christian Association
112 Gatewood Avenue

A theme of New Formalism, inspired by New York architect Edward Durrell Stone, influences the design of the YWCA. Completed in 1961, the two-story facility houses offices, classrooms, a swimming pool and activity spaces. High Point architect Leon Schute designed the structure, which is composed of a one-story slab that floats above the sloping site. An automobile access point is cut from beneath the left-most portion of the building's cantilevered base. A wall of cement block lattice screens the south-facing front façade of the flat roof structure. The screen is supported on a steel skeleton that stands five feet from the façade. Behind the screen are turquoise spandrel panels beneath large plate-glass windows that permit filtered light inside the building. The front yard of the building features mature trees, including live oaks. To the rear are a parking lot and playgrounds.

59. Piedmont Hosiery Mills
410 English Road

For many years, beginning in 1910, Piedmont Hosiery Mills was the largest mill in the city. The mill was combined with others in the city to form Adams-Millis Corporation in 1927, the first company in High Point to be listed on the New York Stock Exchange. The three-story mill structure was stoutly constructed to withstand vibrations of heavy machinery. The brick exterior walls of the building are reinforced with pilasters to further steady the structure from movement. Large windows topped by segmental arches allow natural light, and heavy slow-burn timber posts resist quick collapse in case of fire. The poured concrete frame structure to the west of the Piedmont building was constructed between 1929 and 1931, after the company merged with Adams-Millis Hosiery Company. The mill closed in the 1980s, but the building remains one of the most prominent mill structures in the city. It was adapted for furniture showrooms in 2001–04.

60. Scottish Bank
111 Hayden Place

Lumberton-based Scottish Bank constructed this imposing four-story office building in 1962 for their city offices. High Point's Robert Conner designed the Modernist building that was erected at a cost of $500,000. The bank's off–Main Street location was compensated for by positioning the building's entrance at the visual terminus of West Washington Street. Despite the increased visibility of the building that occurred after Washington Street was extended westward as Kivett Drive, the back street location was an influence in the bank's relocation to Main Street soon after it merged with First Union National Bank in 1963. Since then, the Hayden Place building has been used for the offices of North State Communications.

The building is constructed of a pale gray concrete with banded windows on each floor. The off-center main entry features a two-story glazed curtain wall accentuated by bold green aggregate trim and complemented by small green and red tiles arranged in a textile-like plaid pattern. A broad field of concrete relief in a diagonal pattern extends from the entry to the north corner of the building.

61. REDDING FLATS
100 Hayden Place

The *High Point Enterprise* announced in March 1907 that the newly erected Redding building would feature mixed uses, promising, "The lower floors will be used by wholesale distributors. The upper stories are nicely fitted apartments." J.P. Redding was a well-recognized leader in the city. He started out with the Snow Lumber Company (among the first factories in town) and eventually was an organizer in 1895 of the Alma Furniture Company, which grew into one of the largest companies in High Point.

When constructed, Redding's building was the tallest in the city, rising four stories above College Street across West Broad from the freight depot. For Redding Flats, the as-yet unidentified architect utilized warm golden brick and Mount Airy granite trim to create a classical façade of arched windows and an oversized cornice. The building raised architectural awareness in High Point and paved the way for the design of the classically inspired façade of the North Carolina Savings Bank and Trust Company Building on Main Street a few years later.

By 1909, High Point promoter J.J. Farriss wrote of Redding, "He was the first citizen of High Point to build an up-to-date city flat, which is one of the most imposing in the city." Redding Flats was unusual in several ways. First, although it was one of the city's first major buildings, it was not located on busy Main Street; rather, it was on College Street, today's Hayden Place and still a side street. Secondly, Redding Flats' apartments on the upper floors made it the prototype for later High Point apartment buildings. The building has since been converted to office use and now houses offices for North State Communications. In the early 1990s, the company covered the Neoclassical Revival façade of the Redding building with false siding, which one day could be removed to reveal the building's original appearance.

QUAKER WOODS AND OAKWOOD

62. LINDSAY STREET AND GATEWOOD AVENUE HOUSES

Residences that remain along Lindsay Street and Gatewood Avenue are the remnants of High Point's first subdivision, Quaker Woods. Developed by Homer Wheeler in 1895 on land that once held the meetinghouse of the North Carolina Yearly Meeting of the Society of Friends, this gridded subdivision included today's

Lindsay and Elm Streets, as well as portions of intersecting English, Church, Gatewood and Westwood Boulevards. Early in the development of the neighborhood, frame Queen Anne and Colonial Revival residences lined its streets, complemented in the 1910s and 1920s by Craftsman and period revival houses. Expansion of the central business district into the neighborhood during the 1960s and 1970s resulted in much destruction of original housing stock, though some good examples remain, particularly on Lindsay Street and Gatewood Avenue.

Located at 401 Lindsay Street is the Harmon House, a two-story frame Colonial Revival structure with a wraparound porch, multiple gables and a stamped metal shingle roof. The yard retains some of the original oaks that were part of the grove that surrounded the nearby nineteenth-century Quaker meetinghouse. Dutch Colonial influences can be seen at 221 Lindsay Street, where pebbledash faces the gables of the one-and-a-half-story cross-gambrel-roof house. The Otis E. Mendenhall House blends Dutch influences with Craftsman elements at 409 Gatewood Avenue. Built for the son of prominent Quaker Elihu Mendenhall (see entry #14), the Mendenhall House is a modest gambrel-roof structure with battered post-on-pier porch supports. The R.K. Stewart House at 304 Lindsay is the most complete example of Craftsman design in the neighborhood, featuring battered porch supports, exposed eaves and a wide wraparound porch.

63. OAKWOOD STREET
NR 1991

The collection of residences along Oakwood Street was developed in two phases. The 200 and 300 blocks of the street were platted by Benjamin Best in 1902 and reflect the broad range of popular architectural styles of that time, including the largest collection of Queen Anne–style residences in the city. The earliest buildings share a common appearance, with an off-center front wing of bay windows and shingled gables, coupled with porches supported by Tuscan columns and festooned with decorative sawn and spool work. Other residences in these blocks reflect early Colonial Revival and later Craftsman influences.

Farther south, houses show Craftsman and Colonial Revival influences popular in the 1910s and 1920s. With a wide elliptical median of trees and grass, the 100 block is the later developed section of Oakwood Street. It was platted in 1914 on the site of the R.A. Wheeler house, and the median still contains some of the early trees that surrounded the house. Several notable buildings in this block include the Cecil House, built of quartzite, and the Welborn House, built along the lines of an American Foursquare house. The Oakwood Garden Court Apartments were constructed by Rowland and Ella Gantt around 1935 and contain thirty-three apartments in three brick buildings, each separated by grassy divides and featuring a porch in keeping with most of the houses along the street.

64. HUNT HOTEL
742 English Street

Originally an impressive wedding cake of a building rising three stories and crowned with a cupola, the Hunt Hotel was reduced in stature and detail in the twentieth century. The hotel was named for its owner, Nathan Hunt Jr., the son of a pioneering Quaker and well-known resident of the Bloomington community south of High Point. There, Hunt owned and operated a hotel positioned prominently alongside the Fayetteville and Western Plank Road. However, when the North Carolina Railroad was

Downtown High Point

constructed in 1856, Hunt saw the intersection of the plank road, where downtown High Point would emerge, as a profitable location, and he reopened his hotel there.

The Hunt Hotel was the second hotel in the busy crossroads village, and Hunt spared no expense in erecting a new hotel that would make an impressive statement for the new settlement. Constructed in 1857 at the site of today's Radisson Hotel ballroom, the frame structure towered three stories over Main Street, with broad porches along Main Street and Commerce Avenue. The building was an excellent example of Italianate architecture, featuring a low-pitch roof topped by a prominent cupola, broad overhanging eaves graced with carved brackets, large double-hung windows and a bracketed porch. Black-and-white photographs indicate that the hotel was painted in a variety of colors, and the site was surrounded by graceful elm trees.

The hotel was a popular gathering spot for High Point's citizens. Men, women and children would gather on the shady porch of the hotel and share news, gossip and games. The hotel and its proprietor became so central to the High Point community that in 1860, Nathan Hunt Jr. became High Point's first elected mayor (Dr. R.C. Lindsay had been appointed mayor the year before). The Hunt Hotel remained open as a boardinghouse well into the 1900s. By 1910, its site was identified for the location of the new U.S. Post Office. Instead of being demolished, the old frame building was rolled across town and placed on a new foundation at the corner of English and Chestnut Streets, where it remains today. Many alterations were made to the building as it was converted to apartments. The first floor was turned into an above-ground basement; windows and trim were replaced; the exterior was sheathed in false siding; and the two-tiered porches and cupola were removed. In spite of these changes, the bones of the building remain—the original antebellum timbers that predate the founding of the city.

65. First Reformed United Church of Christ
901 West English Street

This unusual church, dedicated in the fall of 1960, was designed by High Point architect Robert Conner. The sanctuary is sheltered beneath a striking parabolic roofline sheathed in copper that has been allowed to oxidize into a soft verdigris color. The brick façade of the sanctuary, defined by the high arch of the roofline, features a large cross superimposed on a field of stucco. To each side of the sanctuary are low brick structures containing windows and entrances. A freestanding spire rises to the east. The building stands as one of the most architecturally striking and progressive in the West End area.

Southern Suburbs - Map 3

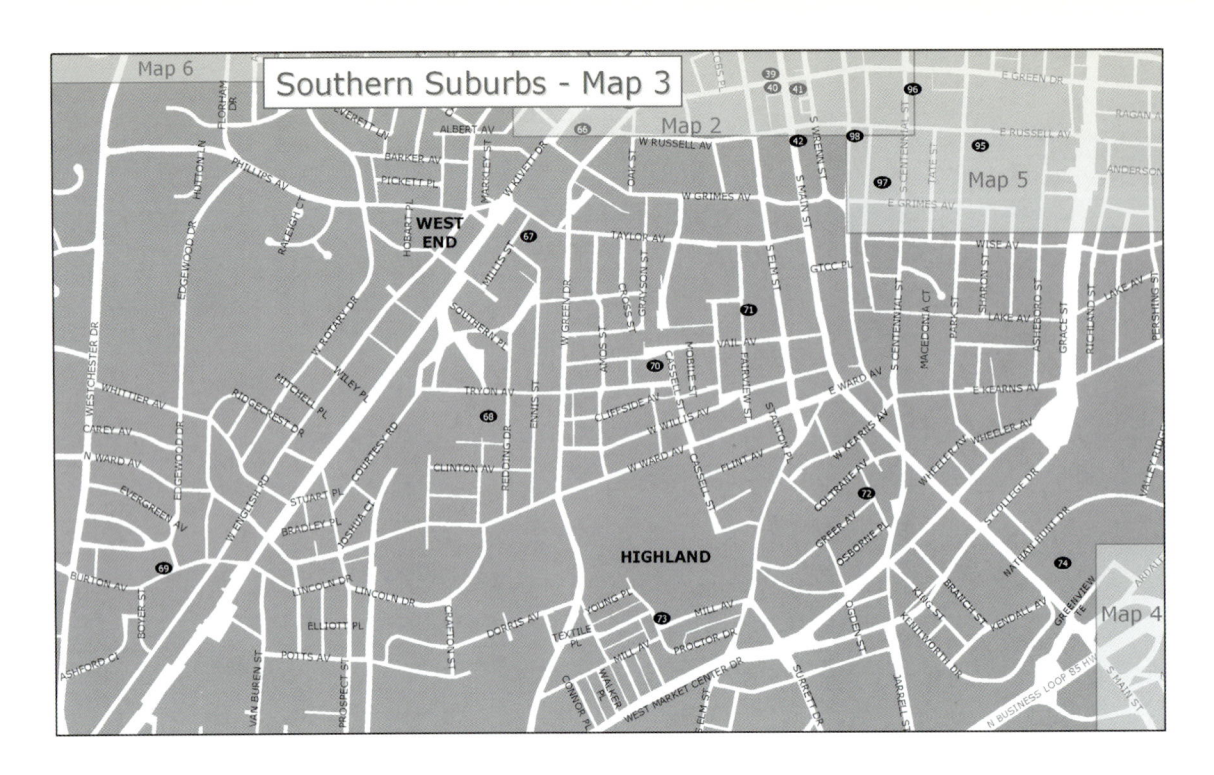

Southeast Suburbs - Map 4

WESTERN AND SOUTHERN NEIGHBORHOODS

West End

With rapid expansion of the city in the 1920s, numerous commercial districts developed around the outskirts of High Point, complementing—but never competing with—downtown. Taking on names such as Southside, West End and Mechanicsville, these shopping areas looked as urban as any small downtown in North Carolina and defined High Point's sprawling neighborhoods. Representative of these compact shopping districts are the one- and two-story brick stores located in the 1500 block of English Drive in West End. Most of these buildings were constructed between 1920 and 1940, with retail space at street level and apartments on their second floors. High Pointers developed increased reliance on cars and shopping centers with parking lots in the 1950s and 1960s. In the process, these small commercial districts lost their convenience and their retail tenants. "Urban renewal," the term used to describe large-scale, government-sponsored redevelopment of inner-city neighborhoods, destroyed many of these commercial centers, including Southside; but West End remains as the best preserved, though not well preserved.

66. Alma Desk Company
614 West Green Drive

Founded by J.P. Redding, A.M. Rankin and Henry Fraser in 1895, Alma Desk Company is situated on a compact site hugging a siding of the Southern Railroad and Grimes Street. Named for Fraser's deceased wife and later owned by J.H. Petty, the company came under the ownership of Charles E. Hayworth and Ralph Parker in 1920. With the death of Hayworth in 1928, the company came under the leadership of his wife, Myrtle Furr Hayworth (later Hayworth-Barthmaier upon her marriage to Herbert Barthmaier). By 1940, it employed 105 skilled and 69 unskilled men and produced annual sales of $952,600 in the days before World War II. The company was spread over nine buildings that included a three-story office, a warehouse, a shipping department and a similar size frame machine and cabinet gluing shop, along with smaller finishing, cutting and storage rooms. Nevertheless, the campus was small compared to other furniture manufacturers in the city. The large frame building that housed manufacturing operations featured side-gable roofs, clapboard siding and large windows to increase interior lighting. Frame buildings were brick veneered in the 1950s. The company produced wood office furniture under the slogan, "Good desks for little money," establishing a price point below sister company Myrtle Desk. By 1970, Alma Desk Company was the largest manufacturer of wooden office furniture in the world.

67. Myrtle Desk Complex
801 Millis Street

Western and Southern Neighborhoods

Located at the junction of the Southern Railway and the High Point, Thomasville and Denton Railroad, Myrtle Desk Company was a mainstay of the West End neighborhood. Formed in 1899 by Henry Fraser, the company was named for his daughter, Ida Myrtle. Charles Hayworth and Ralph Parker purchased the company in 1920, but after Hayworth's death in 1928, the company was run by his wife, Myrtle Furr Hayworth. With assistance from Vice-president Annie Mae Powell, Hayworth had developed the company into a premier manufacturer by World War II. The complex of one-, two- and three-story brick buildings sprawled over 210,000 square feet by 1941, with a workforce of 100 skilled and 153 unskilled men who manufactured wood office furniture, producing $1,138,000 in annual sales. Desks, tables, telephone stands and bookcases were the primary products of an expansive eleven-building campus that included two dry kilns with cooling sheds, a glue room, cabinet rooms, machine rooms, veneer storage, finishing rooms and packing and shipping areas. Many of the buildings were constructed during the rapid expansion of the company in the 1920s, when masonry structures rose as high as three stories to maximize use of land area and featured large metal windows for adequate lighting. The buildings were connected by a series of walkways, electrical lines and water mains designed for efficiency and safety. Myrtle Desk later merged with Alma Desk to form the largest supplier of office furnishings in the world.

68. PICKETT COTTON MILL
1200 Redding Avenue
SL 2001

An enterprising High Pointer, Francis Marion Pickett, saw opportunity in the early twentieth-century trend of electrification of textile mills. Mills were no longer bound to riversides for power; High Point provided the electricity, railroad access and workforce required to operate a mill. Around 1910, F.M. Pickett commissioned the prolific mill architect Lockwood, Green & Company of Boston to design an expansive building on High Point's far western boundary, near present-day Redding Drive. An early account from J.J. Farriss's 1916 promotional pamphlet points out that "the mill construction is of brick with reinforced concrete and iron. The copper guttering and pipe has lead splashings. These modern points of construction make the mill one of the best and safest in every way."

Pickett operated a classic cotton mill, complete with heavy brick walls and an articulated stair tower. Insurance companies at the time operated under strict standards that shaped the distinctive appearance of the cotton mill buildings they insured. For example, stairwells had to be located outside the envelope of the building in order to prevent fire from spreading to higher floors. Therefore, the stair tower at the Pickett mill stands prominently in front of the main building. Expansive windows allowed natural light for task work, and thick wooden beams resisted vibrations of machinery and were slow to fail if fire erupted. J.J. Farriss pointed out these safety features: "Every detail in the construction of the plant has been with a view to permanency and safety, insuring a system in its operation and a safeguard against accidents and fire unequaled in a majority of cotton mills." As a result of the high quality and design of the building, the mill enjoyed the lowest insurance rates available.

Pickett Cotton grew quickly to become one of the major employers in High Point. Though the company was a success at making printed cloth, changing market forces compelled the mill to begin manufacturing yarn by the 1930s. By 1945, the company employed 325 people, many of whom lived in surrounding houses developed by the mill. Pickett's grandsons took over the business in 1953 and continued operations until the plant was liquidated in 1985. Few changes were made to the building over the years, although one of the most notable was the removal of the vast windows when the mill was climate-controlled in the late 1960s. Despite alterations, the Pickett Mill building stands among High Point's most important textile mill structures. Nearby, many houses associated with the mill village have been destroyed, though some well-preserved examples remain in the 1200 blocks of Tank Court and Redding Drive, as well as Tank Avenue.

69. OAK HILL SCHOOL
314 Burton Avenue

Constructed in 1879, Oak Hill School stands among the oldest surviving structures in extreme southwestern Guilford County. Funded by local residents, the schoolhouse was built near the corner of Burton and English Streets to serve a district that extended to the Davidson County line. The simple one-room frame building was heated by two Franklin stoves, fueled by cordwood chopped by older boys and stacked outside the building. The teacher's desk and chair were located on a raised platform opposite the front door. A blackboard extended across the entire wall behind the desk, and a long bench faced the board from which the students would receive their lessons. Upon completion, students would return to double-seated desks in the center of the room to study. Outside of classroom studies, students enjoyed the adjacent playground.

At that time, the surrounding area was farms and woods; High Point's nearest neighborhoods were at least a mile to the east. As the city pressed westward, school enrollment continued to expand and overcrowded an adjacent 1907 addition. A new school was constructed for the Oak Hill community by 1910, and the early schoolhouse was sold. Also in 1910, the original

Western and Southern Neighborhoods

building was separated from the addition. Resident John Wright used a mule, block and tackle and four helpers to roll both sections down Burton Street, where each section was converted into a residence. The 1907 unit was destroyed by fire in the mid-twentieth century, but the 1879 portion remains essentially intact. Alterations such as new windows in the gable walls and plywood panels over the exterior clapboard exemplify the compromises required to adapt early buildings for contemporary use.

Southern Suburban Sites

The southern suburbs of High Point developed quickly in the early twentieth century due to rapid expansion of industry. This sector received the lion's share of new manufacturing facilities that drove the city's economic engine well into the mid-twentieth century. Typical of pre-automobile-era development patterns, services and residences were constructed in and around the factories they served, creating a patchwork of affordable housing interspersed with corner stores and schools. Increasing reliance on cars, independence from public transportation and upgraded building codes have resulted in removal of much of the early residential fabric. In addition, the nature of manufacturing in the United States changed dramatically in the late twentieth century, resulting in a large number of industrial vacancies or underuse. The resulting depopulation of the area has put the neighborhood at risk today; however, its historic resources remain viable records and are an important chapter in High Point's history.

70. Southside Neighborhood

Southside developed as an alternative to the East Washington Drive neighborhood for High Point's African American citizens during the years of the Jim Crow era of segregation. The community was focused along Fairview Street, which featured mixed-use commercial and residential buildings. Modest frame rental houses composed a majority of the community, which became a haven for black citizens to socialize, learn and worship. Much of the community was destroyed during urban renewal efforts in the 1970s. Some simple frame houses remain from the 1910s and 1920s, exhibiting late Victorian, Colonial Revival and Craftsman architectural details.

71. Brooks Memorial Methodist Church
709 Fairview Street
SL 1978

Brooks Memorial Methodist Church was organized in 1907, with Reverend Daniel Brooks as the congregation's first minister. Though they first met in the home of the Gray family at 610 Fairview Street, the congregation celebrated the completion of their new sanctuary on June 26, 1907. The frame church served the growing black population of the Southside neighborhood, who found the new church to be more convenient than churches along Washington Drive. Early leaders included members of the Gray, Gannaway, Nailer and Wright families. Mose Nailer was a prominent member who lived on South Main Street, operated a slaughterhouse and served in a popular brass band.

The simple Gothic-inspired frame church stands as one of the oldest buildings associated with the traditionally African American Southside neighborhood. The temple form structure features a distinctive tower attached to the gabled main façade. Other details include pointed arch windows, clapboard siding and exposed eaves that relate the sanctuary to traditional rural churches of the South.

trim found throughout the North Carolina countryside. Other early houses follow patterns established by early mill villages, including simple one-story plans beneath pyramidal roofs with small, plain front porches. Later houses were constructed along lines of the Craftsman style, featuring one-story plans, battered post-on-pier porch supports and exposed rafter tails. By 1923, the neighborhood had achieved the size to warrant a grand brick city school, named Cloverdale. The school was closed in 1971 and burned in the 1980s. Together, remaining houses portray a once typical mix of High Point's early twentieth-century housing types that are now increasingly rare.

73. HIGHLAND COTTON MILLS VILLAGE
SL 1977

72. CLOVERDALE NEIGHBORHOOD

Situated along Coltrane Avenue, Greer Avenue and Osborne Place, this neighborhood in southern High Point evolved over several decades as a residential area affiliated with the nearby Cloverdale Dye Works. Later, residents were employed in nearby manufacturing and commercial areas along South Main Street and by Highland Mills. The earliest houses follow established rural traditions, including frame triple-A forms with sawn Queen Anne

Highland Cotton Mills was launched in 1913 by the owners of High Point Hosiery Mill in order to supply local hosiery mills with yarn for a specialized knitting process used for socks and underwear. The surrounding neighborhood is High Point's most intact example of a mill village, containing houses and amenities that were necessary to attract workers from rural counties.

Western and Southern Neighborhoods

The HIGHLAND COTTON MILLS at 1014 Mill Avenue is one of an important group of early textile mills in High Point and the only such mill with an extensive, largely intact surrounding mill village. The building exemplifies early twentieth-century textile mills that relied on electricity as a power source, in contrast to earlier mills that derived their power from rivers and conserved energy consumption by using multi-story buildings to shorten the distance from power source to machine. Electric-powered mills, such as Highland, reinvented mill architecture by arranging workspace primarily on one level. Electricity supplied by the city also eventually enabled use of air conditioning, which modified humidity—an important step in the manufacturing process of cotton products. As a result, the large windows of the mill, which were no longer needed for ventilation and light, usually were sealed in the mid-twentieth century.

Mill "Number One," the westernmost portion of the Highland Cotton Mills complex, was constructed in 1913. A later phase, named Mill "One-A," was built between Number One and Proctor Avenue. Horseshoe-shaped mill "Number Two" dates from around 1930 and is located just east of Number One. All buildings are brick, with low roofs and wide eaves; both remain in very good condition. International competition forced the sale of the mill to new owners in the late 1980s. The mill closed in 1995.

HIGHLAND COTTON MILLS VILLAGE demonstrates the utilitarian approach designers took in creating a self-contained community located on the southern outskirts of High Point. The site was likely chosen for its high and level ground adjacent to the Southern Railroad "Belt Line," an urban rail loop surrounding High Point that provided industy access to the main line. From the rail siding north of the factory, raw materials and finished goods were transported to and from the operation, while the village stretched to the south and west.

The village was arranged with public buildings closest to the mill and residences located away at a distance. The church and community building held prominent locations on Mill Avenue across from the mill entrance. The Colonial Revival HIGHLAND METHODIST CHURCH AND PARSONAGE at 1015 Mill Avenue was constructed in 1930 under the direction of Adams-Millis Corporation President John Hampton Adams. The minister's salary was supplemented by the mill in order to maintain a religious presence in the community, and the parsonage was constructed with funds accumulated from proceeds of the mill's sale of Coca-Cola. Church services were originally held in the community building (demolished circa 1965) that was immediately west of the church and contained the company office, gymnasium, clubroom, grocery store, library and bathhouse. A boardinghouse known as Grandma Holbrook's (destroyed), located east of the mill, supplied accommodations for single male workers. The boardinghouse also likely contained the Highland School.

Four large supervisors' houses and workers' housing faced the factory complex along Mill Avenue. Beyond Mill Avenue, streets were oriented along a loose grid system. Proctor, Mill, Textile and Young are oriented nearly east to west; and Fowler, Culler, Walker, Connor and Jordan are oriented roughly north to south. All houses originally were equipped with outhouses and had deep backyards to accommodate private vegetable gardens.

The residential streets around the mill feature the best models of mill housing in the city. The earliest street in the plan was Mill Avenue, which was laid out in 1912. Houses on this street are simple one- and two-story structures with a mix of roof forms. Some pressed metal roofs remain intact. The 1100 block of Mill

Avenue contains a row of nearly identical one-story frame houses with pyramidal roofs, two-over-two windows and attached hip-roofed porches. The residence at 1124 Mill Avenue maintains early pressed metal shingles.

Proctor Drive mimicked Mill Avenue, with essentially identical one-story houses with L-shaped plans and cross-gabled roofs built from 1913 through World War I. Original details included clapboard siding, two-over-two windows, turned porch posts and pressed metal shingles. The residence at 907 Proctor Drive is a well-preserved example of the house form common to the street.

The northern block face of Textile Place contains a row of nearly identical one-story houses with L-shaped plans and cross-gabled roofs built between 1913 and 1925. The residence at 1120 Textile Place has a high degree of integrity, with wood siding, pressed metal roofing and turned porch posts with decorative sawn brackets. Young Place also contains a row of identical one-story, frame Craftsman bungalows built between 1920 and 1935, featuring forward-gable roofs and exposed rafter tails. The street was named for Lee Young, the first engineer and first employee at Highland Mill, who came from South Carolina.

In 1927, Highland Cotton Mill became a supplier to Adams-Millis Corporation, a consortium of mills in the city listed on the New York Stock Exchange. This association brought more work to the mill and began the village's most prosperous period. An article in the *High Point Enterprise* on January 20, 1935, boasted,

> *The mill village on Highland hill is considered a model by sociologists who have frequently praised the cleanliness and attractiveness of the homes and plan and the well directed social program which is maintained there through schools, churches, athletics and the community building. There is, too, a fine degree of loyalty on the part of those who work on the plant as well as those who direct it, for in the general strike of last fall the plant continued to operate despite the efforts of flying squadrons to "pull" the workers and force a shutdown.*

Nearby, the HIGHLAND COTTON MILL OFFICE at 910 Mill Avenue is an academic Colonial Revival structure erected in the 1960s to serve as the administration office for the mill. Constructed of brick and topped by a slate roof, this building reflects the residential styles that were popular in High Point's upscale neighborhoods at the time.

Increasing budgetary pressures in the late 1950s prompted the administrators to sell the individual mill houses in order to free capital necessary to purchase modern equipment. Those who worked in the mill had first choice on buying their houses. Fee-simple ownership of the houses prompted a wave of individualization to the standardized houses. Owners used

Western and Southern Neighborhoods

paint color, landscaping, material choices and sometimes small additions and porch enclosures to meet their needs and differentiate their homes from those of their neighbors. In addition to the effects of privatization, expansion of the High Point city limits entailed alterations to infrastructure. With city sewer service, outhouses were removed, and the city paved, curbed and guttered the streets upon Highland hill. Finally, minimum standards for housing enforced by the municipal building inspections department forced housing upgrades such as solid foundations, storm windows and railings that may have been considered unnecessary before. Most houses are covered in false siding and have replacement windows, but patterns of house forms remain discernable through the alterations.

74. BLAIR PARK
1901 South Main Street

Plans to expand public park space in High Point were initiated during the rapid population growth of the 1920s, but progress halted with the onset of the Great Depression in 1929. Just as the prospect for increasing park space seemed to dim, the David H. Blair family presented the municipality with a gift of seventy-three acres of land along Richland Creek south of the city for use as a public park. City administrators tapped a variety of sources to implement construction plans, including convict labor and Federal Works Progress Administration funds. Blair Park soon featured a playground, municipal golf course and a clubhouse designed by the popular High Point firm Workman, Everhart and Voorhees. The clubhouse was inspired by academic Dutch Colonial architecture, with a magnificent front porch and period detail. Blair Park was dedicated in 1931 as the "initial unit of the city's proposed system of parks." City Lake Park near Jamestown followed a few years later (see entry #197). Though the clubhouse was destroyed in 1990, Blair Park remains important as the city's earliest surviving public park and one of many important examples of Depression-era Works Progress Administration initiatives.

75. MODEL FARM
2045 Brentwood Street
GL 2001, SL 1976

The Model Farm, built in 1866, stands as one of the most important Reconstruction-era historic sites in North Carolina. Established by the Baltimore Association of Friends to Advise and Assist Friends in the Southern States, the demonstration project sought to improve production and prosperity among the state's war-torn farmers by informing them of advances in agricultural practice and procedure. The site had wide-ranging influence across the region and became a center of modern agricultural standards for most of the late nineteenth century. Governor Jonathan Worth stated that the Model Farm was the only green spot in North Carolina in the years after the war.

William A. Sampson of Maine operated the 240-acre farm. Sampson was well-versed in modern agricultural practices and set about demonstrating the use of clover crops for soil fertilization, the sale of seed and the cultivation of grass pastureland. Other initiatives included a barn with running water, "rat-proof" corn cribs, milled bone for fertilization, iron axles on wagons, thoroughbred cattle and registered sheep and hogs. After twenty-five years of service, the Baltimore Association considered its job complete and sold the property for private use in 1891.

Though the outbuildings and barn have been lost, the imposing farmhouse remains. Standing two and a half stories tall, the single-pile frame structure with a steeply sloping triple-A roof features a wide front porch, a large three-sided window bay on the west elevation and arched windows lighting the attic. Interior appointments are simple; however, the plaster walls and ceilings and running water were novel in the South in the years after the Civil War.

76. SPRINGFIELD FRIENDS FOURTH MEETING HOUSE
555 East Springfield Avenue
SL 1977

The fourth Springfield Meeting House was constructed in 1927 according to a design by High Point architect Herbert Hunter. Skilled in Colonial Revival architecture, Hunter created a nostalgic composition that includes a Tuscan portico, a broad entablature and an arched entry with a semicircular fanlight within the tympanum. The brick building's temple form strayed from the traditional side-entry plans that characterized older meetinghouses. Typical of Quaker meetinghouses, the symbolic steeple characteristic of churches is unnecessary. The building is connected to the third meetinghouse (see entry #17) by a colonnade. A chapel stands opposite the colonnade and mimics the main façade of the 1927 meetinghouse with a smaller portico.

Western and Southern Neighborhoods

77. Rock Gymnasium at Allen Jay School
1201 East Fairfield Road

The Rock Gymnasium is a distinctive example of Works Progress Administration projects. In 1937, the Allen Jay School Board and newly hired school Principal Tenor Bennison decided to erect a frame gymnasium behind the Allen Jay School. The board sought to construct the building with their own funds, donated lumber and the labor of neighboring residents. The board was initially discouraged by Guilford County Schools Superintendent Thomas Foust, who was concerned about the cost of such a structure, so the group sought labor assistance from the Works Progress Administration office in Winston-Salem to reduce costs. Though Foust eventually approved of the project, hurdles within the WPA procedure threatened to stall plans. Foust and Bennison made a trip to Washington, D.C., to solicit the help of President Franklin Delano Roosevelt, whom they met in the Oval Office. After Roosevelt cleared the red tape within the WPA, a state engineer recommended the large structure be masonry instead of frame. School board members took advantage of the abundance of stone in the neighborhood and began a drive for rock, which was brought by lunch pail, bag and pickup truck to the site. Construction of the project began in 1938 and was completed by 1939.

The side-gabled gymnasium's fieldstone walls support a wooden truss roof system. In addition to the gymnasium, the board agreed to incorporate a classroom, band room and library in exchange for the county's financing of the heating system. Interior appointments include rough stone walls, maple flooring and large windows that provide natural light. In the 1970s, a new gymnasium was constructed adjacent to the Rock Gym, which today serves as a community center for the Allen Jay neighborhood.

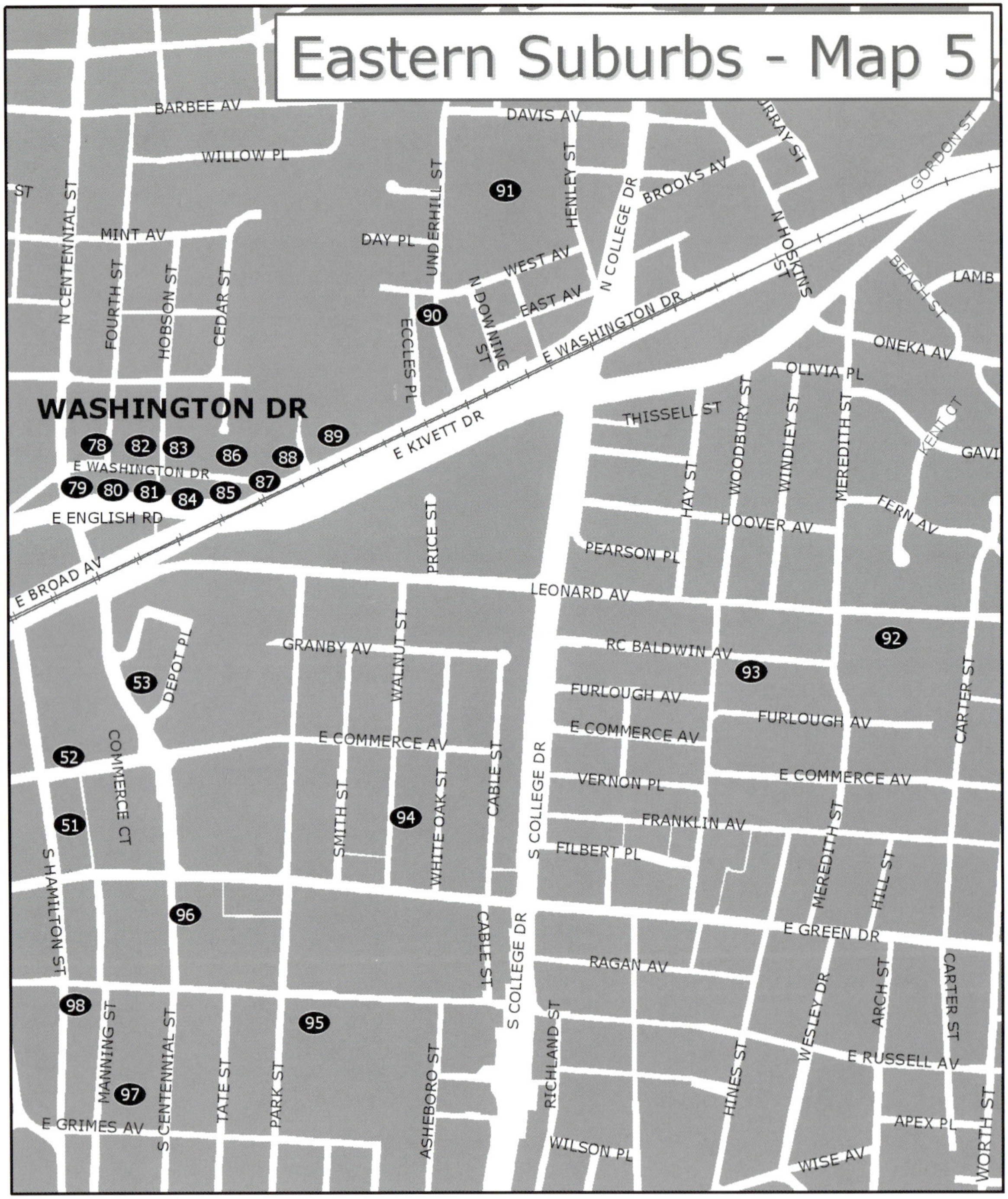
Eastern Suburbs - Map 5
WASHINGTON DR
BARBEE AV
WILLOW PL
MINT AV
DAY PL
DAVIS AV
BROOKS AV
WEST AV
EAST AV
E WASHINGTON DR
E KIVETT DR
E ENGLISH RD
E BROAD AV
N CENTENNIAL ST
FOURTH ST
HOBSON ST
CEDAR ST
UNDERHILL ST
ECCLES PL
N DOWNING ST
HENLEY ST
N COLLEGE DR
N HOSKINS ST
GORDON ST
BEACH ST
LAMB
ONEKA AV
OLIVIA PL
THISSELL ST
WOODBURY ST
WINDLEY ST
MEREDITH ST
KENT CT
GAVI
HAY ST
HOOVER AV
FERN AV
PEARSON PL
PRICE ST
LEONARD AV
GRANBY AV
WALNUT ST
RC BALDWIN AV
FURLOUGH AV
E COMMERCE AV
VERNON PL
FRANKLIN AV
FILBERT PL
CARTER ST
DEPOT PL
COMMERCE CT
S HAMILTON ST
SMITH ST
WHITE OAK ST
CABLE ST
S COLLEGE DR
E GREEN DR
RAGAN AV
HILL ST
ARCH ST
WESLEY DR
E RUSSELL AV
HINES ST
RICHLAND ST
MANNING ST
S CENTENNIAL ST
TATE ST
PARK ST
ASHEBORO ST
E GRIMES AV
WILSON PL
WISE AV
APEX PL
WORTH ST
ST
51
52
53
78
79
80
81
82
83
84
85
86
87
88
89
90
91
92
93
94
95
96
97
98

EASTERN SUBURBS

East Washington Drive
SL 2001

Washington Drive stands today as one of the best preserved of North Carolina's few remaining "black downtowns," most having been destroyed during urban renewal efforts of the mid-twentieth century. The Washington Drive community represents a period when African Americans were segregated from mainstream society and were forced to develop a mixed-use neighborhood that included civic, social, entertainment, educational, religious, health and commercial uses on one avenue. The origins of the mixed-use thoroughfare can be traced to the late nineteenth century, when the 500 through 800 blocks of East Washington Drive were developed by African American citizens after North Carolina voters moved to disenfranchise black citizens through a state constitutional amendment in 1898. This referendum marked the commencement of the Jim Crow laws, named for an antebellum minstrel show character, which created a racial caste system expressed in "separate but equal" facilities for whites and blacks in every facet of society throughout the South by 1914. One result was that blacks developed their own business districts on the fringe of city centers.

East Washington Drive was a logical site for High Point's black downtown because of its proximity to existing institutions such as St. Mark's Methodist Church of 1877 and High Point Normal and Industrial Institute, the African American school that was relocated from Asheboro in 1891. The school was constructed on a knoll overlooking both the busy North Carolina Railroad tracks and Jamestown Street (later East Washington Drive), which was the main eastbound thoroughfare out of High Point. Enrollment during its first year reached 193 students; with the school's success, the adjoining Washington Drive neighborhood naturally became central to High Point's black community. Many of the city's prominent black citizens resided along the street. Religious leaders such as Methodist minister Reverend Daniel Brooks and First Baptist's Reverend O.S. Bullock; entrepreneurs John Robinson, John and Nannie Kilby and Willis Hinton; community physicians Dr. Garron and Dr. Gaylord; and educators A.J. Griffin and O.E. Davis all called East Washington Drive home.

St. Mark's Methodist Church established a presence in the community as early as 1877, and First Baptist Church was constructed at the corner of East Washington and Hobson Streets in 1907. The same year, the Oddfellows built a lodge on East Washington Street. Commercial buildings followed, including Washington Street Grocery in 1910 at 500 East Washington. By the time Charles Hart created his panoramic "aero view" of High Point in 1913, East Washington Drive was lined with a variety of large and small frame houses interspersed with businesses, institutions and churches. The Kilby Hotel, a landmark of the street in spirit as well as presence, was constructed just before World War I to provide accommodations and entertainment for black visitors and residents alike. High Point's black population grew quickly after the war. From 1923 to 1925, black migrants from South Carolina and Georgia sought work in the city's burgeoning industries, resulting in rapid development on East Washington Drive. Many small frame houses were demolished to make way for commercial projects such as the Griffin Building and the Saunders Building.

The period after World War II was perhaps the busiest for East Washington Drive businesses. Not only did the street serve High Point's large and growing black population, but also white citizens patronized some of its popular establishments. Several well-designed structures were erected in this pre–civil rights period, including the Yarborough Law Building, Willard Building and the Washington Drive Branch of the High Point Public Library.

The 1954 United States Supreme Court's decision on *Brown v. Board of Education of Topeka, Kansas*, declared segregation in the public schools unconstitutional. The success of the civil rights movement over the next twenty years contributed to the demise of the East Washington Drive business district as integration encouraged blacks to patronize mainstream establishments. By the mid-1970s, the neighborhood was in decline, in large part due to federally funded urban renewal projects that removed portions of area neighborhoods as well as enforcement of higher standards for building codes citywide. During the last quarter of the twentieth century, nearly a third of the inventory of historic structures in the neighborhood were destroyed. By 2000, community initiatives toward neighborhood renewal began to slow the rate of demolition and abandonment, and shops began to return to the street.

Eastern Suburbs

78. WASHINGTON DRIVE BRANCH/HIGH POINT PUBLIC LIBRARY
201 Fourth Street

Robert Conner designed the Washington Drive Branch of the High Point Public Library around 1958 as a single-story structure with coral-colored Roman brick walls on street elevations broken only by a high band of windows that provide light to the interior. Above the windows are turquoise-colored porcelain enamel spandrel panels that rise to the roofline. On the north elevation, windows are large; on the Fourth Street side, walls of windows frame the well-landscaped covered courtyard that leads to the main entrance. The building is a thoughtfully composed Modernist design that shelters its occupants from the distractions of surrounding city streets, yet floods the interior with natural light.

79. DR. GAYLORD HOUSE
600 East Washington Drive

This residence is important as the home of Sallie and Dr. Cavessa J.H. Gaylord. Dr. Gaylord, a graduate of Shaw University's Leonard Medical School, practiced medicine in High Point for over fifty years, beginning around 1910. A well-respected member of the community, he maintained interests in various civic activities in the neighborhood. This circa 1910 Victorian house has seen numerous additions and alterations, including enclosure of the front porch and the application of replacement siding, but its original form has been preserved. The one-story frame structure is identified by its hip-on-side gable roof and prominent attic gable centered above the main entry.

80. ROBINSON HOUSE
606 East Washington Drive

Early High Point historian Thomas B. Smith remembered, "John Robinson was one of the wealthiest Negroes in High Point from the reconstruction era to the end of the century. He, along with William 'Bill' Robinson, was the best brick mason in High Point. And together, they did the majority of the mason work. All important buildings erected during their active days were at least partly done by them." Smith also remembered that "Robinson owned the entire block on Wrenn Street…later, on account of the business expansion, he sold his Wrenn Street property and erected a home on East Washington Street which is still considered one of the best in the Washington Street section." Robinson maintained his economic status well into the twentieth century, and his house remains as one of the largest dwellings in the neighborhood. Robinson's house is highly important as a reminder of the numerous imposing homes of early black entrepreneurs that once lined Washington Drive. Taking architectural cues from Queen Anne and Neoclassical Revival architecture, this circa 1905 house exhibits a popular mode of its day. Distinctive features include a second-floor balcony located over the front door, a wide front porch supported by Tuscan columns, a front door surrounded by sidelights and transom and a porte-cochere. The house remained in the Robinson family until the 1960s.

81. YARBOROUGH LAW BUILDING
622 East Washington Drive

The Yarborough Law Building is among the most voguish mid-twentieth-century structures in the neighborhood. The building was constructed in the late 1950s by Dr. Martin, husband of Ora Kilby Martin, and features a ground-to-roof glass curtain wall and a projecting fixed awning over the front entry. The glass and blue spandrel panel curtain wall of the Yarborough Law Building is an exemplary component of the style, as is the use of Roman brick. The building's name is depicted in simple metal letters on the façade. The Yarborough Building is among a trio of neighboring buildings that share progressive design features and were likely all constructed around the same time. High Point–based public relations firm B&C Associates was an early occupant of the building.

82. Kilby Hotel
625–627 East Washington Drive
GL 1982, NR 1982

African Americans Nannie and John Kilby came to High Point in the 1890s following their marriage in Alamance County. Born in 1873, John worked for the Southern Railroad. Nannie was a practical nurse and hairdresser, born in 1877. Wisely, the couple invested extra income in real estate. High Point was a booming village at the time with a great deal of promise, and real estate values were increasing quickly.

After the implementation of Jim Crow laws, the Kilbys turned oppression into opportunity by providing High Point's black population a substantial brick hotel and recreation hall. Built in 1914, the Kilby Hotel loomed over the city's "black downtown" of East Washington Drive with three stories containing twenty-one rooms, each with a window and access by hallway to a shared bathroom. The halls were wide and gracious, and the third floor was lit by skylights.

The Kilbys built their hotel in the Romanesque style, with round-arched windows and decorative brickwork. Black business people operated shops on the first floor; the nightclub adjacent to the hotel showcased such legends as Nat King Cole, Ella Fitzgerald and Billy Eckstein. Other shop fronts were used by entrepreneurs, including grocers, beauticians and barbers, as well as physician Otis Tillman.

Nannie Kilby did not stop with the success of her hotel, but continued to invest her profits in real estate, acquiring thirty rental houses on High Point's east side. She earned a reputation for her hard work and superb business acumen, as exhibited by her financial success in spite of the many obstacles placed before her by society. Nannie Kilby passed away in her prime in 1921. Upon her death, the Kilbys' only daughter, Ora Kilby Martin, took over family business matters.

83. First Baptist Church
701 East Washington Drive

With St. Stephen AME Zion and St. Mark's Methodist Episcopal Church, First Baptist Church was one of the most imposing buildings along East Washington Drive. Prominent members of the congregation included Dr. Hoover, Dr. Gaylord, Dr. Tillman and S.E. Burford, who was the first black member of the High Point City Council. Established in 1871, it remains one of the most influential churches in the city, with a deep history of involvement in the community. The 1,200-seat sanctuary was erected in 1907 under the leadership of Reverend O.S. Bullock, who considered the congregation to be the "Little Church with the Big Heart." Measuring fifty feet by seventy feet, the wood frame structure was brick veneered and given its present Gothic theme around 1945. The front façade is anchored on each side by short twin crenellated towers. A high gable roof rises between the towers, culminating in a central bell tower and short pyramidal steeple. Below the bell tower is a large rose window. Other notable features include stained-glass transoms above the double-door entries and a large gothic traceried window directly beneath the rose window. Behind the building is a Sunday school annex, built in 1917.

84. REVEREND SAULTER HOUSE
716 East Washington Drive

This house was the home of Martha and Reverend David S. Saulter, a native of Tarboro, theology graduate of Shaw University and charismatic religious leader in High Point. Its boxy two-story design is exemplary of the American Foursquare and remains in good overall condition on a large lot with a mature red maple in the front yard. It is one of the few remaining residences on East Washington Drive, and its landscaped lot contrasts with the paved or graveled surface lots nearby. Topped by a pyramidal roof with a central-hipped dormer window above the façade, the house exhibits a porch with battered columns sitting on brick pedestals and three-over-one vertical windows. Ample and simply boxed eaves and the low-pitched porch roof evoke the Prairie style, which is often cited as the inspiration for the Foursquare. The house is important to the character of mixed-use development within the East Washington Drive neighborhood.

85. ODDFELLOWS HALL
736 East Washington Drive

The Oddfellows Hall dominates the heart of the East Washington Drive commercial area. The cornerstone of the building states:

GOD of the Morning Lodge
Number 2281 Oddfellows Lodge
erected 1907 Oct 28th Inst. Nov. 11, 1881

The Oddfellow is a worldwide fraternal organization united by a belief in the fatherhood of God and the brotherhood of man. Their three-story lodge of 1907, one of the oldest remaining structures on East Washington Drive, is stucco-over-masonry construction and three bays wide. Each bay holds segmental-arched windows on the second floor and round-arched on the third. Decorative aspects include a patterned brickwork cornice, a molded wooden cornice above the shop fronts and cut-stone windowsills. The building has had minor alterations and its windows are now boarded over. Otherwise, its condition is good and the building commands an imposing presence in the neighborhood.

86. WHITTEN CLINIC
745–751 East Washington Drive

This ensemble of Streamline Moderne–style commercial buildings exemplifies a rare form of architecture in High Point. The storefronts feature Streamline elements, such as a rounded corner with large wraparound windows of glass brick and a stylized stepped parapet gable. Original metal casement windows and a number of plate-glass windows survive. Walls of pressed brick topped by a concrete cap are laid in an English bond. Constructed around 1949, the building was first occupied by physician Clifford Whitten, who operated a popular medical office at 745 East Washington Drive. Other early occupants of adjacent spaces include the Modern Barber Shop, Mae's Beauty Salon and Smith Records and Gifts.

87. (Former) St. Mark's Methodist Church
755 East Washington Drive

88. Dr. Davis Office
761 East Washington Drive

A Methodist church has occupied this site since 1877, when land was purchased by Reverend William Harry Smith to establish Smith Chapel. The original brick sanctuary was replaced in 1928 by the present building, renamed St. Mark's Methodist Church. The congregation moved out of the neighborhood in the late 1970s and sold this property to Mount Zion Baptist Church, the current occupant, in 1982. St. Mark's was one of three imposing churches (along with St. Stephen AME Zion and First Baptist) on East Washington Drive.

The Gothic Revival–style church features two crenellated towers. The three-story east tower dominates the forward-facing gable roof, while the two-story west tower terminates at the spring point of the gable roof. Wire-cut patterned brickwork further embellishes the exterior of the sanctuary. Many windows feature tall, Gothic, pointed arches that contain stained glass. Alterations in recent decades have included removing most of the stained glass on the side elevation for installation at the new St. Mark's sanctuary and covering the window frames and belfry with vinyl siding.

In keeping with the high profile he maintained in his community, Dr. Murray Davis occupied this forward-looking Streamline Moderne–style office throughout the 1940s and 1950s. The circa 1940 building features a projecting two-bay wing with rounded corners. The main entry is recessed within the west setback. The overall form of the building remains intact, although the original glass-brick front windows that face Washington Drive have been replaced with paired double-hung units.

This building is important for its architectural contribution to the East Washington Drive streetscape, as well as being the only tangible reminder of Dr. Davis since his house at 612 East Washington has been demolished. The structure is also one of a small number of Moderne-style buildings in High Point and a good example of a historically African American–owned professional building.

89. William Penn High School, Samuel E. Burford Auditorium
825 East Washington Drive
NR 1978

William Penn High School stands as a symbol of the partnership between African American citizens, members of the Society of Friends and the public school system. It portrays a unique chapter in the history of education in North Carolina, and illustrates a local solution to the difficult circumstances that arose during the Jim Crow era of racial segregation and disenfranchisement.

Increasing racial segregation in the American South attracted the attention of a group of Quakers from New York Yearly Meeting, who sought to found a school in North Carolina devoted solely to the education of African Americans, with an emphasis on teaching young people trades that could be utilized to support themselves upon graduation. Originally established in Asheboro in the 1880s, the school was relocated in 1891 to Solomon Blair's two-room schoolhouse near the intersection of present-day Kivett Drive and Centennial Street. In 1893, the school erected a new campus on the outskirts of High Point, near the newly developing "black downtown" along East Washington Drive. The campus first consisted of only one frame building, but within a year a faculty cottage was added. The institution was renamed the High Point Normal and Industrial School and was administered by a committee of New York Quakers until 1897. In that year, teacher and school administrator Alfred J. Griffin accepted the position of principal and for the next twenty-six years guided the institution through a long period of growth.

At its height in the early twentieth century, the school had a faculty of 9 teachers and 287 local students who maintained a large farm that provided them with pork, wheat, corn and other vegetables. Male students learned brick making, masonry, blacksmithing and furniture making; female students learned food preparation, millinery and other domestic talents. Students also had training in basic academic subjects as well as spiritual training, and they formed several religious organizations. The campus included numerous brick buildings designed in the Romanesque style of architecture.

In 1923, the school was sold by the Quakers to the City of High Point for use as an accredited, segregated public school for blacks. The quality of education continued to improve; the school received an "A" rating by the Southern Association of Colleges and Secondary Schools. When the name of the school was changed in 1929 to honor William Penn (the seventeenth-century Quaker founder of Pennsylvania), the Samuel E. Burford Auditorium of the school was heavily remodeled to its present appearance. The Georgian Revival styling of the brick auditorium facing Washington Drive is evident in the tall, round-arched windows topped with keystones that grace the sides of the building. Similar stone detailing is at other openings, including a small, round "oculus" over the front door. Rising above the entire structure is a tall cupola that acts as a landmark for the neighborhood. In 1954, architect William Henley Deitrick designed a simple brick auditorium for the campus. These two structures are all that remain of the original Penn campus today.

Integration of the public school system in the mid-1960s led to the demise of William Penn School. Though Penn officials had begun to plan for enlarging and remodeling the campus, the city school board decided instead to concentrate efforts on a new high school, today known as T. Wingate Andrews High School.

Closed since the 1960s and once slated for destruction, William Penn High School was renovated and reopened in 2003 as the Penn-Griffin School of Performing Arts within the Guilford County School System.

Eastern Suburban Sites

Although Washington Drive remains the symbolic heart of eastern High Point, sites of historic significance are scattered far beyond its influence. The eastern suburbs of the city chronicle both African American history and white history, industrial growth and the city's forays into social enhancement through improved residential facilities in partnership with the federal government. This sector of the city has contributed to High Point's diverse and inclusive history, and illustrates the growth of the community into one of the largest municipalities in the state.

90. Griffin Park Neighborhood

Griffin Park, which incorporates Underhill Street and segments of West Avenue, Day Place and Eccles Place, became a popular locale for African American merchants, professionals and businessmen to build their homes. The neighborhood was platted in 1922 as a quiet alternative to East Washington Drive, which was then home to most of High Point's middle- and upper-income black families. Residents of Griffin Park chose house styles that were nationally popular, such as Craftsman and Colonial Revival. These residential styles can be found throughout the city, but Griffin Park contains an unusually high number of well-articulated examples built for citizens who participated in various sectors of the city's economy. For example, the house at 131 Underhill Street was built in 1936 for Henry Smith, who worked at Siceloff Ice and Coal and American Ice and Coal companies. This charming Craftsman bungalow features elements common to the style, including exposed rafter tails, tapered wooden posts set upon brick piers and windows featuring three long, vertical panes positioned over one single pane. Architect Fred L. Lander resided at 203 Underhill Avenue in a modest forward-gabled Craftsman-style home. His design studio was located to the rear.

A slightly different story is told just down the street at 118 Underhill Street, the home of the Reverend and Mrs. Walter Blair. Their large extended family lived with them, including their grandson, John Coltrane, who lived in the house throughout his formative years from 1932 until he graduated from William Penn High School in 1943. Coltrane began playing the clarinet in his senior year of high school, but soon switched to alto saxophone and thus started a career as one of America's most gifted jazz musicians.

Eastern Suburbs

91. Daniel Brooks Homes
1431 West Avenue
SL 2001

The solution to overwhelming problems with substandard and crowded housing conditions in High Point came in the form of a local-federal partnership. At the local level, the city established a housing authority in 1940, the first in Guilford County. The authority borrowed funds from the United States Housing Administration to clear "slum" neighborhoods and redevelop them with clean, safe and modern apartments. These federally financed units could then be operated by the local authority on the basis of need.

High Point citizens did not wholly embrace the initiative for housing reform. Some accused government officials and architects of being the true beneficiaries of the effort; others felt that public housing competed unfairly with private landlords. The housing authority—composed originally of J.E. Millis, C.M. Waynick, D.A. Dowdy, O.L. Ruth and L.S. Ross—eventually swayed the community to support the project. As the debate died down, the housing authority was loaned $1,770,000 by the federal government, and the project moved forward.

In accordance with segregation laws of the time, two "separate but equal" projects were planned. To the north, a site was selected near William Penn High School for black citizens. Architect Tyson T. Ferree designed this two-hundred-apartment complex named for Reverend Daniel Brooks, a popular Methodist minister in High Point. Reverend Brooks was active in the community and is best remembered for negotiating the sale of land that became the site of William Penn High School. The second project, located on Park Street, was slightly larger and was reserved for white citizens (see entry #95).

Opened in 1944, Brooks Homes stayed true to social reform ideals of the day. The project was quite revolutionary when compared to traditional urban development in High Point. Instead of the grid plan that characterized the streets of eastern High Point, Ferree chose for the development a gently curving road network with ample parking and landscaped lawns. The "garden city" ideal, as expressed earlier in the Emerywood neighborhood, was brought to the dense older districts in order to lighten the burden of the city. The garden city, conceived in Great Britain, was characterized by clusters of buildings surrounded by open spaces or a village green. It contrasted with the dense urban and industrial landscapes typical of manufacturing cities.

92. Greenhill Cemetery
1700 Leonard Street

This municipal cemetery adjacent to established African American neighborhoods on the east side of town was established in 1910, when the city purchased six acres for $750. African Americans had previously been interred at Oakwood Cemetery, but it is likely that lack of room for expansion and the growing influence of "separate but equal" Jim Crow laws precipitated the creation of a separate burial ground. The cemetery has been expanded and now covers eleven acres containing 1,247 plots. Grave markers range in material from cement to marble and granite, some affixed with porcelain images of the deceased. One stone mausoleum stands for Mary and Thural Ingram, and a prominent plot framed by a milk quartz wall contains the Kilby-Martin family, including Nannie and John Kilby.

93. Rosetta C. Baldwin House
1408 R.C. Baldwin Avenue

Rosetta Cora Baldwin was a prominent educator and director of a private school in the African American neighborhoods of eastern High Point. Teaching children from kindergarten through eighth grade for seventy years, Baldwin left an indelible mark on generations of High Point's black community. Several of her graduates continued on to prominent positions as educators, ministers and power brokers.

Her one-and-a-half-story frame house was also the site of her school. The residence is an excellent example of middle-income housing in the city, featuring Craftsman-era details, including post-on-pier porch supports, wide overhanging eaves and an oversized central dormer window. Interior features are simple, including bead board siding, plank floors and one-over-one windows. The house is well preserved and today stands open to public tours as a museum to honor Miss Baldwin, her family and the African American community.

Eastern Suburbs

94. WHITE OAK NEIGHBORHOOD

Platted by Peoples Realty Company in 1905, this neighborhood of boxy frame houses was one of High Point's earliest suburbs. Comfortable dwellings with simple Colonial Revival, late Queen Anne or Craftsman styles were constructed for the city's rising mechanical, clerical and managerial workers. Early residents of the neighborhood included Mary and C.F. White, a foreman at Globe Furniture; Mary and Jason Shore, a glassworker; Lelia and Robert Young, also a glassworker; Mary and J.G. Thompson, a laborer; and Bettie and Thomas Smith, a furniture maker. Residents enjoyed the convenience of living close to trolley lines along Green Drive that whisked them to work, shopping and social events.

Lining streets just east of downtown, such as Cable, White Oak, Walnut, Smith and Park, many houses were built with two stories containing parlors, two or three bedrooms and a one-story rear kitchen ell, much in alignment with contemporary farmhouses within the region. Finish inside these houses was often simple plaster or bead board, with mass-produced appointments such as mantels. The survival of numerous early houses, despite redevelopment initiatives targeting the neighborhood, attests to the high quality of the construction.

95. CLARA COX HOMES
615 Park Street
SL 2001

Constructed using federal funds in 1944 at the same time as Daniel Brooks Homes on West Avenue (see entry #91), the slightly larger Clara Cox Homes was reserved for whites, in accordance with segregation laws of the time. Residential buildings were intended to replace deteriorated housing classified by the city as slums. Designed by High Point architects Voorhees and Everhart with Colonial Revival details, the structures were integrated into a well-landscaped campus by local landscape architect R.D. Tillson. Designers incorporated garden city ideals of the day by arranging one- and two-story multi-unit residential buildings in groups overlooking a pedestrian-only space of playgrounds and lawns. The complex contrasted with dense industrial and commercial landscapes found on surrounding streets. The complex was named for Clara Ione Cox, minister of Springfield Friends Meeting and champion of social issues in High Point. Clara Cox Homes became a victim of the passing fads of urban housing models in 2005, when the complex was razed by the City of High Point to be replaced by a neotraditional arrangement of housing.

96. SLANE HOSIERY MILLS
309 South Centennial Street

This two-story, masonry mill building erected around 1915 exemplifies early twentieth-century urban textile mills in North Carolina, featuring large windows to allow light for task work, brick pilasters to resist vibrations from large machinery and two-story construction to minimize land acquisition. The utilitarian building was joined in 1924 by a 200-foot by 115-foot brick addition designed by architect Herbert Hunter and built by Greensboro industrial contractor J.O. Connor. Slane Hosiery Mills, started by Willis H. Slane, manufactured men's fancy half hose.

97. THOMAS MILLS, INC.
423 Manning Drive

Established by William B. Thomas to manufacture men's fancy half hose, including well-known brands Retrievers and Ho-Boy, this three-story masonry building, featuring an impressive stepped-gable, was built around 1925. The mill is unusually substantial for High Point, rising higher than most and constructed entirely of masonry, in contrast to masonry and slow-burn timber beam construction. Large windows allowed natural light into the building for task work. After W.B. Thomas Jr. moved the company to Pilot Mountain in the late 1940s, the building was used as a warehouse.

Eastern Suburbs

98. Silver Knit Hosiery Mills, Inc.
401 South Hamilton Street

In 1933, the Silver family moved their hosiery operations to High Point from Kingsport, Tennessee. The company manufactured men's fancy rayon and silk hose in a substantial two-story brick facility on South Hamilton Street, an avenue known a generation earlier as an upper-income residential neighborhood. As families with means moved out to the leafy neighborhoods northwest of the city, industry replaced residential uses along the street. The Silver Knit Hosiery Mills, owned by brothers Milton and Robert Silver, departs from established utilitarian mill design by incorporating fine architectural details into the building, such as Flemish bond brickwork, cast-cement water table and cement-topped pilasters positioned between the large windows. The mill building represents a high-water mark in industrial architecture in the city and occupies a high-profile position at the corner of two major thoroughfares. The building was renovated in 2002 for use as the Center Point furniture showrooms.

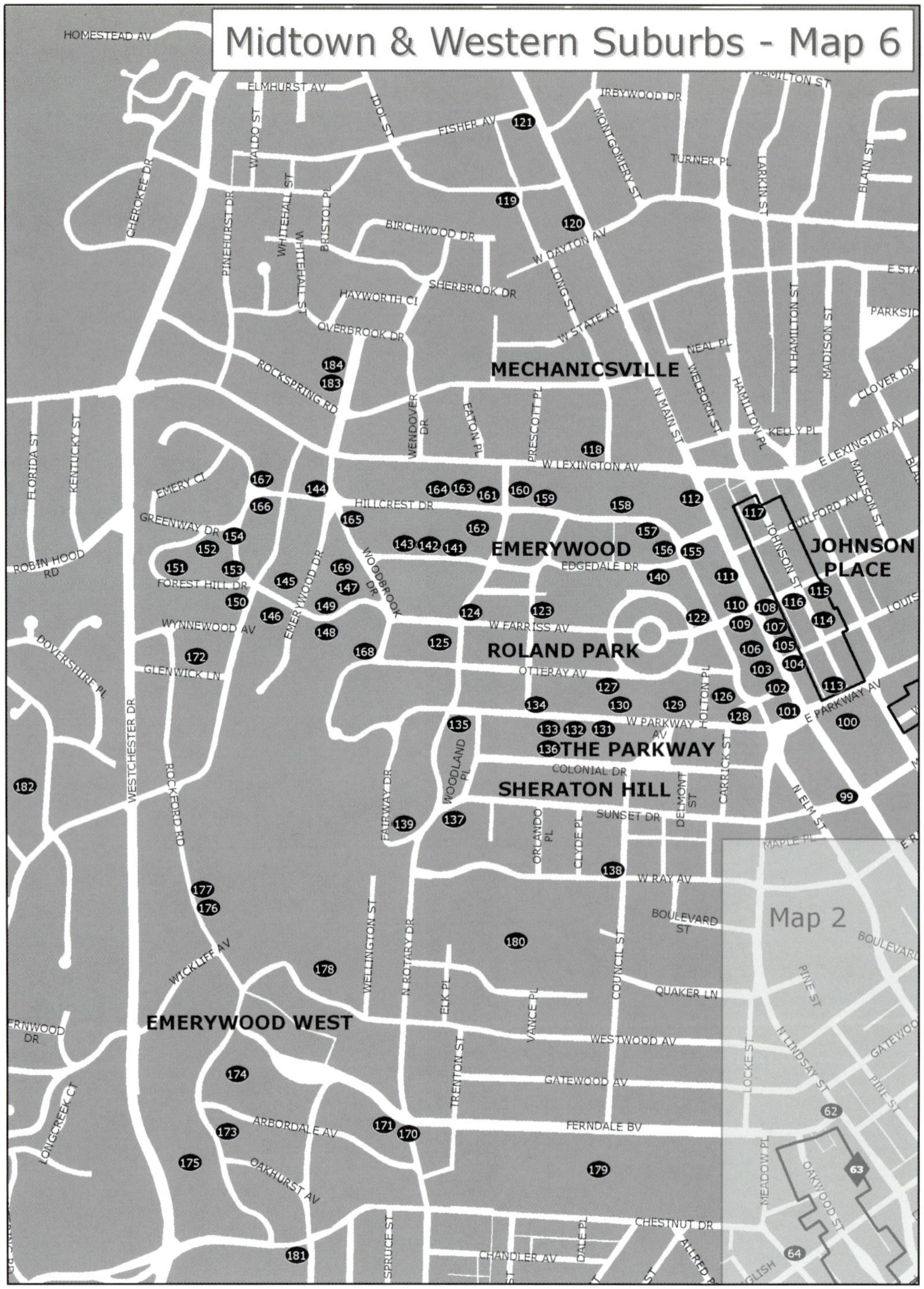
Midtown & Western Suburbs - Map 6
MECHANICSVILLE
EMERYWOOD
JOHNSON PLACE
ROLAND PARK
THE PARKWAY
SHERATON HILL
EMERYWOOD WEST
Map 2
HOMESTEAD AV
ELMHURST AV
FISHER AV
IRBYWOOD DR
TURNER PL
MONTGOMERY ST
LARKIN ST
BLAIN ST
CHEROKEE DR
WALDO ST
IDOL ST
PINEHURST DR
WHITEFALL ST
BRISTOL PL
BIRCHWOOD DR
W DAYTON AV
HAYWORTH CI
SHERBROOK DR
OVERBROOK DR
LONG ST
W STATE AV
NEAL PL
N HAMILTON ST
MADISON ST
ROCKSPRING RD
WENDOVER DR
EATON PL
PRESCOTT PL
N MAIN ST
WELBORN ST
HAMILTON PL
KELLY PL
CLOVER DR
E LEXINGTON AV
FLORIDA ST
KENTUCKY ST
W LEXINGTON AV
EMERY CI
HILLCREST DR
GREENWAY DR
GUILFORD AV
MADISON ST
JOHNSON ST
ROBIN HOOD RD
EDGEDALE DR
FOREST HILL DR
WOODBROOK DR
EMERYWOOD DR
WYNNEWOOD AV
W FARRISS AV
DOVERSHIRE PL
GLENWICK LN
OTTERAY AV
HOLTON PL
W PARKWAY AV
E PARKWAY AV
WESTCHESTER DR
ROCKFORD RD
WOODLAND PL
COLONIAL DR
CARRICK ST
DELMONT ST
FAIRWAY DR
ORLANDO PL
CLYDE PL
SUNSET DR
N ELM ST
MAPLE PL
W RAY AV
BOULEVARD ST
BOULEVARD
WICKLIFF AV
WELLINGTON ST
N ROTARY DR
ELK PL
COUNCIL ST
QUAKER LN
PINE ST
VANCE PL
WESTWOOD AV
N LINDSAY ST
LOCKE ST
FERNWOOD DR
TRENTON ST
GATEWOOD AV
LONGCREEK CT
ARBORDALE AV
FERNDALE BV
MEADOW PL
OAKWOOD ST
OAKHURST AV
SPRUCE ST
CHESTNUT DR
CHANDLER AV
DALE PL
ALLRED PL
99
100
101
102
103
104
105
106
107
108
109
110
111
112
113
114
115
116
117
118
119
120
121
122
123
124
125
126
127
128
129
130
131
132
133
134
135
136
137
138
139
140
141
142
143
144
145
146
147
148
149
150
151
152
153
154
155
156
157
158
159
160
161
162
163
164
165
166
167
168
169
170
171
172
173
174
175
176
177
178
179
180
181
182
183
184
62
63
64

MIDTOWN AND WESTERN SUBURBS

Midtown

North Main Street contains the greatest collection of early twentieth-century mansions in the city, recalling the beginning of a movement among wealthy industrialists to establish residences outside dense older neighborhoods of central High Point, a pattern continued later with Emerywood. Nearly all residences in the midtown area were constructed between 1907 and 1925, as streetcar lines and automobiles allowed upper-income families to enjoy the conveniences of the city as well as the pastoral setting of the countryside. The earliest houses were constructed with Neoclassical Revival influences, but residences erected after 1910 in association with Homer Wheeler's Johnson Place development east of Main Street were built in Prairie style, Colonial Revival style or with Mediterranean influences. First Presbyterian Church and St. Mary's Episcopal Church added prestige to the neighborhood when they were constructed in the late 1920s. Multifamily housing was constructed along North Main Street during the high growth period of the 1920s and 1930s, resulting in the city's best collection of Art Deco apartment buildings. Though the neighborhood lost appeal during the mid-twentieth century, renewed interest in historic preservation fueled restoration projects and infill that brought institutions and commercial establishments to the area. The area remains popular, containing many of the city's notable institutions, businesses and boutiques.

99. HIGH POINT PUBLIC LIBRARY
901 North Main Street

This three-story masonry building, constructed in 1990–92, plays an important visual role in the North Main Street corridor just north of downtown. The design by High Point architect Clayton Mays was conceived by analyzing usage, departmental relationships and services within the library. This information was translated into the current half-circle-plan building that takes advantage of indirect northern light, controlled views of the city skyline and adjacent strip development and ease of access. The rounded lobe of the half-circle presses south, and its elevation contains little glazing. In contrast, the north-facing cross section of the circle features extensive windows overlooking a courtyard and masonry screen. The building was sheathed with a reflective white masonry that resonates with classical architecture of the Mediterranean within the context of a progressive and modern structure.

100. FIRST PRESBYTERIAN CHURCH
918 North Main Street
SL 2001

Hobart Upjohn of New York City, in consultation with Harry Barton of Greensboro, designed this important church that was the first of a number of well-designed High Point sanctuaries by regionally or nationally known architects. The church site occupies a prominent location chosen by the designers and members of the building committee, at the corner of Main Street and East Parkway, within a grove of sizable oaks. The architects and committee agreed that a style reminiscent of an English Gothic cathedral was most suitable for the congregation and their site. The congregation required a six-hundred-seat sanctuary, which the architects designed with steel construction, Crab Orchard stone walls, limestone trim and slate roof. Crab Orchard stone, a light brown sandstone quarried near Crab Orchard, Tennessee, is sought for its red and orange swirls from high iron content, as well as a sheen caused by a large quantity of mica crystals. Construction began on Thanksgiving Day 1926 and ended by April 1, 1928. The building was recognized by the North Carolina Chapter of the American Institute of Architects in 1929, the first year such citations were administered.

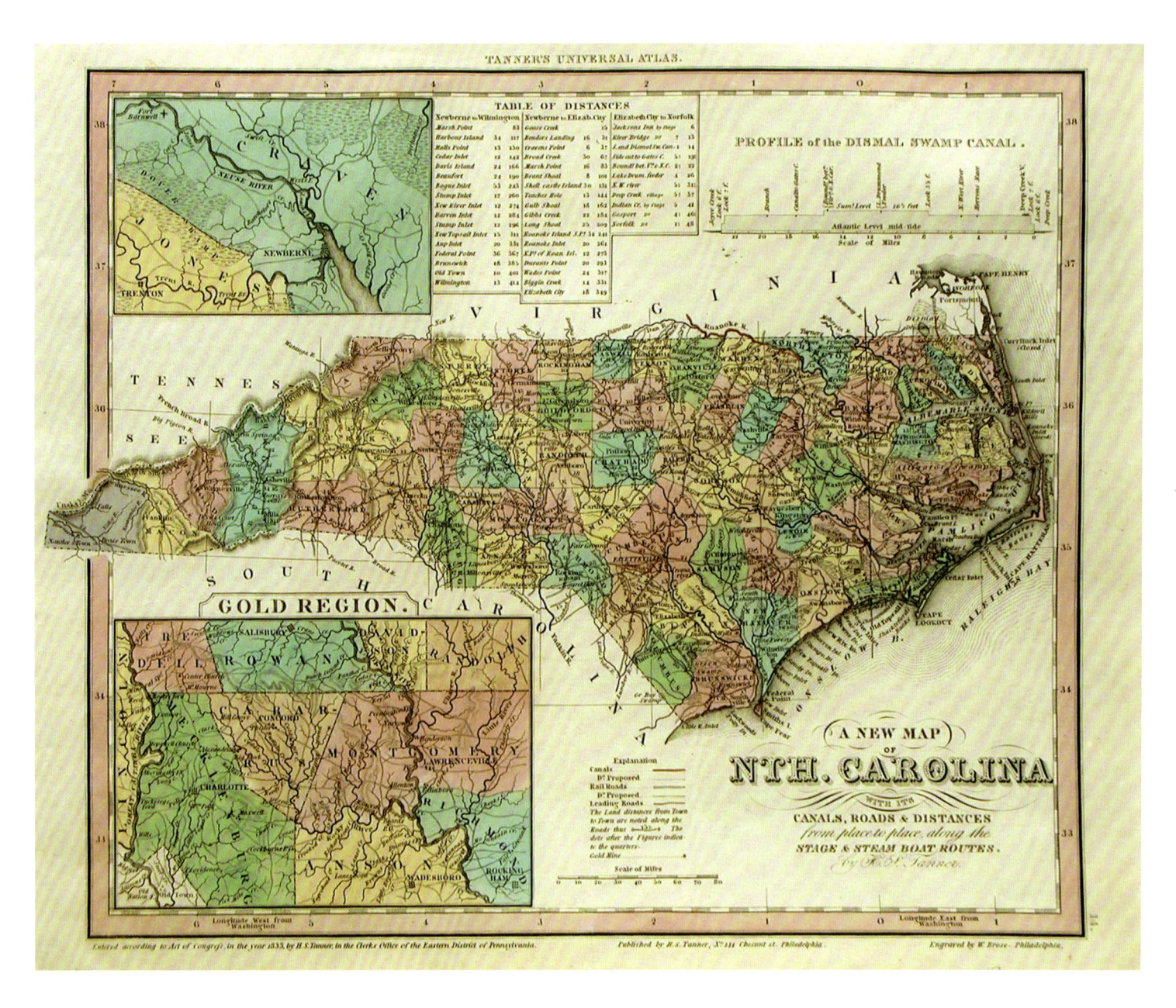

1. Map of North Carolina, H. Tanner, 1833. *Property of Benjamin Briggs.*

2. Southern Railway Passenger Depot.

3. Ecker House.

4. Jamestown Indulged Meeting House.

5. Deep River Meeting House.

6. Coggin House.

7. Hayworth House.

8. J.H. Adams House.

9. First Presbyterian Church.

10. Little Red School House.

11. Pennybyrne.

12. Conner House.

13. Armentrout House.

14. High Point (Central) High School.

15. Three Musketeers.

16. Amos House.

17. Denny House.

18. Deep River Cabin.

19. Harper House.

20. Perry House.

21. Roberts Hall, High Point University.

22. Hoggatt House.

23. Haley House.

24. Mendenhall Store.

Midtown and Western Suburbs

The T-plan building features a large nave housing the sanctuary, flanked by a stepped down ambulatory. The façade features a tall, pointed arch window above two sets of wooden doors. To the rear is a perpendicular wing of Sunday school rooms and offices. The structure is dominated by a tall tower situated in the corner of the northern junction of the "T" that rises above the sanctuary's roofline and culminates in four corner spires in an English Gothic fashion. Landscaping designed by church member R.D. Tillson includes a low wall surrounding the site, walkways, evergreen shrubbery and native trees.

101. Rowella Apartments
1003 North Main Street
SL 2001

Named for its builders Rowland and Ella Gantt, the Rowella Apartments were completed in 1935 and instantly developed a reputation for upscale urban living. The two-story brick and cast-cement building was designed by Tyson T. Ferree around an inner courtyard accessed through a passage from the rear parking areas. Additional entry to the building is gained through twin entrances directly off Main Street. The Art Deco theme and interior courtyard are reminiscent of garden apartments of the West Coast. The front and rear elevations of the building display numerous decorative elements, such as cast-cement surrounds topped by stylized cartouches at each front door, as well as metal light fixtures. Design motifs formed into the cement include zigzags, a draped effect and fluted pilasters. A dogwood feature is repeated in each spandrel between the first- and second-floor windows. Two second-floor units facing Main Street have French doors with metal railings in a geometric design. The twenty-four units vary from simple studio apartments to one- and two-bedroom arrangements, most with oak flooring, plaster walls and ceramic tile bathrooms.

102. Grayson House
1009 North Main Street
NR 1994

Dr. C.S. Grayson and his wife, Bertha Crawford, commissioned this house of Mount Airy granite. Grayson, an obstetrician and gynecologist, arrived in High Point in 1907 and practiced in the city his entire career. In addition, he served four terms as mayor from 1931 to 1939, a time of both economic crisis and public projects such as the lowering of the railroad tracks through downtown. Greensboro architect Harry Barton designed the house, which was completed by Waldensian stonemasons in 1925. The Waldenses are skilled artisans in stone who came to High Point from northwestern Italy via Valdese, North Carolina, and served on many building projects in the city. The two-story house features an eclectic mix of Colonial Revival and Craftsman details. Three dormer windows top the three-bay house, while battered stone supports indicative of the Craftsman style support the broad front porch that extends to a porte-cochere. Other Craftsman details include the carved false rafters of the wide eaves of the roof, which is covered in red French tiles. The house was adapted in 1970 for use as the BERNICE BIENENSTOCK FURNITURE LIBRARY, a comprehensive collection of seven thousand volumes on the history of furniture, from ancient Egypt to Bauhaus.

103. ECKER APARTMENTS
1011 North Main Street
SL 2001

One of a series of early apartment buildings constructed along North Main Street in the 1930s, the Ecker Apartments represent a period in the city's history when quality affordable housing was at a premium. The building was built as a real estate investment by Elizabeth Kalte, daughter of entrepreneur Ferdinand Ecker, upon her father's death in 1932. The three-story, brick, Art Deco–style building was a fashionable location for many High Point newlyweds, who often lived here before acquiring their first homes. Apartments include appointments such as hardwood floors, closets, tiled bathrooms and kitchenettes. A wooden carport stands to the rear of the property.

104. SHERROD HOUSE
1100 North Main Street
SL 2001

By 1915, prominent High Point businessman Archibald Sherrod and his wife Lizzie moved into this impressive Prairie-style house. Sherrod was originally from Martin County in eastern North Carolina and relocated to High Point in 1898 after purchasing the High Point Chair Company. An active businessman, Sherrod held interests in the Sherrod Shirt Factory on North Main Street, as well as real estate and insurance ventures. He was the principal developer of Sherrod Park, a fashionable subdivision centered on Woodrow Avenue.

Considering the confidence and practicality that Sherrod seemed to exude in his business practice, it comes as no surprise that he would have his residence executed in the Prairie style, a mode popularized in the Midwest by Frank Lloyd Wright and rarely seen in North Carolina. The house likely caused a stir among High Point society when it was constructed during World War I, due to its stark, modern appearance that stood in sharp contrast to the staid Colonial Revival styles being constructed nearby on Main Street. Despite renovations, the Sherrod House retains a surprising number of its original Prairie features. The exterior is enveloped by a wide porch set upon a foundation of Mount Airy granite, the material of choice for fashionable early twentieth-century houses, while the broad, green slab tile roof adds gravity as well as beauty to the overall composition. Wide overhanging eaves block the strong vertical summer sun yet allow volumes of low winter sunlight into the house by way of large windows. Interior details continue the Prairie theme within a more traditional framework. Unlike Wright's open floor plans, formal parlors open to the right and left of a broad reception room. A grand staircase distinguished by a simple, straight-cut balustrade rises from the rear of the reception area to the second floor. The dining room exhibits handmade paneling of American cherry, and oak floors unite the first-floor ensemble of rooms.

105. HARDEE APARTMENTS
1102 North Main Street
NR 1991

Constance Charles Hardee had these apartments erected around 1924 to provide housing for High Point's growing number of upper-level managers and professionals. Designed in the exotic Mission style, the apartment building contained elements that were unusual for rental units: large floor plans, porches and private parking. Mission details include plaster walls, a coped parapet roofline and heavy square porch supports. Interior appointments were equally impressive: hardwood floors, plastered walls and generous exposure to sunlight by many windows.

106. BRILES HOUSE
1103 North Main Street
SL 2001

Erected in 1907, the Briles House was one of the earliest houses built along North Main Street. Though High Pointers initially teased the Brileses that their home was located halfway to Winston-Salem, the Briles House inspired the construction of a parade of magnificent houses along upper Main Street, many of which remain today along with their prototype. The house was built by Bertie Wallace and Lee Briles, who returned to the area from Florida in order for Lee to take the position of head cashier at the North Carolina Savings Bank and Trust Company. Lee Briles passed away early in life, but his family remained in the house for nearly one hundred years, until the death of Ruth Briles in 2002.

Ruth Briles recalled that her parents retained an unidentified Greensboro architect to design their large Southern Colonial mansion. The resulting residence stands today as an excellent example of Neoclassical Revival architecture, demonstrated by its monumental Ionic entrance portico, the full modillion cornice and tripartite windows on the main façade. The city once contained more than twenty houses constructed before 1920 with monumental porticoes, but the Briles House remains today the sole survivor of this group of grand High Point houses. The house also is notable for its foundation of Mount Airy granite and its cypress siding. The main entrance features hand-crafted lead glass windows that were cut and formed to fill the front hall transom and sidelights. Above the front door, the beveled glass forms the face of a lion. The interior features a center-hall plan, quarter-sawn oak floors and trim, pocket doors, wainscoting and anaglypta wallpaper.

107. SICELOFF HOUSE
1104 North Main Street
NR 1991

This residence was constructed around 1920 for Mattie V. and Jonathan Clarence Siceloff, the owner of Siceloff Hardware Company and the Sunnyside Ice and Fuel Company. The house was a good example of the Mission style, featuring a symmetrical façade with an eye-catching ogee (now removed) centered atop the roofline. Mission-style architecture borrowed from other popular styles, as witnessed in the unusual features of the house: Prairie-style porch supports and wide overhanging eaves, Spanish-inspired rough stucco walls and shaped parapets and porch railings. The porte-cochere extending to the south of the residence was a popular feature for houses built during that time period. The Siceloff House represents typical upper-income dwellings built in the city after World War I and is one of the few remaining residences along North Main Street.

108. ADAMS HOUSE
1108 North Main Street
GL 2002, NR 2001

Elizabeth Barnes and John Hampton Adams, both natives of South Carolina, commissioned this grand expression of the Italianate Renaissance Revival style that was completed by 1918. The Adamses came to High Point in 1900, when John Adams established the Piedmont Hosiery Mills with J. Henry Millis to produce black stockings (see entry #59). Adams and Millis went on to create other companies, including Highland Cotton Mills and Cloverdale Dye Works. As North Carolina's hosiery industry grew in national prominence, so did Adams and Millis's interests, which were consolidated in 1928 under their shared name. Adams-Millis Corporation was High Point's first company publicly traded on the New York Stock Exchange, and the men briefly lived just two blocks apart from each other on North Main Street.

The Adamses' splendid residence exceeded in grandeur any other private residence constructed in the city, setting a new standard for opulence and luxury that was unmatched for several years. The house rises two and a half stories above Main Street, with masonry walls covered with rough stucco and embellished with decorative cast-stone details such as shields, modillions and pediments. Additional features typical of the Italian Renaissance Revival style are the entrance pavilion with a colonnaded loggia on the second floor and the mosaic tile floor of the front terrace. A foliated face of a "Green Man" presides over the main entry. Small elliptical windows provide natural light to the third floor, and wide eaves with wooden brackets support a green Spanish tile roof. Interior appointments are equally lavish, including oak parquet floors, elaborate cast-plaster crown moldings, a music room with rounded corners, French doors, mosaic tiles and a grand staircase lighted by a bank of windows at the landing. The classical appearance of the interior presented a formal context for the public rooms; however, private spaces within the house enjoyed equally high standards. Servants' quarters were located to the rear.

The Adamses lived here with their two daughters until 1931, when they moved to their estate Adamsleigh in Sedgefield. Thereafter, the house was leased as a private residence for several years and subsequently accommodated the YWCA of High Point until 1961 and then the Chapel of Flowers until 1996. Threatened with demolition for a Burger King franchise in 1997, the Adams House ultimately was preserved for use as an inn in 2000. A wing containing dining space was added to the rear, and a three-story building with additional accommodations designed by High Point architect Greg Mercer was built beside the house.

109. Mary and H. Albion Millis House
1109 North Main Street
SL 2001

This two-story, brick, Georgian Revival–style house was designed circa 1920 by the firm of Greensboro architect Harry Barton for H. Albion Millis and his wife, Mary Lewis. Millis was the son of Adams-Millis cofounder J. Henry Millis and held a position as cashier at the Bank of Commerce at the time the house was constructed. The finely detailed house on a corner lot is attributed to Barton's chief draftsman, Lorenzo S. Winslow, architect of the White House from 1933 to 1952. The two-story house is sheathed in a buff-colored brick that accentuates a green French tile roof. The five-bay façade is centered upon an entry with a flat-roof porch topped by a metal balustrade. First-floor windows serve as French doors, each pair topped by a lunette with a keystone. Additional Neoclassical details include a heavy modillion cornice and stylized Corinthian porch columns. Following threats to destroy the property for use as the city's first McDonald's franchise in 1976, the house was adaptively restored as Millis Square, a collection of specialty shops.

110. St. Mary's Episcopal Church
108 Farriss Avenue
SL 2001

Architect Herbert Hunter collaborated with the High Point firm of Louis Voorhees and Eccles B. Everhart for the design of this cruciform church in 1928 for the city's Episcopal congregation. The church takes the modest appearance of an ancient English parish church, featuring stone walls and a slender copper-clad spire. Defining features of its Gothic style include modest buttresses that support parapet end walls, a slate roof and tall and narrow lancet windows with stained glass. R.K. Stewart and Sons was the contractor.

To the rear of the sanctuary are two buildings. The earliest was constructed shortly after the sanctuary and features Tudor appointments such as half-timbering filled with nogging of brickwork laid in a herringbone pattern. The later structure was designed by Voorhees, Everhart and Conner and erected in 1961–62. It presents an innovative and progressive addition to the otherwise staid historical theme of the complex in its Modern style.

Midtown and Western Suburbs

111. Emerywood Court
1203 North Main Street
SL 2001

Emerywood Court was constructed adjacent to the popular Emerywood neighborhood around 1936. The ten-building apartment complex held a reputation as the largest multifamily housing in town and attracted high-income residents. The complex is fashioned on the garden apartment model initiated by housing reformers in New York in the 1920s and features three-story brick buildings clustered around a well-landscaped central courtyard. The complex provided efficient and private urban living in buildings exhibiting streamlined classical motifs. Details include molded entrance surrounds, metal casement windows, brick quoins at corners and a balustrade relief at the roof parapet. Substantial and well constructed, Emerywood Court represents the culmination of Depression-era multiple-unit housing in High Point, and is among the last residential buildings in the city to enjoy an urban context adjacent to busy North Main Street.

112. Fire Station Number 4
1329 North Main Street
GL 1986, SL 1985

Growth of High Point's northern neighborhoods prompted construction of Fire Station Number 4 in 1925. Respecting the residential context of nearby Emerywood, the station was built in a Dutch Colonial style, featuring a slate-covered gambrel roofline with the gambrel end turned to the street to accommodate a truck bay. The bay was originally mirrored with a matching door to the rear alley to allow trucks to pass through the building from back to front. Original interior appointments include a masonry floor, sleeping quarters on the second floor and a brass pole used to provide quick access to the first floor in emergencies.

JOHNSON PLACE
HD 1986, SL 2001

A remarkably well-preserved collection of early twentieth-century houses, Johnson Place was also High Point's first locally designated historic district. The primary avenue of the subdivision is Johnson Street, named after the Johnson family, whose farm was used for the development. Covering sixty-eight acres east of North Main Street, the subdivision was developed by J. Homer Wheeler, a prominent High Point entrepreneur with a history of success in developing the Quaker Woods neighborhood in 1895. In 1907, Wheeler laid out the Johnson Place neighborhood in a grid of twelve rectangular blocks. The largest lots were close to Main Street, a route that later became the city's main streetcar line. Leading High Point lawyers, politicians and industrialists purchased these grand sites to enjoy a strong presence on the fashionable avenue. These sixty-foot-wide lots accommodated large houses serviced by rear alleys. Advertising from the period touts the neighborhood's "highest location, beautiful outlook, strictly city property, with city conveniences." Amenities included city water, sewerage, electric lights, cement sidewalks and shade trees. The neighborhood was briefly the center of High Point society before the suburban setting of Emerywood drew captains of industry and finance to its leafy surroundings.

Johnson Street developed more slowly than North Main Street. Though a few lots were sold earlier, most property on Johnson Street did not garner attention from buyers until the city's streetcar line began service in 1910. By 1915, land along the street was nearly sold out. Early Johnson Street residents included industrialists, elected officials, doctors and attorneys. House styles range from the Queen Anne to the Prairie style. Aside from the uniformity of consistent setbacks and wide porches, the distinguishing characteristic of Johnson Street remains the nearly continuous canopy of sugar maples planted by historian John Blair in the 1920s. The trees remain, as observed by *High Point Enterprise* editor Holt McPherson in the 1960s, "one of the best investments of public funds in municipal history." Nearby, a trio of houses on Louise Avenue feature Neoclassical designs. The houses were built between 1909 and 1911 by general contractor John A. Young, who was the builder of the United States Post Office downtown.

113. ECKER HOUSE
901 Johnson Street
EA

Constructed in 1908 for Frenchman Ferdinand Ecker, this house was the first on Johnson Street and became a landmark as soon as it was built. Ecker brought his family to High Point by way of Brooklyn and established Ecker Glass Company, which supplied the city's rapidly growing furniture industry. Newspaper editor J.J. Farriss wrote in 1909, "Recently Mr. Ecker has built a beautiful home in the Northern part of the city which is attracting attention on account of its substantial beauty." Erected by builder Alfred Abijah Moore of Davidson County, the design of the two-and-a-half-story frame house blends late Victorian details, such as the wrought-iron rails and cast-iron roof cresting, with Colonial Revival elements, such as the dormer windows, modillion cornice and paired Tuscan columns. Originally, the shingles of the roof and second floor were stained a deep green that contrasted with a mustard shade on the first-floor clapboards. The oversized windows featured plate glass from crosstown rival Pittsburgh Plate Glass Company, which sent its best material in order to impress its competitor. Interior appointments include quarter-sawn oak, hand-cut lead glass windows, massive pocket doors and handsome mantels.

Midtown and Western Suburbs

The two-story frame carriage house at the rear of the property was constructed around 1908 and is the largest carriage house remaining in the city. It features German siding, a clipped gable roof and hipped dormer windows. Restoration work on the building in 2004 identified evidence of four horse stables on the north side of the building.

The preservation of the house came into question in November 1989, when a fire roared through the attic and nearly incinerated the entire structure. Local historic district regulations delayed demolition of the house, permitting the property to be sold and restored in 1991.

and was an advocate of High Point's Burris Memorial Hospital. The house blends clapboard siding on the first floor with wood shingles on the second. The somewhat irregular form—with a two-story polygonal window bay on the south elevation, a broad wraparound porch with a pedimented entrance bay and paired Doric columns and large alternating arched and pedimented dormers with windows of diamond-shaped glass—identifies the house as an early example of Colonial Revival style. The modillion cornice of the roof and porch and the front door with sidelights and rectangular transom also are trademarks of the style. The carriage house to the rear was constructed in 1947.

114. ODELL LINDSAY HOUSE
1002 Johnson Street

The Odell Lindsay House was constructed in 1912 in the Colonial Revival style. R. Odell Lindsay arrived in High Point in order to manage Consolidated Hosiery Mills, which had been established by J.H. Millis around 1910. In 1912, Lindsay married Frances Gordon, secretary to the president of Commercial National Bank. Upon the creation of Adams-Millis Corporation in 1928, Lindsay was named vice-president of the new firm. He also ran his own company, Guilford Hosiery Mills,

115. BURNETT-MCCAIN HOUSE
1008 Johnson Street

This well-sited house at the corner of Johnson Street and East Farriss Avenue stands as an excellent example of Prairie-style architecture. The house was constructed in 1912 by W.G. Burnett, who was the secretary treasurer for High Point Ice and Coal Company. Burnett lived in the house only briefly before he sold it to Dr. H.W. McCain, a prominent physician from Union County. McCain was trained in Chapel Hill and Philadelphia and was a stockholder in High Point's first hospital. The house is framed by mature shade trees and a lush lawn. Identifying elements of the Prairie style include broad plank balusters along the front porch railings, wide masonry piers that support the low-pitched roof of the porch and wide, clean overhanging eaves at the porch and main pyramidal roofline. Additional period details include narrow weatherboard sheathing on the first floor of the house, in contrast to the shingles on the second floor. Unusual panels of stucco flank a forward-facing feature window, embellished with tiles in a fluted design. Double-hung windows feature multiple panes of glass above single-pane sashes, and a stained-glass window illuminates the staircase. Interior details include oak floors, classically inspired columns and plaster walls.

116. DALTON HOUSE
1013 Johnson Street
EA

Perhaps the first residence in High Point to fully articulate the Craftsman style, the Dalton House was constructed in 1913–14 for Mary Land Dalton and her husband Carter. Carter Dalton enjoyed a distinguished career in the city, with notable service as an attorney. He later held civic roles as a municipal judge, a state representative (1916–18) and an advocate for greater commerce and improved education. The two-story house features a gable-front design with shingle siding, exposed rafter tails, diagonal bracing beneath the eaves and decoratively sawn raking boards. All of these details became highly popular in High Point as Craftsman-style houses were built in every sector of the city for the next twenty years. Features that set the Dalton House apart from most other Craftsman houses include the Mount Airy granite foundation with large planters flanking the front stairs, large twelve-over-one double-hung windows and fine interior appointments such as hardwood flooring and tile fireplace surrounds. A cross gable wing was added around 1918 and continued the Craftsman details. Typical of the style, the siding of the house was originally stained a dark color to call attention to the light painted features expressing structural elements.

117. ZOLLICOFFER HOUSE
1207 Johnson Street

Perhaps the city's best example of the Prairie style is this house built for Robah Bencini and Dallas Zollicoffer in 1912. The architect for the Zollicoffer House is not known; it is possible that the design was selected from a popular magazine or plan book of the day. Dallas Zollicoffer was a Wake Forest College–trained lawyer who ran unsuccessfully for the United States House of Representatives in 1914. Dallas was the son of a prominent doctor from Northhampton County, North Carolina. Robah was the daughter of E.A. Bencini, the cashier and bookkeeper of the local Snow Lumber Company. With its stucco walls, low-hipped roofline and casement windows—some of which appear to wrap around the second-story corners—the two-story house is a pure interpretation of the Prairie theme. Additional features inspired by designs of Chicago architect Frank Lloyd Wright are the solid balustrade-framed porch overlooking Johnson Street, the side entry and the extremely deep and unadorned eaves.

MECHANICSVILLE

In his *Collection of Historical Remembrances*, High Point historian Stephen C. Clark described the development of Mechanicsville beginning in the early part of the twentieth century. According to Clark, several families who were mechanics in city mills grew discontent over the idea of paying higher city taxes to fund a variety of costly municipal initiatives. In protest, they moved just north of the city limits and established an unincorporated community that they named Mechanicsville. Led by the Montgomery and Crouch families, Mechanicsville was one mile north of the depot, near the crossroads of Lexington Avenue and North Main Street. Previously known as Welborn's Crossroads, the heart of the new settlement soon boasted a service station, a grocery store, a drugstore and churches. Because it was outside the city limits, Mechanicsville did not have the benefit of city services, such as police and fire protection, and many High Pointers remember conflagrations that burned houses just outside the limits, sometimes in the presence of firefighters who could not assist because the properties were outside their jurisdiction. Without police protection, Mechanicsville developed a reputation of poker games gone awry, shady characters and sometimes murder. Little remains of Mechanicsville today. A few one- and two-story brick commercial buildings of the 1920s and 1930s survive along North Main Street and West Lexington Avenue, as well as several modest frame houses with front porches primarily along Long, Welborn and Idol Streets; but many of the early properties have been destroyed to make way for commercial development.

118. GODWIN HOUSE
202 West Lexington Avenue

Located just west of the intersection of North Main Street and Lexington Avenue, the Godwin House possibly stands as one of the oldest in the midtown of High Point. The house sits well back from the street behind a wide front yard graced with mature trees. It was likely constructed before the turn of the twentieth century and veneered with brick by physician Jason Godwin and his wife Beulah around the 1920s. Perhaps the most telling signs of the building's age are its symmetrically arranged one-room-deep, two-story form with a center hall and the two-tiered entrance porch with turned posts and balusters at the upper level.

119. LONG STREET NEIGHBORHOOD

Centered on the intersection of Long Street and Idol Street is a collection of early twentieth-century residences that reflect early suburbanization of High Point's northern outskirts. The intimate scale, mature vegetation and historic architecture of the neighborhood today stand in stark contrast to strip development of nearby North Main Street and Westchester Drive.

The neighborhood is anchored by two historic churches. At the terminus of West State Street stands the PRIMITIVE BAPTIST CHURCH at 1405 Hicks Place. Founded in 1906, the church features a cemetery containing stylish markers—some in the form of cut trees, others sporting Art Deco motifs. The frame sanctuary likely dates from the early twentieth century and was sheathed in brick a few decades later. LEBANON UNITED METHODIST CHURCH, established in 1865, anchors the western end of Idol Street. The original sanctuary has been destroyed, but the large cemetery containing graves from the Reconstruction era remains.

Many comfortable one-story Craftsman-style bungalows of the 1910s and 1920s, featuring wide porches and lush gardens, line the primary streets of the neighborhood. The house at 1511 Long Street features an unusual pyramidal roof, and its neighbors at 1515 and 1517 Long Street are identical twins. These early houses take the appearance of mill housing and may be associated with the Sherrod Shirt Factory that stood nearby at North Main Street and State Street.

A few notable residences stand out, including the YOKLEY HOUSE at 1615 Long Street. This one-story Queen Anne–style house was likely constructed around 1910 and features a side-gable roof with a gable aligned over the front door. A fourth gable extends toward the front of the house to the right of the entry and features a cutaway bay window with decorative sawn shingles and turned pendants. A full-width porch with sawn trim work and turned porch supports extends across the façade.

Midtown and Western Suburbs

Likely constructed around 1920, the two-story residence at 209 Idol Street is among the largest in the neighborhood. The house has a triple-A roof, boxed eaves, shingled gables, one-over-one windows and a full-width front porch supported by square posts. Rear chimneys and a one-story rear ell complete this design that reflects rural architectural traditions brought to the city in the early part of the twentieth century.

120. BENNETT BUILDING
1813 North Main Street

The two-story office building designed around 1958 by architect Robert Conner for Harold C. Bennett, owner of Bennett Advertising, features a façade of multiple surfaces and shapes. The second floor dominates the composition, featuring a masonry-framed border surrounding a recessed tile wall containing four ceiling-to-floor windows. Beneath the cantilevered second floor, the ground level is faced with Roman brick and features windows around the entry. An automobile passage supported by columns that widen as they rise skirts north of the building. Parking is located beyond the passage to the rear. In all, the building presents a remarkably modern face in the midst of later strip development of the 1960s and 1970s. The firm offered a broad range of advertising services to the community, but specialized in furniture advertising and catalogues.

121. BIVENS AND CALDWELL BUILDING
1923 North Main Street

Constructed for the early computer service company Bivens and Caldwell, this innovative one-story office building was designed in 1957 by newly arrived High Point architects Mays and Parks, Associates. It enjoys a corner location amid a sea of suburban sprawl. A simple Solite masonry block façade is broken by narrow bands of windows with transoms. A glazed lobby area opens onto an enclosed patio for staff. Inside, fluorescent lighting is fitted within a novel system of laminated roof beams. The form of the building follows interior functions: low ceilings of a wing containing offices and a lounge are contrasted with the high ceilings of a laboratory and machine rooms.

ROLAND PARK
SL

The Roland Park subdivision was announced to the public in March 1912 by the Roland Park Company, a group of Winston-based investors led by T.V. Edmunds. The company purchased land west of North Main Street, opposite the highly successful Johnson Place subdivision begun in 1908. Johnson Place and Quaker Woods had established northern High Point as "the favored locality for the location of the Best Homes," according to developer Stephen Clark. The introduction of the municipal trolley system in 1910 reinforced the northward trend of development.

Roland Park was platted by J.N. Ambler of Winston and constructed under the supervision of H.H. Riddle. Stephen C. Clark, who later developed nearby Parkway, Sheraton Hill and Emerywood, established himself in the field as selling agent for the development. Early schemes for the design of Roland Park planned the development's centerpiece as Brentley (later Brantley) Circle, a circular "court" including grass, flowers and a fountain. However, this formal Beaux Arts landscaping plan gave way to a casual English treatment focusing on monumental native oaks and hickories that were already in place. Paved sidewalks, lighting fixtures and water and sewer systems characterized the subdivision from the beginning.

The first homes in Roland Park were built in the winter and spring of 1913 on Brantley Circle. Clark quickly developed a program that brought homeownership to a broad audience of customers. Financing arrangements encouraged lot sales through a $10 deposit and payment of $1.25 per week. Free life insurance, a sixty-day return policy and even a 5 percent cash discount encouraged rapid sales of prime property around the central circle. Property sales languished on side streets, however, perhaps due to the perception of those areas as secondary. As a result, speculators purchased a great deal of property on side streets, and many houses were not constructed until the 1920s. By 1920, the Roland Park Company had been sold to Atlantic Coast Development of Lynchburg, Virginia, and Greenville, North Carolina. At that time, today's Farriss Avenue was known as Rockwell Avenue west of Brantley Circle and as Wexler Avenue to the east. Clark maintained his association with the development and continued to sell lots.

Those who purchased properties around the park represented High Point's emerging managerial class. Debbie and Robert R. Morrow purchased the handsome Craftsman-style house at 104 Brantley Circle circa 1912. Morrow worked for High Point Insurance and Real Estate at the time they bought the house. In contrast, Joseph T. Weaver was a traveling salesman with High Point Hosiery Mills when he and his wife Elizabeth purchased their home at 106 Brantley Circle circa 1912. Etta and Dr. J.W. Austin, an eye, ear, nose and throat specialist, purchased the exotic Mediterranean-style house at 119 Brantley Circle.

Midtown and Western Suburbs

Houses constructed in Roland Park feature the styles most popular at the time. Eclectic styles began to make an appearance on the prestigious Brantley Circle shortly after it opened. Craftsman, Colonial Revival, Dutch Colonial and even Mediterranean and Mission styles parade around the circle in what must be one of the most impressive early twentieth-century urban streetscapes in North Carolina. Side streets such as West Farriss Avenue, Ardmore Circle and Otteray Avenue contain more restrained designs, with most houses designed with either Craftsman influences or the Colonial Revival in mind.

Two important houses constructed at the very rear of the property helped to determine the future of development in High Point for years to come. Joe D. Cox and W.B. McEwen both built sprawling frame residences in the Colonial Revival style. Their large tracts were left naturally wooded, with a small stream running through the property. These houses would set the pace for estates built in eclectic styles in nearby Emerywood and, later, Emerywood West.

Foursquares, Minimal Traditional and Ranch houses also appeared in Roland Park. A few Dutch Colonial houses were also built. An interesting circa 1915 example of the Dutch style stands at 602 West Farriss Avenue, where the designer may have tried to evoke the gambrel roofline of a barn instead of a Dutch house.

Today, Roland Park remains a desirable place to live. All houses are in good condition and there is a strong sense of place. Perhaps an unfortunate result of the later success of the Emerywood subdivision to the north is that Roland Park lost its individual identity and is now considered part of Emerywood by real estate agents and residents alike. The name Roland Park, which was borrowed from Baltimore, has disappeared from the consciousness of the city.

122. TERRY HOUSE
200 West Farriss Avenue

Nancy and Randall B. Terry had this house constructed around 1912. It is likely one of the earliest houses in Roland Park, as well as one of the first Tudor Revival–style houses in High Point. Tudor period features, evocative of ancient and picturesque British houses, include heavy brick porch supports, false half-timbering on the second floor, the slightly cantilevered attic gable of the front pavilion and massive corbelled chimneys above the side-gabled roofline. Landscaping around the house includes several mature oaks, dogwoods and feature shrubs. Terry was president of High Point Underwear Company at the time of construction and later was an investor in Dalton Furniture, Atlantic Bank and Trust and the *High Point Enterprise*.

123. Parsons Residence
614 West Farriss Avenue

124. Willard House
718 West Farriss Avenue

Agnes Lowe and David H. Parsons built this American Foursquare around 1916. Parsons was a prominent attorney, judge of the Recorder's Court and president of High Point Realty Investment Company at the time the house was constructed. A pyramidal roof is accented by a hipped-roof attic dormer window. Other features of the brick house include paired windows, a bracketed cornice, a full-width front porch supported by brick piers and sidelights flanking the front door. The house stands as one of the most substantial and best-preserved Foursquares in High Point.

This Spanish Eclectic house was likely constructed around 1925 for Ann Russell and R.M. Willard. Prominently sited on Rotary Drive, its unique design contains elements of Mediterranean-inspired architecture, including elaborate iron strap hinges on the front door, stucco walls, segmental-arched openings, casement windows, a leaded-glass window, iron lighting fixtures and a low-pitched roof. Spanish tiles originally covered the roof, but they were replaced circa 1990 with a red fiberglass shingle roof. A distinctive ogee arched buttress of stucco extends west of the house. The Willard House illustrates the growing enthusiasm of eclectic housing styles in High Point during the 1920s.

125. Cox House
803 West Farriss Avenue

126. Holton House
1006 Holton Place

Constructed in 1916 for May and Joseph D. Cox, this two-and-a-half-story frame house is locally important as one of the first in High Point to be sited within a natural landscape without regard for the context of the street grid. Designed by Greensboro architect Harry Barton, the Colonial Revival–style house was said by Stephen C. Clark, developer of Emerywood, to be the catalyst that sparked new life for the Roland Park development once the cream lots around Brantley Circle were sold. The house has two fronts. The Otteray front is more formal, with a circular drive in a grassy lawn and a large Palladian window and main entrance flanked by sidelights and protected by a shed roof supported by columns. The Farris façade is more casual, with dormer windows overlooking woods and Pretty Branch. An open porch looks westward; to the east is an attached garage. At the time of construction, Joseph Cox was secretary treasurer of J. Elwood Cox Manufacturing Company, which made shuttleblocks and bobbinheads for textile manufacturing (see entry #52).

This two-story frame house may predate the development of the Roland Park and Parkway neighborhoods. The house sits atop a hill, looking west, and is surrounded by mature oaks. Perhaps dating from circa 1910, it was the residence of E. Letitia and Julius Frank as early as 1920. A. Julius Holton, a carpenter, possibly built the house. The traditional nineteenth-century I-house form has a hipped roof, rear chimneys, a wide hipped-roof front porch supported by attenuated Tuscan columns and a one-story frame ell to the rear. Decoration is minimal, limited to molded cornices, and the main entrance is plain. The house is an unusual example of a rural housing type popular with middle-income residents that was brought into High Point's increasingly affluent suburbs.

127. "My California Bungalow"
303 Otteray Avenue

Bessie Prince remembered with great fondness the years living in this house, which she called "my California bungalow." Her description was appropriate, for the house in certain respects indeed resembles period housing found in the Golden State. Distinctive features include a low-hipped roofline with very wide overhanging eaves that lack the diagonal braces or rafter tails of the Craftsman style commonly associated with California bungalows. Instead, the deep, unadorned eaves evoke the Prairie style, as do the full-length, slightly tapered porch posts. The projecting bay windows are capped with pent hoods and feature diagonal muntins. Bessie and C.C. Prince, vice-president of the *Southern Furniture Journal*, were the first residents of the house around 1920.

The Parkway and Sheraton Hill
SL

The success of Roland Park must have impressed Stephen C. Clark, who embarked on his own development, named the Parkway, in 1915. Constructed immediately south of Roland Park, the Parkway consisted of a single wide avenue extending from an established neighborhood on North Elm Street west to Palatka Street. Originally known simply as Parkway, this avenue was renamed West Parkway Avenue and featured sidewalks set far from the road and nearly seventy lots.

Within a year after the opening of the Parkway, Clark embarked upon the slightly larger development known as Sheraton Hill. While Roland Park took its name from the well-known Baltimore neighborhood and the Parkway took its name from the broad avenue at its center, Sheraton Hill took a new approach. Clark wrote, "In casting about for an appropriate and distinctive name for High Point's most exclusive residential subdivision the thought occurred 'Why not link it with the town's distinctive industry?'" Accordingly, he developed a system of streets named for prominent styles of furniture. "Colonial" gave its name to the main street of the subdivision and connected to West Parkway Avenue via Queen Anne Court. Jacobean Court and Chippendale Drive eventually were renamed Colonial Place and Sunset Drive, respectively, and soon the theme of the development was lost. Like nearby Roland Park with its circular green space, Sheraton Hill had as its centerpiece a triangular park created by the diagonal branch of Colonial Drive off West Parkway Avenue. Queen Anne Court and Jacobean Court formed the two other edges of the park. Originally, a pergola and shelter overlooked a wading pond, but these features have been removed.

Sales were brisk for both developments. The first house on West Parkway Avenue was occupied in July 1915. In April 1917, twenty months later, Clark reported that eight houses were completed, and four were in various stages of construction. Sixty-three additional lots were sold, ranging in price from $500 to $1,000. Clark made the claim that "this selling and building record…has never been equaled during the first 20 months of any residential real estate development known to us, except one, that of Roland Park, Baltimore Md."

House types on West Parkway Avenue range from early twentieth-century Queen Anne and Colonial Revival designs to late-century contemporary styles. The most impressive residences date from 1916 to 1925, when Parkway was the most prestigious avenue in High Point. Early houses such as the D.N. Welborn and Bascom Hoskins Houses feature Craftsman details, but the Colonial Revival was present from the beginning of development, as exemplified in the Dutch Colonial that Clark built for himself. English-influenced Tudor Revival houses were added to the eclectic designs of the neighborhood by 1930.

By the start of World War II, most of the lots along West Parkway Avenue had been developed. A few undeveloped lots were built on during the last half of the twentieth century. Most of the postwar houses, though only a small number of the total neighborhood, are Ranch style or Modernist.

128. Pardue House
208 West Parkway Avenue

This house was likely constructed for Dora and David L. Pardue around 1915 and may predate the development of the Parkway neighborhood. David Pardue was the clerk at Gilmer's store in downtown High Point. The two-story frame house has a three-bay façade with a projecting wing. The porch across the entire façade has been partially enclosed and its supports replaced. A few Victorian details remain, including a shingled pediment in the gable, a modillion cornice and two-story polygonal bay windows on the east elevation. The Pardue House is one of a small number of houses in the city exhibiting Queen Anne detail.

129. A.E. Taplin Apartment Building
408 West Parkway Avenue
GL 1995, NR 1996

Constructed in 1920, the A.E. Taplin Apartment Building is a rare example of multifamily housing integrated into a High Point neighborhood otherwise composed of single-family houses, although the trend of peppering upscale residential neighborhoods with some apartment buildings was popular in other North Carolina cities during this period. In order to blend with neighboring residences, the apartment building mimics a single-family house in its massing, its orientation with a narrow façade addressing the street and its modest scale and decorative detail. The Spanish Colonial Revival structure stands three stories high, topped by a hipped roof and covered in stucco. On the main façade, a rounded-arch entry is centered on the first story; triple French doors at an iron balcony distinguish the second story; the third story has only four simple casement windows. Other details evocative of the style include the exposed rafter tails of the eaves. Constructed by contractor and civil engineer A.E. Taplin, the five apartments were occupied through the years by an architect, attorneys, salespersons, mill foremen, teachers and doctors, as well as Taplin and his wife until 1923.

130. Welborn House
516 West Parkway Avenue

Blending Craftsman design with Colonial Revival features, this house was constructed in 1916 for Nancy P. and David N. Welborn. Among the earliest residences constructed in the Parkway, the two-story frame house features salient Craftsman design elements, such as shingle siding, tripartite double-hung windows and a shed dormer centered on the roof. These features are complemented with Colonial Revival details, including the symmetrical fenestration and sidelights and fanlight surrounding the front door. Double-hung windows with shutters are on the second floor. The lot is high, and terracing of the front yard helps to mitigate the otherwise steep slope. A detached garage stands to the rear of the property. Welborn was president of Blair Hoskins Shoe Company on Main Street.

131. HOSKINS HOUSE
521 West Parkway Avenue

132. MARY L. AND CHARLES F. TOMLINSON HOUSE
529 West Parkway Avenue

Constructed in 1916 for Alice and Bascom Hoskins, this house was later long associated with the Durland family. Bascom Hoskins was president of Citizens Real Estate and Insurance Company when he and Alice moved into their house. This unusually picturesque one-and-a-half-story dwelling features a cross-gable roof with a prominent asymmetrical front gable and a shed-roofed front dormer. Decorative elements include a stickwork sunburst in the gable peak, exposed rafter tails and diagonal braces under the wide eaves. Unusually heavy masonry columns support the flat roof of a wraparound porch. Originally, the porch roof was an open trellis, and there was no connection between the front and side porches. In the west gable end, prominent hipped and shed hoods shelter small bands of windows.

In 1921, one of the most substantial houses on West Parkway Avenue was designed by Greensboro architect Harry Barton for High Point Public Schools Superintendent Charles F. Tomlinson and his wife Mary. Barton and Tomlinson forged a friendship that later resulted in projects such as Tomlynhurst (see entry #163) and High Point (Central) High School (see entry #179). Barton's design for this house was influenced heavily by the Dutch Colonial style of architecture, as indicated by the green slab-tile gambrel roof of the one-and-a-half-story brick and frame dwelling. Other period features include a graceful arched entry supported by paired, attenuated columns and shutters with cut-out designs. A one-and-a-half-story wing extends to the left of the façade, with complementary details such as a shed dormer and ribbon windows topped by transoms. A sweeping lawn graces the large side yard that terminates in a natural wooded area.

133. Murray House
533 West Parkway Avenue

134. Clark House
538 West Parkway Avenue

This residence was constructed for Marguerite and Forest Murray around 1925 in the Eclectic style. It is distinguished by a low-pitched hip roof with shallow eaves, a decorative wrought-iron panel over the front door and a wide, slightly recessed segmental-arched main entrance with double doors. The stuccoed house has large windows on the first floor topped by relief panels and paired double-hung windows on the second floor. A two-story extension to the left of the house continues the overall design theme. As secretary treasurer of Giant Furniture, Forest Murray exemplified the upper-middle-income managers who sought to live on West Parkway Avenue. The Murray House portrays the increasing sophistication of eclectic design seen in High Point's neighborhoods by the mid-1920s.

Neighborhood developer Stephen C. Clark and his wife Daisy Ogburn built this two-story frame and stucco house in 1916, and it stands today as one of the earliest residences on Parkway. Topped by a gambrel roof and full-width shed dormer, the house is a good example of Dutch Colonial architecture. Additional details include paired and tripartite double-hung windows and a small gable framing the fanlight above the main entry. Originally, the second floor featured banded shingles. The house is said to have been designed by the prominent Winston-Salem architectural firm Northup and O'Brien, who were later commissioned to plan several other notable homes in the city.

Midtown and Western Suburbs

135. Hudson House
701 West Parkway Avenue

136. Walter Thomas House
622 Colonial Drive

This Neoclassical Revival residence was constructed around 1920 by Homer T. Hudson and his wife Lola. Hudson was owner of Anvil Brands, manufacturer of overalls. As one of the most substantial houses on the avenue, this two-story, side-gabled brick house features a dentil cornice and a monumental portico with stylized Corinthian columns and a lunette within the tympanum. The main entry to the house sports an elliptical fanlight topped by a narrow balcony with a wrought-iron railing. The lot occupies a full block along West Parkway Avenue. To the west (right) of the house are formal gardens, featuring retaining walls and pathways developed when neighbor D.B. Carrick subdivided his suburban estate Carrickmoor in the 1940s. A thorough renovation carried out circa 1993 left the house substantially intact.

A gambrel roof with a full-width shed dormer identifies the Dutch Colonial style of this two-story frame house constructed around 1925 by Alice and Walter B. Thomas. A full-width porch is supported by attenuated Tuscan columns and has a small gable over the front door; two small feature windows are located in the middle of the second-floor dormer; and an addition to the left of the main house is a frame porch. The large lot with its traditional landscaping is one of the highest lots in the subdivision. The Thomases came to High Point from Birmingham, Alabama, to work with Tomlinson Chair Company. In 1910, Walter took a position with his brother Fred Thomas at Union Furniture, which was destroyed by fire around 1925. Thomas then organized Thomas Hosiery Mills to manufacture men's fancy half hose.

137. TAPLIN HOUSE
1214 Woodland Place

138. WHITSELL HOUSE
1101 Council Street

Contractor and civil engineer A.E. Taplin constructed this Spanish Colonial house in 1923. Taplin and his wife Ruth moved to the house from their apartment building on Parkway, which he had built a few years earlier in the same style (see entry #129). The stuccoed house stands atop a high hill overlooking Woodland Place in a yard richly landscaped with mature oaks and boxwoods. The two-story house features a hipped roof covered with red Spanish tiles and a main façade with a centered, slightly projecting gabled pavilion highlighted by a Palladian arcade for the main entry. The house is among a notable number of houses in High Point influenced by Mediterranean architecture.

High Point's best residential example of the International style was built for W.K. Whitsell in 1951. The International style is distinguished by an absence of ornament, a theme played out with features such as flat roofs of various heights, white-painted plaster walls, curved surfaces, use of glass brick and windows wrapped around corners, all of which characterize the Whitsell House. Whitsell was an industrial arts instructor at High Point (Central) High School, and he constructed the house with assistance from members of his family. The close similarity of this house to others in Durham, Weldon and elsewhere across the state suggest that it was derived from a design published in a popular magazine. The unusual house stands as part of a small collection of architecturally progressive High Point houses that include the Zollicoffer House of 1912 (see entry #117) and the Frank Dalton House of 1949 (see entry #164).

Midtown and Western Suburbs

139. JUDGE HAWORTH HOUSE
902 Fairway Drive

This Modern-style house was designed by High Point firm Mays and Parks, Associates around 1958 for Sarah C. and Judge Byron Haworth. The house consists of two low-pitched gabled units of equal size facing the street and joined by a courtyard recessed into the façade. A wood-framed roofline in the shape of a shallow inverted V covers the courtyard. Gabled wings are solid brick on the front, but windows line each side. A wooden screen along the south-facing windows filters incoming light. The entire site is well landscaped and sits comfortably surrounded by Eclectic-style houses of the 1920s.

EMERYWOOD
SL

Earl Sumner Draper, the nationally known landscape architect and town planner, once predicted that Emerywood would "rank among the finest in the country, among which are such well known developments as Roland Park, Baltimore, Md., the Country Club district in Kansas City, Mo., Shaker Heights, Cleveland, Ohio, etc." Draper, who planned comparable neighborhoods such as Myers Park in Charlotte and Forest Hills in Durham, designed portions of Emerywood in 1923.

Riding on the success of Roland Park, the Parkway and Sheraton Hill, developer Stephen C. Clark observed a growing appetite among wealthy High Pointers for exclusive and well-landscaped lots with controlled social settings. Since his first development project of Roland Park in 1912, Clark was involved in bringing increasingly sophisticated levels of urban planning to the growing city. Roland Park was the first High Point subdivision to incorporate public space into its layout, using a broad circle as a focal point for its fashionable homes. The Parkway featured a wide avenue and houses set well back from wide sidewalks. A triangular park was the focus of Sheraton Hill, where the main avenue, Colonial Drive, traversed a relatively high hill featuring a mature stand of indigenous oaks and hickories.

In 1922, land owned by the widow of Emery Bencini just north and west of Roland Park was available for purchase. The Bencinis had planned a large suburban estate on the property, with a mansion on the hill on which Tomlynhurst (see entry #163) is located today. Upon the premature death of Emery Bencini in 1917, plans for the estate were cancelled, and Clark paid Mrs. Bencini $35,000 for fifty acres located west of Main Street for a grand new subdivision. Clark named the new subdivision Emerywood after Emery Bencini and declared in 1923, "It is now common knowledge that High Pointers, to secure homes of the better class…with no distracting views and unpolluted atmosphere, must go northwest." High Point industrialist Joe D. Cox had already confirmed an appetite for large estates in natural settings in the late 1910s when he established his residence on land at the rear of Roland Park. Cox's house and the McEwen residence just to its north proved there was demand for large parcels of land in an upscale and natural setting.

It is unclear whether Clark hired premier landscape architect Earl Sumner Draper of Charlotte to design the first phase of Emerywood, although his later role is firmly documented. In any event, from the beginning Emerywood was quite different from earlier High Point subdivisions. Hillcrest Place accessed North Main Street as a landscaped avenue featuring a median along the center that terminated at Pickett Avenue; it was later renamed Hillcrest Drive. Both Hillcrest Drive and its sister street, Edgedale Drive, meandered casually westward, crossing Hurdover Street to end temporarily at Palatka Street.

High Point Enterprise editor Holt McPherson remembered that in bringing higher standards of development to High Point, Clark "lighted and installed streets, planted trees and shrubs by the thousands, all at his own cost." Hillcrest seemed to elicit the greatest attention from Clark, who bragged, "For the present, only Hillcrest Drive will be improved, but those improvements are to be the most pretentious ever attempted in any development in North Carolina." Lots on Hillcrest were a minimum of one hundred feet wide, and restrictions prevented construction of any house costing less than $10,000. Hillcrest was designed to be twenty-six feet wide, topped with asphalt and bordered by an "oval" curb and gutter. Water and sewer lines were included in the original plan, as were gas lines. As for the lighting, Clark speculated that Hillcrest Drive, when lighted, would "amaze High Pointers."

Plans for the second phase of Emerywood prominently display architect Earl Sumner Draper's name. The curvilinear streets of Emerywood departed from the rigid grid of earlier models and maximized linear street frontage of building lots, a determining element for property value. Intersections often included triangles, circles and even Y-shaped junctions that avoided standard patterns. A variety of trees were planted to enhance the property. Emerywood was described in promotional material as "an exquisite suburban district. The winding roads and attractive sylvan localities lend much to the artistry of the development. The magnificent oaks, the fine North Carolina pines and other trees were largely left undisturbed." The adjacent High Point Country Club golf course was added in 1928, with designs drawn by High Point landscape architect R.D. Tillson. Later extensions of the neighborhood westward were known as Emerywood West (1928), Emerywood Forest (1957–67) and Emerywood Estates (circa 1930).

Promotional literature of the period indicates Emerywood was known for its "great variety of architecture…some of the most charming dwellings of the old world, especially of Normandy and Brittany, have furnished the design for attractive homes here, and there is also seen the picturesque peasant type of rural France, together with the best examples of Colonial architecture and other American types." Clark once wrote that "a photographer representing one of the leading home and garden magazines in this country stated upon a recent visit to High Point that he was able to get more pictures of pure, interesting and unique architecture in High Point than in all the rest of the states combined."

The earliest houses constructed in Emerywood followed the lines of rectilinear Foursquares and Craftsman bungalows. In 1924, however, the S.H. Tomlinson residence, known as Tomlynhurst, was completed. Harry Barton of Greensboro was the architect for the mansion, which heralded the arrival of the Tudor Revival style to the neighborhood.

Popular styles in the neighborhood soon included Colonial Revival and Mediterranean styles. The Italian Renaissance Revival Edwards House and the Gurney H. Kearns House joined exotic styles such as Norman, Welsh Cottage and Mission to develop a rich mix of architecture.

Styles of Emerywood houses built after the Great Depression followed general patterns seen across the nation, as Ranch houses were erected on scattered undeveloped lots. A notable Japanese-style house was constructed for Ruth Ellis at 605 Hillcrest Drive in the mid-1960s that attracted national attention. Since 1970, a few noteworthy houses have been built, some on previously developed lots after their first residences were demolished. Thus far, these "tear downs" have targeted the neighborhood's more modest houses and have not resulted in the loss of the landmark architecture for which Emerywood is renowned.

Midtown and Western Suburbs

140. ROLAND HOLTON HOUSE
205 Edgedale Drive

141. CUMMINS HOUSE
410 Edgedale Drive

This two-story stuccoed house features design elements common to Mission architecture of the American Southwest. Constructed around 1930 for Nell and Roland T. Holton, then vice-president of Continental Furniture, the house is characterized by a flat roof delineated by a parapet above a tiled pent roof. The parapet culminates in an ogee in the center of the façade. Other identifying elements include segmental-arched openings at the lower façade, with metal grilles, a front terrace with decorative metal railings and a round-arched window above the front door. The house stands among a small group of eclectic houses in High Point that depart from popular Tudor Revival and Colonial Revival prototypes to evoke the more unusual Mission style.

Built circa 1923 for Claude J. Cummins, secretary treasurer and eventually president of Carolina Veneer, and his wife Mecca, this two-story house resembles an English Cottage illustrated in "Gordon-Van Tine Home No. 602," a homebuilder's plan book of the 1920s. Typical of the mode, the house is stuccoed and has a clipped gable roof with wide overhangs and shed dormers. A gentle segmental-arched roof covers the front door, which is flanked by tripartite double-hung windows. A screened porch is attached to the side elevation, and a matching detached garage stands to the rear. An unusual concrete curb surrounds the front lawn. The Cummins House illustrates the national influence on local house styles and is one of many Emerywood houses derived from popular architectural publications of the day.

142. Hayes House
418 Edgedale Drive

143. Armentrout House
420 Edgedale Drive

Dr. William A. Hayes, a dentist, and his wife Helen had this Renaissance Revival–style residence constructed around 1925. The grand two-story, hipped-roof house has an imposing presence on Edgedale Drive due to its large scale and its position atop a hill. The white brick residence sits behind a wide terrace that is overlooked by French doors with transoms and entablatures, and the main arched entry is defined by Ionic columns. The green slab tiled roof extends with deep eaves with modillions. The house is flanked by one-story wings sporting Tuscan columns flanking large brick piers, both originally used as open porches. The interior is arranged around a central stair hall, featuring a large Palladian window on the landing overlooking the backyard.

This two-story stuccoed house, constructed for Winnifred and Hirum M. Armentrout around 1925, stands as one of the most detailed Spanish Revival–style houses in the city and illustrates the extent designers of the period sought to incorporate authentic handcrafted elements, such as the wrought-iron balcony and wrought-iron porch supports of the bellcast-hipped entrance porch. The asymmetrical massing and Spanish tile roof features a gable. A pair of tall arched windows to the left of the front door complements the two-tiered casement windows to the right of the main façade. Spanish tile tops a wall extending west from the house and pierced by a decorative iron gate. Hirum M. Armentrout was employed as secretary of Snow Lumber Company.

Midtown and Western Suburbs

144. RANKIN HOUSE
427 Edgedale Drive

Adele and Alex M. Rankin were the first occupants of this sprawling Tudor Revival residence. Constructed around 1925, the two-story brick and half-timbered house is a variation of the medieval-inspired residences that were constructed throughout Emerywood in the 1920s. The Rankin House takes advantage of a large lot, resulting in a somewhat rambling residence with an irregular slate-covered roofline and rear wing that extends at an acute angle from the main house to an attached garage. Tudor details include the cantilevered second story of false half-timbered walls, rough-hewn porch posts with decorative up-bracing and the strong vertical orientation of windows. A gable visually breaks up the main façade, and a partial-width front porch shelters the simple front door. Rankin was secretary treasurer of Consolidated Mirror Company.

145. GIBSON HOUSE
412 Emerywood Drive

Designed by High Point architecture firm Mays and Park, Associates, the sleek, ground-hugging residence built around 1958 for Geneva F. and Sloan Gibson, owners of Gibson Ice Cream on North Main Street, is among a small group of progressive Modernist houses erected within Emerywood. The architects overcame difficulties posed by the shallow, wide lot by creating a classic Ranch house with a low-pitched, uninterrupted roofline and deep eaves. The salmon-colored brick was the choice of the owner; however, the blue spandrel panels beneath the windows were the architect's choice. In an effort to conserve energy, the Gibson House was among the first in the South to utilize a heat pump. Landscaping is integrated into the site, and foundation plantings have been incorporated into the design of the house to maximize privacy. Most of the concrete on the site was tinted green to minimize its visual impact.

146. Shadowlawn
514 Emerywood Drive

147. Tate House/Kearnwood
600 Emerywood Drive

By the late 1920s, the tone and quality of housing in Emerywood had been set, and prospective builders sought increasingly grand and sophisticated designs for their residences. No house better illustrates this new level of residential construction than Shadowlawn, erected by contractor R.K. Stewart for J. Elwood Cox and his wife Bertha Snow in 1926 to designs by Winston-Salem architects Northup and O'Brien. The two-story, steel-frame house sheathed in brick was designed in a variation of the Tudor Revival style, using details such as patterned brickwork over the front door, scalloped timber lintels, copper gutters, lead glass casement windows and limestone trim around the doors and windows. Materials utilized in the construction of the house exceeded anything previously seen in High Point, including the Vermont slate on the steep-pitched roof and the stone living room fireplace featuring a relief of a hunting scene that came from Chambord in the Loire Valley. The lot on which the house sits once occupied half of the block and remained largely natural, cleared only around the house. A large matching carriage house to the rear of the property, complementing the main house in its brickwork and slate roof, was converted to a separate residence around 1980. Cox was a leading citizen of High Point, president of the Commercial National Bank and 1908 gubernatorial candidate.

Constructed for Fred N. Tate, former mayor and owner of Continental Furniture, and his wife Estelle Field, this house was later named Kearnwood by subsequent owner Amos R. Kearns of Crown Hosiery. The impressive residence was designed by Winston-Salem–based Northup and O'Brien and constructed by contractor R.K. Stewart around 1930 in the Colonial Revival style, standing two stories with masonry walls finished in stucco and a slate roof. The rambling house is composed of a four-bay main block, a one-story porch to the right and two two-story wings to the left. The motif of paired columns characterizes all of the porches. A distinguishing element is the large arched window with a wrought-iron balcony located left of the main entry. A large portion of the front yard has been left wooded, although more formal areas exist on the northwestern grounds. A detached two-story garage with wall dormers stands to the rear. The house, along with a handful of others, represents a prolific and ambitious period of construction in Emerywood, characterized by regionally celebrated architects and great economic wealth.

Midtown and Western Suburbs

148. AMOS HOUSE
902 Forest Hill Drive

Though attributed to Greensboro's Charles Hartmann, the design of this two-story Colonial Revival–style house—constructed for Robert T. Amos, founder of Amos Hosiery Mills, Inc., and his wife Charlotte in 1925—exhibits the influence of Philadelphia architect Charles Barton Keen and the Philadelphia "country house" movement. Typical of Keen's work are the robust porch columns, stuccoed walls and a green slab tile roof punctuated by brick chimneys with decorative clay pots and a broad shed dormer. Here, the main roof blends into an engaged front porch that is supported by cantilevered joists. A hood shelters the main entry, flanked by sidelights and pairs of floor-length windows. Forward-facing pediments containing round windows terminate the front porch roofline. Two-story wings extend the house at gentle angles toward the rear. The rear façade is more formal than the front, featuring an elaborate Palladian window above the rear entrance as well as numerous fanlights, balconies and dormer windows. The front yard includes a sweeping lawn with mature trees, while the backyard contains more formal garden areas and terraces, as well as a matching garage.

149. J. ED MILLIS HOUSE
905 Forest Hill Drive

This house was constructed for J. Ed Millis, son of Adams-Millis Corporation co-founder J. Henry Millis and an officer in the company, and his wife Helen Brooks. It was designed by the prominent Winston-Salem–based architectural firm Northup and O'Brien and erected by contractor R.K. Stewart in 1925. The Millis residence stands as one of the most impressive in the city, with period detail that evokes a rambling medieval English manor house. The house is a distinctive variation of the Tudor Revival style in its incorporation of stuccoed walls throughout, rather than the more typical brick and false half-timbering. The two-story house has a tall slate-covered roofline featuring stuccoed chimneys with decorative round clay pots, multiple gables and varied eave lines. Elements of historic English architecture include cast-stone label molding around the front door and feature window, diamond glass and casement windows with lead cames, wall dormers and an oriel and a bay window. An auto court to the right provides access to a large garage. The rear of the property is equally detailed and overlooks the High Point Country Club golf course.

150. Thomas House
906 Forest Hill Drive

151. Jackson House
1101 Forest Hill Drive

The frame residence designed by High Point architect Louis Voorhees for Frances C. and Fred A. Thomas around 1930 evokes a grand Southern Colonial mansion with its full-height portico, French doors with entablatures and front door topped by a broken ogee pediment. Three dormers containing arched windows punctuate the slate-covered, side-gabled roof. A decorative Chippendale-style balustrade was removed from the top of the flat portico roof around 1990. Landscaping is traditional, with many mature native trees in the yard and little in the way of additional foundation plantings. With his brother W.B. Thomas, Fred Thomas owned Union Furniture Company, which was destroyed by fire around 1925. He then established a warehousing business, served on the first board of trustees of Burris Memorial Hospital and eventually reopened Thomas Furniture Company, manufacturers of high-quality leather office chairs, in the 1920s.

Dr. Walter Leo Jackson and his wife Celeste built this impressive Georgian Revival–style house around 1930. Dr. Jackson was a physician, principal investor in Guilford General Hospital and president of Jackson Hosiery Mills. The two-story, symmetrical, seven-bay brick house is designed along the lines of Colonial Georgian architecture, as seen in details such as the heavy modillion cornice, the tall hipped roof and the central, three-bay pedimented pavilion carrying the entrance porch with heavy entablature. The original slate roof remains intact. To the east is a porte-cochere. The rear of the house looks quite different from the front, with a two-story glass window overlooking a formally landscaped yard. The house is prominently sited at the intersection of Forest Hill Drive and Country Club. Landscaping includes a brick driveway and extensive brick fencing behind the house.

152. Rones House
1112 Forest Hill Drive

153. Voorhees House
1132 Forest Hill Drive

Constructed around 1927, this two-story, three-bay stone house was one of the first constructed in Emerywood Addition No. 4. Fannie L. and Max Rones were early residents of the house. Built in the Colonial Revival style with Crab Orchard stone from middle Tennessee, it was one of only a few houses in High Point that used the material. The main block of the house displays a simple symmetrical façade centered on the main entry recessed in a round arch framed by a classical surround. An unusual feature of the house is the broken and stepped cornice of the house. The original slate roof has been replaced with standard shingles. Large twelve-over-twelve windows on the first floor and eight-over-eight sash on the second floor, all topped with flat stone arches and keystones, contribute to the Colonial Revival theme. The surrounding property was once extensive, but has been reduced as lots were sold for development. A number of outbuildings survive behind the house, however, and remain well maintained.

Prolific High Point architect Louis Voorhees designed this house for himself and his wife, Elizabeth Peyton, around 1927. The irregularly massed, two-story frame house, one of the earliest built on the street, displays multiple side-gabled roofs, wall dormers and a gable-front wing composed of a second-floor overhang with a sculpted pendant at each end. The house stands as one of the finest examples of "interpretive Colonial Revival" in High Point, since Voorhees used New England colonial elements in an imaginative design rather than as an academic approximation of a Colonial house. Elizabeth Voorhees's kindergarten classroom building, also designed by her husband, remains in the backyard.

154. Cottam-Wall House
1101 Greenway Drive
EA

This unusual Welsh-style house was built on speculation by contractor Robert Cottam in 1926. The two-story main block is veneered in historic brick recycled from a nineteenth-century house located on the Plank Road in Forsyth County. The house combines features thought to be common in Wales, including a cantilevered second floor, rough-hewn timbers for side porch supports and window lintels on the second story, a slate roof, a prominent straight-stack chimney and doors containing diamond leaded-glass panes. The house remained a rental property for several years after construction. Early occupants were Minnie and Guy Henry, who owned Henry Motor Sales, but the house is most associated with later owners Elizabeth Bowne (Bonie) and Matt Wall of Froelich and Wall Veneer, who lived in the house for nearly thirty years. The Walls added a two-level porch to the west, designed by architect Louis Voorhees. The steep topography of the lot was utilized to make an intimate setting for the house. The result is a heavily landscaped and terraced yard, featuring flagstone walkways, a brick driveway and a distinctive sunken garden encircled by old brick retaining walls, topped by a wrought-iron fence.

155. Emerywood Section 4 Showhouse
1107 Greenway Drive

This two-story house originally served as a model for Emerywood Addition No. 4. It was constructed by builder David McJester, who purchased the lot from developer Stephen C. Clark on February 10, 1927. The house opened Wednesday, June 15, 1927, fully furnished. Using the model, McJester attempted to set the tone for design in the newly opened addition to the neighborhood. The style chosen for the L-shaped house was the romantic French Eclectic, or Norman, style that featured steeply pitched roofs and an entrance tower, stuccoed façade and casement windows. Prominently sited on a high corner lot, the property has a winding walk to Greenway and a retaining wall near the driveway and garage. A porch along the east gable end overlooks Greenway and the yard to the east. S.T. Bryan, circulation manager of the *High Point Enterprise*, was an early occupant of the house.

156. Edwards House
11 Hillcrest Place

This two-story brick house at the entrance to Emerywood was constructed for Charles C. Edwards and his wife Alice around 1935 in the Italian Renaissance Revival style. The first story is of wire-cut brick, the second is stuccoed with brick trim around the windows and corners and the whole is topped by a hipped, Spanish tile roof of variegated colors. Distinctive features include a pair of narrow, round-arched windows over the arched front entry and keystones over the first-floor windows. A matching garage stands to the rear. Charles Edwards was an instructor and director of Edwards Business College on West Commerce Street.

157. Woodruff House
205 Hillcrest Drive

This one-and-a-half- and two-story residence constructed around 1925 for physician Fred Woodruff and his wife Bert is exceptional as an academic rendition of Tudor Revival architecture. Topped by a hipped roofline of slate, the house has a stucco exterior, casement windows, asymmetrical forward-facing wall dormers, false half-timbering in the gable and a conical roof over the round-arched main entry. The most remarkable detail of the house is a small window placed within a massive chimney located on the southeast end of the house, a feature that has become a landmark of the neighborhood.

158. DENNY HOUSE
207 Hillcrest Drive

159. ALVIN S. PARKER HOUSE
212 Hillcrest Drive

This residence constructed around 1925 stands with the Woodruff House next door as an exceptional academic rendition of Tudor Revival architecture. Varying in height from one and a half to two stories tall, with a hipped roofline of slate, the house has stucco exterior walls, casement windows and exposed joist tails. On the main façade, the hipped roof sweeps down to engage a front wing with recessed porch and large gabled dormer with false half-timbering and diamond-paned windows. A prominent tall chimney rises over the façade featuring decorative brickwork and articulated double flues. The first occupant was K.C. Denny.

This imposing Georgian Revival–style house, constructed around 1925 for Alvin S. and Deborah Tomlinson Parker, is a good example of its style in its massing and decoration. The main block of the house features a parapet gable-end roof covered in slate and a central front door with heavy surround topped by a broken pediment. Windows also are heavily accentuated: those at the first story of the main façade have aprons and molded architraves; those at the second story have keystones in brick flat arches. A distinctive feature is the roofline balustrade of brick that opens with classical turned balusters at each of the three dormer windows. The main block of the house is flanked by one-story wings: an enclosed sunroom to the east and a porte-cochere to the west. Parker was the first president and treasurer of the local Snow Lumber Company.

160. Murray House
306 Hillcrest Drive

161. Kearns House
308 Hillcrest Drive

Among the earliest houses in Emerywood, the stuccoed Dutch Colonial–style residence built for Lucille and Walter L. Murray in 1923 has a characteristic gambrel roof and wide frame shed dormer. Sidelights flank the front door, and a convex porch with a balustrade shelters the entry. The house illustrated a growing interest in academic detail in period buildings, and helped to set the pace for subsequent development in the neighborhood. Walter L. Murray was a sales manager at Giant Furniture Company, self-advertised as "manufacturers of suites, odd dressers, and chiffoniers."

This brick house, constructed for Kate Harmon and Gurney H. Kearns circa 1925, is among the landmark houses in Emerywood due to its Italian Renaissance style as well as its relatively early date. Few Italian-style houses were constructed in High Point, and this house is an important representation, due to its grand presentation. Topped by a hipped roof with deep modillion eaves, the beige brick Kearns House is five bays wide, flanked by one-story wings. The façade is dominated by the main entrance, which is imposing with a balustraded pent-roof porch with Tuscan columns supported by a segmental-arched ceiling that frames an elliptical fanlight and sidelights. Red Spanish barrel tile sheathes all of the roofs. First-floor windows are capped by stucco-filled arches. A terrace with turned balustrade matching that of the entrance porch extends the full width of the façade. Landscaping is dominated by an ancient willow oak in the front yard. Otherwise, foundation plantings are traditional. A matching garage stands in the backyard. Kearns founded Crown Hosiery Mills in High Point in 1912. Later owners added the tennis court around 1980.

162. KING HOUSE
402 Hillcrest Drive

Constructed around 1930 for Alice Carr and Rufus King, this house was designed by Greensboro architect Harry Barton. The frame house features a distinctive green slab tile hipped roof. Essentially a five-bay house, the frame structure features a forward-facing gable to the right of the front door, complementing a small eyebrow attic vent to the left. Shutters with decorative cutouts flank six-over-one windows and provide visual detail to the façade. A sunroom is engaged within the house to the right. An open porch extends to the left with robust columns that support a flat roof. A Colonial Revival entry porch with attenuated columns and elliptical ceiling sits amid the pent roof that extends across the width of the façade between the first and second floors. A distinctive terrace and brick walkways embellish the grounds, as do several dogwoods and oaks. The house is important as a member of a small group of residences stylistically related to the English Arts and Crafts movement popularized by Philadelphia architect Charles Barton Keen, a style that enjoyed a brief period of popularity in the 1910s and 1920s. It is characterized by green tile roofs, light-colored stucco walls, massive porch supports and sunrooms. Rufus King was a colorful Quaker minister with a reputation for travel, heartfelt sermons and religious service. His wife Alice Carr King, a native of Great Britain, became a longtime member of St. Mary's Episcopal Church. The house remained the home of their youngest daughter Annabella until her death in 1980.

163. TOMLYNHURST
403 Hillcrest Drive

Constructed in 1924 to designs rendered by Greensboro's prolific architect Harry Barton, Tomlynhurst is one of the earliest and most architecturally distinctive residences in Emerywood. Located on a generous lot, the masonry Tudor Revival–style house was constructed on a knoll originally intended for the country estate of Emery Bencini. Bencini's premature death halted these grand plans, but the prime site caught the eye of furniture entrepreneur Sidney Halstead Tomlinson and his wife Ethel Diffee, who erected this grand house. Tomlynhurst, its name inscribed in script on a crest on the porte-cochere, displays an array of features and details identified with medieval English houses, including asymmetrical massing and roofline, elaborate cast-stone trim around the main entry, casement windows with cast-stone mullions and trim, first-story walls of brickwork, a false half-timbered second story featuring rough stucco infill and framed quatrefoils, a masonry porte-cochere featuring battlements and a slate-covered roof. The interior features unusually fine paneling, molding and trim. To the rear of the house is a two-story garage with details that mimic the main house. To the east, at the crest of a steep slope overlooking a ravine, is an elaborate and classically inspired gazebo with five colonettes and an open wrought-iron dome. These elements contributed to an academic period design that represents the high-water mark of the Tudor Revival style in High Point, and established a standard in Emerywood that designers of numerous houses in a variety of eclectic styles aspired to meet and surpass over the next decade.

164. Margaret and Frank Dalton House
406 Hillcrest Drive

Constructed in 1949, the house built for Margaret Hayworth and Frank Dalton is likely the earliest example of Modernist architecture in High Point. The single-story, flat-roofed house was first arranged in an L-shaped plan attributed to Greensboro architect Edward Loewenstein. The house was expanded to a U-shape with an addition by Clayton Mays in 1959, and a greenhouse was added in 1978. The original portion of the house features board and batten siding of redwood, contrasted with cobalt blue shingles on the roof and great spans of casement windows. The interior has an open plan for the public spaces, a large stone fireplace and Vermont flagstone floors. To the rear is an enclosed breezeway that connects a two-car garage and screened porch. A courtyard is located at the back of the house, bordered by a low Crab Orchard stone wall and lush plantings.

The house is notable as one of Emerywood's most progressive, a sharp contrast to the historically inspired houses around it. In marked contrast to residences erected a generation earlier that seized attention with high-profile, historically inspired styles, the design of the Dalton House sought to blend harmoniously with the existing landscape. Landscaping is naturalistic, with native trees left intact so that the structure is as unobtrusive as possible. Additional plant material has been added, such as ivy and rhododendron, to enhance its woodland setting.

165. BOWNE HOUSE
410 Hillcrest Drive

166. WILSON HOUSE
425 Hillcrest Drive
NR 2005

Reverend Henry Norwood Bowne of St. Mary's Episcopal Church and his wife, Marie Antoinette Wood, were the first residents of this academically rendered Dutch Colonial residence, completed in 1924. The two-story house features a sweeping, steeply pitched gable-end roof, a full-width shed dormer and a front slope that flares to engage a full-façade porch supported by columns. Sidelights flank the front door and paired windows balance the lower façade. The house resembles seventeenth- and eighteenth-century dwellings found in the Dutch settlements of the Hudson River Valley in New York and may have been designed by popular High Point architect Louis Voorhees. A notable departure from the gambrel roof form of Dutch Colonial architecture, this house represents an effort to redefine the vocabulary of Colonial Revival design with an eye toward authenticity and detail.

The 1926 Wilson House continues an exploration of authentic Colonial Revival architecture, this time likely using the 1816 Tudor Place in Georgetown, Washington, D.C., as a model. Tudor Place—featuring a domed demilune porch, blind arches above first-floor windows, a hipped-roof and flanking wings—was built for Martha Custis and Thomas Peter. It is recognized as one of the hallmarks of America's Federal Period. In the High Point house designed for J. Vassie Wilson of Furniture City Upholstery and his wife Lucy Kirkman, Fred Klein reinterpreted Tudor Place by reducing the scale of the building and adding elements such as the green slab tile hipped-roof, garland relief within the blind arches, keystones above first-floor windows and a modillion cornice. The demilune porch features four Corinthian columns and a balustrade with a center grille. Hipped dormers pierce the roofline; the main body of the house is flanked by one-story projections, a porte-cochere to the west and an enclosed porch to the east.

Midtown and Western Suburbs

167. ELLIS HOUSE
605 Hillcrest Drive

168. KLEIN HOUSE
606 Hillcrest Drive

Constructed around 1964 for Ruth P. Ellis, the owner of clothing retailer Collier Ellis, this unusually progressive house was designed by High Point firm Mays and Park, Associates. Named for Ruth Ellis's deceased husband, Collier Ellis was a prominent upscale clothing store in the city. The cruciform-plan single-story house, blending Japanese and Modernist influences, illustrated voguish architectural design for the time. The exterior and interior design incorporate a blend of muted earth tones, such as redwood framing and tan brick, laid in a patterned protruding bond. Entry is from a side door that opens off a small patio framed by wood studs and rafters. Large areas of glazing flood the public spaces with light. The landscape design is modern, with natural areas incorporated into the architecture of the house by using gravel-filled planters and retaining walls along with parking in the front of the narrow lot.

Fred Klein, the original owner and designer of this house, was the architect of several residences in Emerywood. The house was built for him and his wife Beatrice around 1927, early in the third phase of Emerywood, and established a context for the street through its eclectic and detailed English Cottage styling. The two-story, steep multiple-gabled, smooth stuccoed house combines typical architectural features, such as wall dormers and a bay window, with distinctively English details, such as the front gable containing the main entrance and the arched entry framed quoins. The Klein House is notable for exploring English architecture without using hallmark features like false half-timbering, a massive forward facing chimney or exposed brickwork. Instead, it takes an academic approach to the style, mimicking masonry residences rendered in plaster throughout England during the nineteenth century.

169. Eunice and Ralph Parker House
401 Woodbrook Drive

This Colonial Revival–style house was erected around 1925 for Eunice and Ralph Parker. The two-story house sheathed in white painted clapboards is unusual in its close approximation of a specific type of Colonial residence, in this case a southeastern Pennsylvania farmhouse, exemplified by the pent across the symmetrical façade above the first story. Other, more typical Colonial Revival details include sidelights flanking the front door and the wooden lunette above it, tripartite windows and quarter-round attic windows in the gable ends. More recent wings extend each end of the main block. Ralph Parker was the vice-president of Tate Furniture Company and part owner and general manager of Alma Desk.

Emerywood West

Continued economic success of textiles, furnishings and related support industries encouraged developer Stephen Clark to continue the momentum experienced with Emerywood toward opening Emerywood West in 1928. This area is located west of the adjacent High Point Country Club golf course, on hilly terrain centered upon Pretty Branch Creek. High Point landscape architect R.D. Tillson continued themes brought to the city five years earlier by Earl Sumner Draper, including curving roadways, sidewalks, large lots and eye-catching infrastructure like a stone bridge carrying Rockford Road over Pretty Branch. The development was chosen for palatial Eclectic-style residences that took advantage of commanding sites, interspersed with Colonial Revival–, Regency- and International-style middle-income housing along Ferndale Boulevard and Rockford Road, most constructed in the 1930s and 1940s.

170. Vuncannon House
1001 Ferndale Boulevard

The Pearl M. and S. Colon Vuncannon House is among High Point's best examples of the International style, a mode of design popular during the 1930s with progressive architects. This example was designed around 1935 by local firm Voorhees and Everhart, which had a long reputation for introducing nationally popular styles to the city. A.E. Taplin was the contractor for this house that features details such as a curving wall of glass brick, cleanly incised windows with metal casements wrapping around

Midtown and Western Suburbs

corners and smooth, stucco-covered walls. Certain aspects, such as the low-pitched roof and shallow eaves, depart from the style's broadly recognized characteristics of flat roofs with no overhang. The overall austere and machined appearance of this corner house stands in contrast to the traditional houses surrounding it. Vuncannon operated a grocery store on West Green Street.

171. SHELTON HOUSE
1007 Ferndale Boulevard

In tandem with the Vuncannon House next door, the Mildred and Roy E. Shelton House of circa 1935 represents a rare but stylish example of Depression-era design. The Shelton House is one of the city's best examples of the historically inspired Regency Revival style, an interpretation of late eighteenth-century English residential architecture, with its wooden panels beneath the large multi-paned first-floor windows, awning-style metal roof above the front door and a low roofline. Additional features of the brick house include delicate dentil molding, quoins, a transom above the front door and shutters. Shelton was a building contractor.

172. WHITE HOUSE
1106 Glenwick

One of the earliest examples of Modern architecture in the city is this residence constructed in 1954 for Nancy and Gib White. Designed by Winston-Salem architect Lamar Northup, the house was influenced by the German-born Mies van der Rohe, a leader of the Modernist movement who directed the Bauhaus in Dessau and later taught at the Massachusetts Institute of Technology. Northup attended classes taught by van der Rohe while attending MIT and developed an appreciation for his "less is more" philosophy of design. This one-story house is identified by its flat roof, regularly spaced buttressed mullions across the façade, fire-resistant fiberboard "cemesto" siding and a floor plan featuring curved brick walls. White was a contractor who admired Northup's own home in Winston-Salem, of which this house is a nearly identical copy.

173. MYRTLEWOOD
800 Rockford Road

174. HILLBROOK
900 Rockford Road

Constructed by Myrtle Furr Hayworth-Barthmaier and her family in 1951, Myrtlewood was designed in the Georgian Revival style by architect William Roy Wallace of Winston-Salem. The imposing two-story house sits amid a stand of mature native hardwoods atop a steep bluff overlooking Rockford Road. The steel frame house was constructed by R.K. Stewart and Sons with Flemish bond brickwork, a slate roof and a projecting gabled pavilion containing the main entry, topped by an arched window centered upon the symmetrical main façade. Other details of the façade include a gabled front porch, segmental-arched windows, a heavy cornice and flanking wings with wall dormers. Refined Neoclassical Revival moldings and décor designed by New York designer Rose Talmey and Greensboro's Otto Zenke highlight the interior. Myrtle Hayworth-Barthmaier is remembered as one of a small number of female furniture company executives, successfully managing Alma Desk, Myrtle Desk and Hayworth Roll and Panel after the death of her husband in 1928. This house is one of the few in High Point designed by Wallace and illustrates the increasing popularity of restrained Neoclassical architecture over the exuberant Eclectic styles of the 1920s and 1930s.

Situated on a rambling estate of highly variegated topography, Hillbrook was constructed for Elizabeth Harriss and W. Comer Covington in 1929 to 1931 by contractor R.K. Stewart, according to a design by Luther Lashmit of Northup and O'Brien in Winston-Salem. Lashmit's work included the Gray family estate Graylyn in Winston-Salem. Covington established Harriss and Covington Hosiery Mills with his father-in-law, Julius Ward Harriss, in 1920 to manufacture mercerized cotton and artificial silk men's and women's hosiery. Covington also founded Triangle Hosiery Company in 1928 with John H. Adams.

The imposing steel frame house blends English Cotswold and Norman Revival styles. Cotswold features, such as Duke stone cladding, limestone trim, plain clay tile roof and massive chimneys, were combined with Norman details, such as an entryway with label mold with dropped and returned ends, Tudor arches and a conical tower. Other notable details include casement windows, a multi-car garage and an extensive New England–slate covered terrace. The interior of the house includes a grand "double cube" living room, a spiral stair within the tower, wood paneling, rippled plaster walls and parquet flooring.

Noted Philadelphia landscape architect Thomas Sears designed the grounds to resemble a mountain setting, using plants native to high elevations such as rhododendron, mountain laurel, white pines and hemlocks. Close to the house was a formal parterre de pieces coupes garden of paths and distinct planting beds featuring roses, sculpture and fountains. Terraces adjacent to the house overlook the woodland ravine containing the brook for which the private house was named. With its hilltop setting, high-grade materials, quality craftsmanship and skilled composition, Hillbrook may be viewed as the culmination of a grand era of lavish residences built in North Carolina as a result of the growth of the textile industry during the 1920s.

175. BRIGHTWELL
903 Rockford Road

Occupying a knoll overlooking a vast grassy lawn, Brightwell is notable as one of a series of suburban estates constructed during the late 1920s and 1930s in Emerywood West. Constructed for Lillian Jordan and Earl N. Phillips around 1939–40, Brightwell displays a Neoclassical Revival theme in its south façade, with an impressive full-height portico topped by a Chippendale balustrade, a broken pediment above the main entry and a symmetrical façade with flanking wings. The primary five-bay block is flanked by two-story wings featuring wall-dormers; additional wings extend beyond, culminating in gabled pavilions. The north façade features a single-bay portico with four Ionic columns. Brightwell was designed by Luther Lashmit of Winston-Salem–based architectural firm Northup and O'Brien and was constructed by High Point contractor R.K. Stewart and Son. Phillips owned Phillips-Davis, Inc., a successful fabric converting firm that brokered large quantities of fabric from mills to furniture upholsterers. He also served as mayor of High Point in the late 1940s. The walled garden north of the house was designed by notable landscape architect Ellen Biddle Shipman in 1946–47, incorporating native fieldstone stone walls and planting beds of perennials. Brightwell stands as one of the largest residences in the city and maintains a rural setting with extensive and well-landscaped grounds.

176. JONES HOUSE
1030 Rockford Road

177. COGGIN HOUSE
1032 Rockford Road

This impressive Dutch Colonial house was designed by architect Louis Voorhees, who had studied under architectural historian Fiske Kimball at the University of Virginia. Kimball's influence may be manifested in the historical accuracy of the Jones residence. In contrast to the gambrel-roofed interpretations of Dutch style popular throughout the city at the time, Voorhees employed wood-shingled sweeping rooflines, flared eaves, stone walls and an extended front porch, all hallmarks of seventeenth- and eighteenth-century Dutch architecture in New York's Hudson Valley. The house was constructed around 1940 by Wilber Jones, who operated the local division of the Troy, New York–based abrasives supplier Behr-Manning Corporation. He shared his home with his mother, Minnie Jones, and sister, Valette Harris Walsh, an accomplished artist, musician and world traveler.

Erected for Dot and Thayer Coggin, this Modernist residence was designed by Salt Lake City architect Fred Babcock, who developed a reputation for designing stylish residences in the Rocky Mountain states. Babcock had collaborated with interior designer Milo Baughman, who designed a line of modern furniture manufactured by Thayer Coggin's furniture company. Through their professional relationships, the three men grew acquainted with one another's work, and the stage was set for the design of the Coggin House. Built in 1972, the low masonry house is oriented away from Rockford Road and toward the Emerywood golf course to the rear of the property. Public spaces in the house take advantage of the view overlooking the golf course with expansive glazing. In contrast, private spaces are located toward the street and are screened by high-banded windows. Materials include dark brick tones and a copper roof. Landscaping is lush, with birch trees and shrubs. Though modern, the house blends harmoniously with the traditional houses of the neighborhood in scale, color and attention to detail.

178. Three Musketeers
1204 Westwood
GL 1990, SL 1990

The "Three Musketeers" was built as the home of Meredith Clark and Willis H. Slane. Willis Slane came to High Point in 1913 and purchased High Point Machine Works; however, his attention soon turned to the textile industry, and he established Slane Hosiery Mill in 1915 to manufacture men's and women's cotton and mercerized hosiery. Meredith Slane was active with the Arts Council, North Carolina Symphony Society and Historical Book Club, and was a founding member of the Junior League of High Point.

Three Musketeers was completed in 1930 according to plans by Luther Lashmit, an architect with Northup and O'Brien of Winston-Salem. The sprawling twenty-one-room mansion was constructed by R.K. Stuart of High Point. Lashmit designed the house to resemble a French chateau, with the round towers topped by conical roofs often found in Normandy. Among other features common to the style are thick masonry walls covered in stucco, a steeply pitched slate roof with flared eaves, arched dormer windows and numerous French doors. Interior appointments include murals by interior decorating contractors W. & J. Sloane of New York depicting the Three Musketeers departing for England, four hand-carved marble mantels, plaster crown moldings, hand-painted paneled walls and hand-painted Eglomise mirrors in the sunroom. Whimsical details include a weathervane depicting the Three Musketeers in silhouette atop a turret and the face of the Slanes' daughter, Meredith Slane Finch, over the front door.

Sited on a prominent knoll that Emerywood developer Stephen C. Clark considered the best location in the neighborhood, Three Musketeers is one of the most notable residences constructed in North Carolina. The 3.8-acre lot overlooks rock-strewn Pretty Branch Creek in a forest of mature oaks and hickories to the west. On the east side of the house the landscape is refined, including a broad traffic circle and flat lawn surrounded by plantings. A four-car garage and service area is attached to the north side, accessed by a drive.

Western Suburban Sites

179. High Point Central High School, Ferndale Middle School and Charles F. Tomlinson School
801 Ferndale Boulevard
SL

In response to High Point's rapid growth during the 1920s and increasingly demanding educational requirements, the High Point School Board commissioned Greensboro's Harry Barton to design a new high school west of downtown. Civic pride encouraged lavish spending on the project, which cost the city $750,000. It grew to become a symbol of the growing prosperity and sophistication of the city.

High Point's 1927 high school stands as one of the most impressive campuses in the state because of the collaborative efforts of its two designers. Charlotte landscape architect Earl Sumner Draper provided distinguished context for Barton's three-story building that blends the historic English Gothic style with the then-new Art Deco to produce a style known as "Neo-Gothic." Low squared towers and gothic arches are combined with spandrel panels and relief sculpture to create a style unique to the period. With its auditorium and cafeteria wings, the horseshoe-shaped building ranked among the largest schools in the state.

A few years later, Barton designed Ferndale Middle School, built on the east side of the campus in 1931. The two-story middle school incorporates details from the high school to create a unified campus theme. In 1958, Raleigh architect William Henley Deitrick designed a brick shared athletic facility between the two schools, adjacent to the athletic fields, featuring a boxy form and broad expanses of metal windows.

The last educational facility added to the campus was Tomlinson Elementary School, built in 1952–53 at 700 Chestnut Street. The school was named in honor of High Point School System Superintendent Charles F. Tomlinson, who led High Point's public schools after arriving from Winston in

Midtown and Western Suburbs

1904. One of the most influential acts of Tomlinson's career was his involvement with the development of the High Point Central campus.

Tomlinson Elementary was constructed on the western edge of the Central campus. Raleigh architect William Henley Deitrick took advantage of the wooded and rolling site, integrating the two-story brick building with the variegated topography and mature trees. Large windows looked out into the trees, and the building was oriented to give many rooms a sunny exposure. The form of the spare, flat-roofed school building follows the function of its uses, resulting in separately articulated classroom and cafeteria spaces. Doors and certain windows are framed in concrete; classrooms are identified by their triple windows recessed between full-height brick piers. Tomlinson Elementary represents a radical departure from the historically inspired school campuses previously built in High Point by using the forms that would define school designs for the remainder of the twentieth century.

180. HIGH POINT FRIENDS MEETING HOUSE
800 Quaker Lane

This Georgian Revival–style meetinghouse was constructed in 1955–56 according to a design by meeting member Howard Olive with the local architectural firm Voorhees and Everhart. The conservative treatment suggests early Georgian-style Friends meetinghouses around Philadelphia and is comparable to other prominent contemporary meetinghouses in the state. Sometimes dubbed "the Quaker Vatican," the complex is regarded as one of the most expansive Quaker campuses in North Carolina. Elements of the rambling building include Ragan Hall, the Haworth Chapel, a library, Sunday school rooms, classrooms and offices. Landscape architect R.D. Tillson provided a gracious greensward of pin oaks to buffer the meetinghouse from nearby Quaker Lane. Later improvements include a columbarium by William Freeman in 1990 and the Lower School by his son Peter Freeman in 2003.

181. Wesley Memorial Methodist Church
1101 Chestnut Avenue

Harold E. Wagoner, a nationally recognized church architect from Philadelphia, designed the sanctuary, chapel, offices and classrooms of Wesley Memorial Methodist Church in 1958, with assistance from Charles C. Hartmann of Greensboro. Wagoner chose to blend modern and Gothic architectural features to create a Neo-Gothic–style campus. A large stone sanctuary is the focus of the campus, comprising a long nave of stone topped by a slate roof and illuminated with stained-glass windows by Philadelphia craftsman Henry Willet. The nave is flanked by a tower of stone that rises in multiple stepped-back tiers to culminate in a copper-sheathed spire. The tower houses a carillon of antique Belgian-made bells. The main entry displays unusually fine wrought iron and delicate carved stonework. To the west of the sanctuary is a chapel topped by a complementary spire, as well as an array of one- and two-story buildings sheathed in stone that constitute various Sunday school classrooms, meeting rooms and offices. Located on Chestnut Street, the campus of stone structures and lush landscaping is the last of High Point's great twentieth-century religious complexes that demonstrates hand craftsmanship, historical precedence and monumentality.

182. B'nai Israel Synagogue
1207 Kensington Drive

B'Nai Israel Synagogue is High Point's main place of worship for those of Jewish faith and is the most progressive study in the city of modern architecture for a religious building. The congregation formed in 1911 and relocated to this new suburban site in Emerywood Forest northwest of the city around 1965. The unique Modernist-style building was designed by High Point architect Robert Conner. An unusual serrated roofline cut with beveled edges accentuates the main sanctuary; a menorah and the name of the congregation in Hebrew highlight the concave brick façade. To the north of the sanctuary extends a wing of classrooms and offices.

Midtown and Western Suburbs

183. Freeman House
1403 Rockspring Road

Architect William F. Freeman designed this residence for his own family's use. Built in 1955–56, it displays a flat roofline and alternating panels of glass and Philippine mahogany flanked by massive brick piers on each side of the structure. A covered parking area dominates the façade of the house, and entry is gained by way of a cantilevered platform. Interior public spaces are arranged openly, and private spaces are situated to the rear of the house. Freeman sought to contrast his family's residence with its wooded site by designing an abstracted cubical structure that was respectful but did not blend with the setting.

184. Conner House
1405 Emerywood Drive

Robert Conner designed his family's 1956 residence to blend with its forested environment through use of rough-cut Western Red Cedar sheathing. Rising to maximize vistas into the nearby trees, the broad, angled roofline incorporates a carport. Interior features include broad expanses of south-facing windows, skylights, open public spaces and walls constructed of historic bricks salvaged from a demolished downtown building.

Northern Suburbs - Map 7a

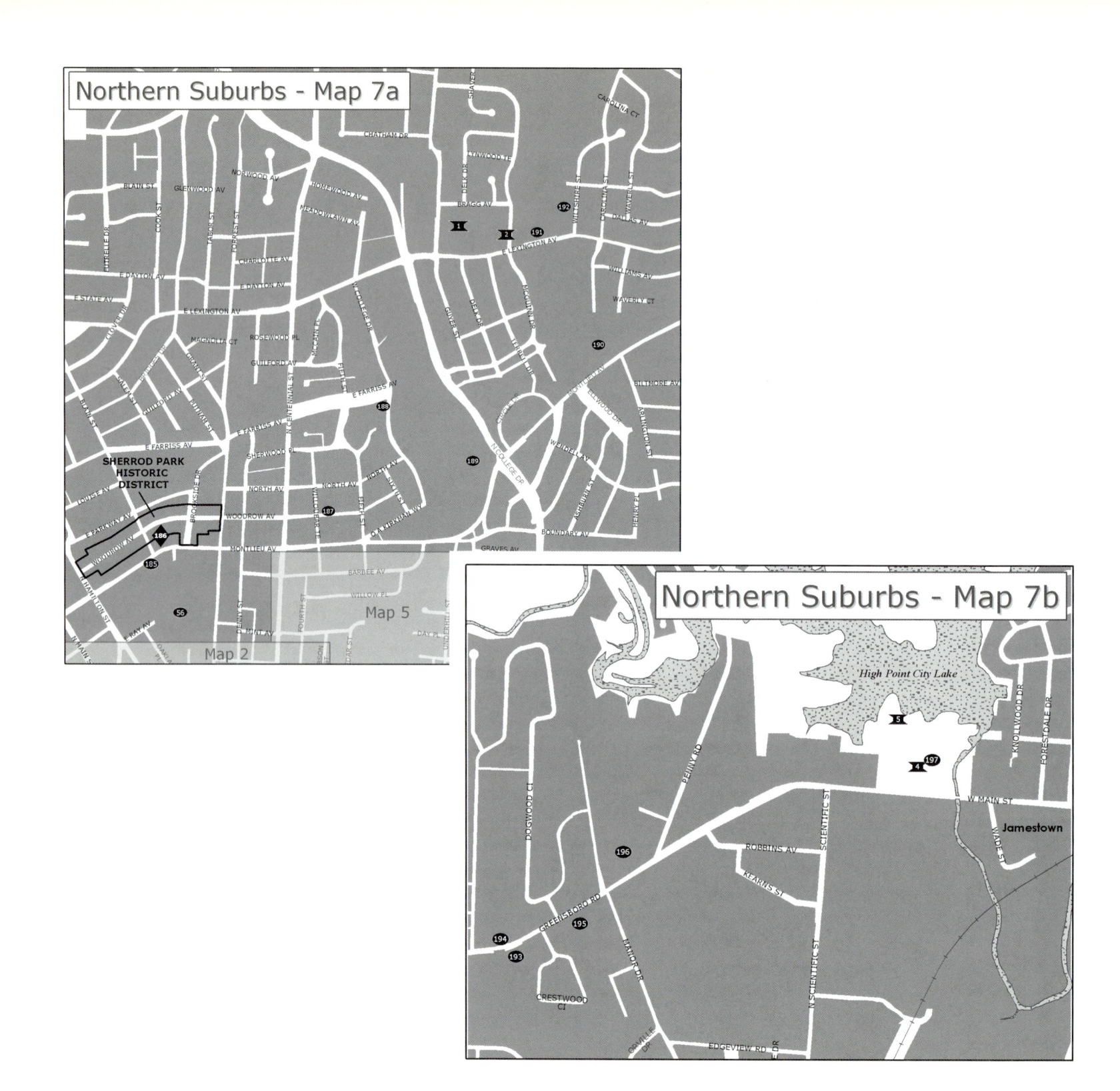

Northern Suburbs - Map 7b

NORTHERN SUBURBS

Early Northern Suburban Resources

High Point expanded rapidly in the second quarter of the twentieth century—with much of that growth focused northward—and most development was built under the close scrutiny of zoning laws that segregated land use by category. As a result, High Point's northern suburbs grew in an orderly manner, with few intrusions of manufacturing facilities or commercial areas. This sector of the city was born within the era of the automobile, and its sweeping residential streets, coordinated shopping centers and dispersed parks, schools and churches catered to those with access to cars. This model, first set forth in the 1920s, remains popular into the twenty-first century. Subdivisions that developed independently from each other are accessed by arterial thoroughfares, at which commercial development is found primarily at intersections. Institutions are scattered randomly throughout the landscape, sometimes taking advantage of adjacent parkland. The area remains popular today due to its planned character and proximity to transportation routes. This portion of the city has also benefited from the placement of several key institutions, most of which have worked to stabilize their surrounding neighborhoods.

185. Montlieu Avenue
SL

The Montlieu Avenue subdivision likely took its name from the late nineteenth-century Montlieu Dairy Farm, located adjacent to the thoroughfare on the southwest corner of Montlieu and Centennial Avenues. Montlieu Avenue (loosely translated from French as "high point") was created around the turn of the century as an alternative route to Greensboro from central High Point to bypass the growing East Washington Drive neighborhood.

The Montlieu Avenue subdivision was platted and advertised in May 1924 by Own-A-Home Co. This was Own-A-Home's third project, the first two having been located off East Green Drive in High Point's more moderate-income eastern neighborhoods. Stephen C. Clark, who was responsible independently for several exclusive real estate developments in High Point through the Great Depression (see the Parkway, Sheraton Hill and Emerywood), owned Own-A-Home with associates R.E. Snow and C.M. Kephart. Sixty-three lots were offered in the development, and sales started briskly during the summer of 1924. Advertisements in the *High Point Enterprise* touted the subdivision's close proximity to amenities such as a public school and newly founded High Point College, proclaiming how "mother may sit on her front porch and watch her baby boy or girl go to and from the Ray Street school and then in after years as that child grows into young manhood and womanhood, watch with eager interest his career through a high grade college located within a stone's throw of mother's porch." Lot prices ranged from $2,000 for the largest tracts to $1,000 for the smallest and most remote tracts.

Most houses were constructed soon after land was purchased from the development company. Styles popular at the time are represented on the street, including examples of Craftsman and Colonial Revival architecture. Several other styles, all built around 1925, are rare to High Point: the one-and-a-half-story brick and frame English Cottage with a false thatched roof built for optometrist Dr. J.F. Tesh and his wife Ruth at 209 Montlieu Avenue; the one-and-a-half-story brick Craftsman Airplane Bungalow at 212 Montlieu Avenue occupied by Lucien Long; and the stuccoed Spanish hacienda at 302 Montlieu Avenue built for East Green Service Station employee Lawrence Maupin and his wife Mamie. Stehli Silk Mill supervisor Fred Young and his wife Lola lived in the brick American Foursquare with Craftsman detailing at 217 Montlieu Avenue, which is more typical of the neighborhood house types and styles.

A point of interest in the neighborhood is a memorial dogwood tree at the corner of the drive to Oakwood Cemetery and Montlieu Avenue. A stone at the base of the tree features a bronze plaque that states, "May 30 1939 This Tree is in Memory of all World War Veterans."

186. SHERROD PARK
NR 1991, HD

Sherrod Park, extending along both sides of Woodrow Avenue off Hamilton Street, was developed during the economic prosperity of the 1920s. Seeing opportunity in the growth of the city, entrepreneur Archibald Sherrod left his manufacturing roots to found the High Point Insurance and Real Estate Company. Sherrod acquired eighteen acres of land between the highly successful Johnson Place subdivision to the north and the Montlieu Avenue neighborhood to the south. In 1926, he commissioned landscape architect and engineer A.E. Taplin to plat the subdivision as sixty-six lots mostly arranged along Woodrow Avenue, a curved street lined with sidewalks. Sherrod went a step further, though, in adding amenities to his subdivision. In 1928, he commissioned J. Van Lindley, a well-known landscape designer from Greensboro, to plant pin oaks and crepe myrtles along the drive. Pin oaks are known for their rapid growth, and crepe myrtle trees were popular for their colorful summer flowers. Along Brookside Street, a cross street straddling a small brook that runs through the development, Lindley planted various shrubs and trees to create a natural area reminiscent of the countryside.

The lots in Sherrod Park sold quickly; around one-third of the homesites were filled by the onset of the Depression. Houses were constructed in the many fashions popular at the time, but the Craftsman and especially Tudor Revival styles to late 1930s, many in the Colonial Revival style, and later a few Ranch houses were added. The Chernault-Proctor House at 321 Woodrow Avenue is an early example of Colonial Revival design in the neighborhood. Features of the simple, side-gabled house include stone veneer, an arched front door and twelve-over-twelve windows. Chernualt was a clerk at Quality Shoe Store. The Horney House at 225 Woodrow, by contrast, is a later and simpler version of the style, featuring gabled dormers and a full-width front porch. The "Colonial Cape Cod" plans for the house were advertised as the house of the month in a 1934 *McCall's Magazine*. Horney was employed with the High Point Fire Department.

predominated. The late Victorian Sydney Tomlinson House at 213 Woodrow Avenue was moved to the neighborhood from Main Street in the 1930s. Constructed in 1907 for the owner of Tomlinson Furniture, the building is the oldest on the street and is a style anomaly. Otherwise, most of these homes were constructed of brick and were modestly scaled yet carefully detailed, and almost all had generous front porches. Tudor Revival cottages feature steep roofs, half-timbering and diamond glass windows; Craftsman homes were known for their low rooflines, large windows and exposed rafter ends. The Byrum House at 311 Woodrow Avenue is a good example of the Tudor Revival style, featuring a prominent front chimney, stucco-covered walls and kicked roof peaks. The house was the model for the neighborhood and served as the sales office until 1929. Byrum was vice-president and superintendent of Robbins Knitting Company. The Ellison House at 320 Woodrow Avenue is another brick variation of the Tudor Revival style, exchanging stuccoed walls for an exuberant yellow-and-red patterned brick exterior and kicked peaks for a steep pyramidal roof. Ellison was superintendent of Perry Plywood Corporation. More homes were built when the pace of construction increased in the mid-

187. Willoubar Terrace

Once part of the vast Barbee Dairy that covered much of the territory around the intersection of Centennial and Montlieu Avenues extending toward High Point University, Willoubar Terrace was planned by landscape architect and engineer A.E. Taplin in 1914 after heirs of William G. and Louise Barbee (Wil-Lou-Bar) sold the dairy to a consortium including the Penny brothers. The neighborhood was filled with well-designed examples of Craftsman residences constructed in a variety of materials, including fieldstone and oversized brick. Other common details include wide porches carried by battered post-on-pier supports, low rooflines and wide eaves featuring diagonal brackets. Among the subdivision's most architecturally interesting houses are several that exhibit influences of the Spanish Eclectic style, the best examples of which stand at 800 and 802 Willoubar Terrace, and 707 and 710 Woodrow Avenue. The houses share features such as masonry walls, castellated parapet rooflines and a mix of segmental, rounded and square openings. Together, this collection of houses represents an exotic trend in North Carolina's diverse early twentieth-century architectural history.

Northern Suburban Sites

188. West College Drive Neighborhood

The West College Drive neighborhood enjoyed a burst of momentum during the post–World War II building boom, due to the area's prime location across the street from High Point College and the increasing convenience of the area to shopping districts such as nearby College Village Shopping Center. The suburban location and nearby college fostered some of the earliest examples of modern architecture in the city.

The earliest residences in the area were constructed in the 1950s, including the ECCLES B. EVERHART HOUSE, designed for himself in 1952 at 923 West College Drive in the Modernist style, featuring clean horizontal lines, broad expanses of windows facing away from the street for privacy and a flat roofline, all within the context of a richly vegetated lot. In the same year, contractor Everette Hill constructed the Modernist BILL STRONICH HOUSE for the High Point parks and recreation director at 1001 West College Drive. In contrast to the Everhart House, it features a high-cantilevered gable that protects a dramatic floor-to-ceiling wraparound corner window that addresses the street. The house is sheathed with natural wood siding above a rough stone raised basement and takes a commanding angled presence on its corner lot surrounded by lush landscaping. Hill constructed several other houses adjacent to the Stronich House, including his own EVERETTE HILL HOUSE at 1007 West College. The Hill House takes design cues from Frank Lloyd Wright's later designs, including a low-pitch roof supported by large exposed roof beams and natural cladding of wood and brick. The West College Drive neighborhood represents High Point's most unified and well-preserved collection of Modernist residences, all designed or constructed by notable regional names in the field.

189. HIGH POINT UNIVERSITY
SL 2001

In 1921, the Chamber of Commerce initiated a High Point College Campaign to solicit funds to attract the attention of the North Carolina Methodist Protestant denomination, a group that had sought to establish a college in their name for decades. The city aspired to establish the college as a remedy to a long-perceived civic shortcoming that it had no institution of higher learning. High Point succeeded in attracting the college over rivals Greensboro and Burlington with a gift of sixty acres and $100,000 in pledges from leading citizens. High Point College opened in 1924 with pledges and support of funds from numerous civic organizations, including the Rotary, Kiwanis, Civitan and the American Business Club.

Washington, D.C. architect R.E. Mitchell partnered with local architect Herbert Hunter and adopted a Georgian Revival theme to provide ready charm for the new campus. The classically inspired architecture lent an air of dignity and erudition for an institution that had yet to cultivate a reputation. The most impressive building on the campus is ROBERTS HALL, among the first triad of buildings, which demonstrates the British Renaissance ideals that inspired Georgian architecture in its tall multi-tiered tower and imposing front portico of Corinthian columns. The 1923 building may have been loosely modeled on Independence Hall in Philadelphia. Other Georgian attributes include round-arched dormers, a modillion cornice, an oculus (replaced by a clock face in 2005), twelve-over-twelve windows topped with keystones and handsome Flemish bond brickwork. WOMEN'S HALL, also designed by Herbert Hunter in 1923, continues the architectural theme of Roberts Hall, including keystone-topped feature windows, a strong cornice and rows of dormers (in this case pedimented). In addition, Women's Hall sports an elaborate cupola centered over the heart of the building. WRENN HALL, originally constructed as the M.J. Wrenn Library, was completed in 1937 and progressed the Georgian dialogue of early campus buildings with an elaborate elliptical transom window, a broken ogee frontispiece, Ionic pilasters, a full entablature with a modillion cornice and parapet side gables with chimneys.

Breaking free of the Georgian theme, architect Leon Schute contributed a number of Modernist designs to the campus. The HORACE S. HAWORTH HALL OF SCIENCE opened in 1967 and featured a two-story masonry façade that was broken at regular intervals by concrete pilasters. Each post was flanked by narrow windows and trimmed with concrete to provide the effect of a classical colonnade. Broad bands of concrete at the top and visual floor of the building completed the façade, detail that is still visible despite an addition in 1999. Schute was also the designer of the SLANE UNIVERSITY CENTER (formerly the McPherson Campus Center) in 1972, which continued the window-flanking-post theme for which he was well known. Recent additions to the campus have revisited historically inspired architecture, including the HAYWORTH FINE ARTS CENTER, a domed structure with a Tuscan portico designed in consultation with London-based architect Christopher Smallwood. This is Smallwood's only project in the United States outside the Northeastern states.

190. Montlieu Avenue Elementary School
1105 Montlieu Avenue

191. Little Red Schoolhouse
East Lexington Avenue at the High Point Greenway
GL 1988

Designed in 1957 by William Henley Deitrick of Raleigh, the Montlieu Avenue Elementary School continued a trend that saw public school buildings turn away from historically inspired designs to single-level structures that recognized the unique functional needs of a school. Deitrick was well known in Raleigh for his associations with Dorton Arena and numerous other projects, including schools in the eastern part of the state. His High Point projects were among his few commissions in the Piedmont Triad. Montlieu Avenue Elementary School adopts an irregular plan that reflects the use of space within the building. The main entry leads directly to offices as well as common spaces, such as the large cafeteria and library. Glazed breezeways connect these shared spaces to classroom wings. The entire complex is veneered in pressed brick and expanses of plate glass and embraces a horizontal orientation emphasized by its single story. Restrained detail exists in the form of a brick feature wall adjacent to the entry that is laid in a parquet pattern. The grounds originally included shaded low-maintenance natural areas, but these have been lost over time to expanses of grass.

This single-classroom building was designed in 1930 by High Point architect Louis Voorhees for use by his wife Elizabeth, who was then the first-grade teacher at Ray Street School. The building housed approximately thirty students and was erected to alleviate overcrowding in the main building. Though the main building fell to arson in 1961, the Little Red Schoolhouse, as it became known, remained intact and was adapted for commercial use before being relocated to land owned by the city around 1988. The building features a broad bank of windows that originally faced west. The entrance is through a small, clipped corner porch adjacent to a polygonal bay. The porch features lattice supports trimmed in white, which contrast with the red color of the German siding.

192. Forest Park and the Perry Estate

This collection of stylish middle-income residences expresses a variety of period Revival and Craftsman styles. The neighborhood represents a prosperous period in High Point's history in its high quality of design and execution. A.E. Taplin laid out Forest Park in 1926, beginning with Wiltshire Street. The success of Emerywood siphoned middle-income home buyers away from Forest Park, and lower-income areas that grew up around the subdivision at the end of the Great Depression rendered the neighborhood an island of distinctive architecture detached from other examples of period housing.

Foremost among the Wiltshire Street residences of the street is the Margaret and Henry D. Perry House built around 1923 at 1403 Wiltshire Street. Shortly after arriving from Alabama, Henry Perry took a position as a public works director. The residence he and his wife built represents a high-water mark of Craftsman design in its skillful incorporation of so many of the mode's characteristic elements. Heavy, square, brick piers support the wide porch, and non-structural but picturesque studded trusses decorate the gables of the house. Exposed rafters, banded windows and hand-crafted stained glass appear throughout. The landscaping is among the best of the period, featuring irregular stone walls, extensive iron fencing, a stone footbridge and grand masonry piers that hold forged iron lanterns. Mature hemlocks, walnut trees and boxwoods round out this well-preserved property.

Other houses in Forest Park display an array of period designs. The residence at 1503 Wiltshire circa 1926 is among the best examples in the city of the Mission style, featuring fanciful scalloped parapets, a pyramidal roof covered in Spanish tiles, stuccoed walls and wide overhanging eaves supported by exposed rafters. As a rare example of its style, the house illustrates an adventurous period in the design of residences in the city.

193. Williard House
1000 Greensboro Road

194. Modern Upholstery Company
1101 Greensboro Road

Dairyman Lewis Orville Williard built this fine Craftsman house around 1920. Today it stands as High Point's best example of an airplane bungalow. The identifying feature of the form is the small, upper-level single room that projects cleanly above the much larger first floor so that it resembles the raised cockpit of an early twentieth-century airplane. At the Williard House, the broad sweep of the side-gabled first-story roofline evokes an airplane's wings. In a warm climate such as North Carolina, the upper room with windows on three or four sides was prized for its ability to catch cooling breezes. Craftsman features of the house include battered post-on-pier supports for the porch, exposed rafter ends, diagonal eave bracing and vertically divided upper-window sashes. The house was retained when self-storage units were erected to the rear in 2002.

Ann E. and John E. Trexler operated Modern Upholstery, a manufacturer of upholstered living room furniture that was sold both wholesale and retail from this late example of Streamline Moderne architecture. The two-story building was erected in 1955 with a yellow brick façade and large picture windows. It was built just outside the city limits to avoid restrictions and encumbrances of municipal regulations and taxes. Streamline details include rounded corners with tall panels of glass brick and vertical bands of glass brick flanking the large picture windows of the second floor and lining the curved walls at the recessed entrance. It stands as one of the best examples of Streamline Moderne architecture in the city.

195. Harper and Welch Houses
1212 and 1214 Greensboro Road
SL

In the early 1920s, two High Point friends, Terry Harper and J.C. Welch, married a pair of attractive showgirls they had met in Chicago. The future Peggy Harper was from Chicago, and the future Wilna Welch hailed from New Orleans. Both couples settled in High Point and commenced construction of two eccentric houses on adjacent lots on the outskirts of town. Both residences were designed in 1926 by Clarence D. Tedford of Burbank, California, and were the talk of the town not only for their exotic out-of-town inhabitants, but also for their architecture as well.

The Terry and Peggy Harper House has an Arabian theme expressed in the turban-domed front porch supported by spiral colonettes. The J.C. and Wilna Welch House is a bit more subdued in its Spanish theme, which enjoyed popularity in California with film stars. Both houses were finished in stucco and originally painted pink, which accentuated their stage presence on Greensboro Road. They were the site of memorable parties and quickly gained a reputation as a place to see and be seen.

In 1931, tragedy brought good times to an end when Terry Harper discovered his wife's paramour, Charles Holton, in the living room of their home and shot him. Peggy Harper contended that she tried to stop the confrontation; Holton, in a statement before he died, claimed that Mrs. Harper asked him to the Harper residence to meet with her husband to discuss a divorce and was ambushed by Harper. Harper asserted that he shot Holton in self-defense. Charges against Peggy Harper were soon dropped, and Terry Harper was acquitted of charges by a jury just twenty-seven minutes after the judge completed his one-hour charge.

The sensational trial captured High Point's attention for days. Once it ended, there was a great deal of speculation about the Harpers' plans. Much to everyone's surprise, the couple reconciled and remained in their house for almost thirteen years before selling it in 1945 and moving to south Florida. Happy times did not prevail at the Welch House either, as the Welches divorced in the mid-1940s and Wilna moved home to New Orleans.

196. PENNYBYRNE
1315 Greensboro Road
SL 1976

George T. Penny (the T is rumored to stand for "Trade") was born in Randleman, North Carolina, in 1877. From his simple beginning as a horse trader, he and his brother Jim attained the reputation of "The World's Original Twin Auctioneers." The colorful pair specialized in buying and selling real estate to great profit, sometimes at the expense of other investors. By the mid-1920s George Penny and his wife Lena had amassed the financial resources to construct a home that broke all previous standards in the city. Penny commissioned Greensboro architect Raleigh James Hughes to design the imposing mansion at a cost of $126,000. Local contractor R.K. Stewart and Sons completed the house in 1927. The estate was named Pennybyrn and included ten acres of woodland and lawns landscaped by Charles Mackintosh, who also did work in Emerywood.

Pennybyrn is arguably the grandest home ever built in High Point. Its elaborate façade is festooned with medallions, arches and balustrades, all elements of the Italian Renaissance Revival architecture that was a popular choice for wealthy clients in major metropolitan areas. The Adams House on North Main Street in High Point is a smaller but equally detailed example.

Discontent with residing in what was then a rural location, Lena Penny enjoyed the estate for only five years. The couple moved to Greensboro and leased their country home to others. It was rented twice but remained empty most of the time. The first lessee used the home as a furniture store and design center; the second, as a nightclub known as the Chateau.

In 1947, five sisters from the Irish order of the Poor Servants of the Mother of God arrived in High Point at the invitation of His Excellency Vincent S. Waters, bishop of the Catholic Diocese of Raleigh, and Reverend Father Robert MacMillan of High Point's Immaculate Heart of Mary Church. High Point was selected as the location for a new hospital and nursing home administered by Catholics. Pennybyrn, commodious enough to offer sufficient space for start-up facilities, was purchased by the order in 1950. Though the order abandoned their grand plans for a new hospital complex on West Lexington Avenue when the city's public hospital upgraded in the 1950s, the sisters retained the Penny estate. The order renamed the campus Maryfield and focused their efforts on establishing a skilled nursing facility on the grounds. The mansion took on a new role as a convent for the sisters. In 2005, an expansion on the site was initiated, and named Pennybyrne in honor of the historic manor.

197. CITY LAKE PARK
602 West Main Street, Jamestown

When High Point's City Lake Park opened in 1934, it was among the grandest municipal parks in the state and featured one of the largest swimming pools in the South. Other amenities found in this sprawling park included an amphitheater for two thousand, two large playgrounds, a field house with exterior fireplaces, a large picnic ground with tables and barbeque pits, two tennis courts and a small museum in the Mendenhall Store. The centerpiece of the 340-acre park was the massive swimming pool, bathhouse and terrace. Modeled on the Wheelen Swimming Pool in Chicago, the pool was constructed 270 feet long and 165 feet wide and remains one of the largest outdoor pools in North Carolina. Federal Works Progress Administration grants covered most project costs by employing local workers during the pressing years of the Great Depression. Many High Pointers found employment constructing City Lake Park, along with other projects such as the Blair Park Clubhouse and the railroad cut through downtown.

City Lake Park became known as the "Playground of the Piedmont," and in a single day in 1935 it set a record for admitting 2,150 swimmers. According to the National Park Service, High Point led the state by 1937 in terms of acreage dedicated as municipal park space, nearly double the amount of the closest rival Greensboro and quadruple that of much larger cities such as Winston-Salem and Charlotte.

City Lake Park has benefited from several upgrades through the years, including the addition of a gymnasium (where the bathhouse and terrace originally stood) in 1961, and later improvements such as a water slide and a miniature train. It remains a landmark of the Triad and a central meeting point for statewide swim meets and social gatherings.

198. NATHAN WRIGHT HOUSE
1634 Penny Road

This house is notable as an amalgam of at least three early residences, including the mid-nineteenth-century two-story frame house of Nathan Spencer, Mary Couch's log house of the same period and a one-and-a-half-story frame wing erected by Nathan Wright. The Spencer House was moved from a site now occupied by Park Hill subdivision; the Couch and Wright components were erected nearby or on-site. Wright was a noted gunsmith in the Deep River area before 1858. The resulting amalgam was assembled around 1880 and united with period architectural detail, including brickwork, trim and mantels. The house was purchased by Quaker buggy manufacturer Henry Clay Briggs and his wife Isla Horney around 1880, in whose family it remains today.

199. Deep River Friends Meeting
5300 West Wendover Avenue
NR 1995

Established in 1753 by members of the Society of Friends, the Deep River Friends Meeting was near the end of the trail for a steady stream of settlers to the region from northern states and the Tidewater. Quakers are said to have chosen the site of the meetinghouse due to its high and dry savannah-like location. A large wood frame meetinghouse was erected in 1758, remarkable in the fact that it never burned despite wood-burning stoves vented directly into the attic, where smoke escaped by wafting through cracks in the shingles.

By 1871, a movement began to replace the original frame meetinghouse, which was then nearly 120 years old. Construction began two years later on a new building that measured sixty-five feet long and thirty-five feet wide. All materials were secured locally, including 133,000 bricks that were made and fired in a field located near today's intersection of Samet and Tinsley Drives. On the first Sunday in November 1875, Friends met for worship for the first time in their new meetinghouse. Distinctive features of the building include the iron face plates in the shape of stars that can be seen on the façade, which are evidence of structural shifting caused by the 1886 earthquake that required the insertion of long, iron rods to stabilize the exterior walls. The meetinghouse was among the earliest Quaker sanctuaries in the region to position its main entry on the gable wall as opposite the minister's lectern. Subtle Italianate details include molded hoods above windows and doors and raking eaves. Little original interior detail remains except for plastered walls and pine flooring.

The cemetery located to the north of the meetinghouse contains graves dating to the mid-eighteenth century, though many remain unmarked. Early Quakers avoided "superfluous monuments" characteristic of contemporary cemeteries. Three British soldiers were reported to have been buried here when Cornwallis's army passed through Deep River in 1781. More recent graves include elaborate markers of non-Quakers from Jamestown and the surrounding countryside. At least twelve former members of the North Carolina State Legislature are buried in the once rural graveyard.

Northern Suburbs

200. Williams House
Deep River Road

Originally constructed as a two-bay, two-story house around 1870, the Williams House was later extended first by a single-bay addition to the south and later by a two-story rear ell for a new kitchen, dining room and bedrooms. Marion Banner Williams is thought to have constructed this balloon-frame house set upon a fieldstone foundation with simple details such as raking eaves, circular sawn lumber and mass-produced windows, doors and sawn brackets. The interior finish is also simple, utilizing wide board sheathing, bead board siding and pine floors later overlain with oak. To the rear of the house is a collection of outbuildings, including a smokehouse, a carriage house for buggies and a barn. The loom house and two outhouses no longer remain. The Williams farm was surrounded by rail fences that enclosed sheep and cattle.

201. Oakview Community

This collection of early twentieth-century houses is clustered along Old Winston Road, an early portion of the highway bypassed in the 1950s when Main Street was realigned to the west. Houses include well-executed Craftsman designs, Colonial Revival styles and one Spanish hacienda with stuccoed walls and a flat parapet roof. Despite increasing pressures of urbanization, the community retains its semi-rural nature and stands as one of the city's few well-preserved residential neighborhoods clustered on a major thoroughfare.

202. Dyer House
121 Old Mill Road

One of a handful of rustic log houses in High Point built during the 1920s and 1930s, this house constructed for Dr. John Wesley Dyer represents an unusual chapter in period revival architecture. Dr. Dyer was an avid hunter who took a particular interest in breeding excellent hunting dogs. Likely constructed around 1925, this log house is a product of the Eclectic Revival period in American architecture, in which "romantic" styles were designed to infer simpler and more exotic periods in history. Log house construction was popular in Guilford County during the nineteenth century and enjoyed a long association with its history. Rustic Revival log houses differ from earlier log structures in their use of rounded logs and complex floor plans. Of the log houses in the county, the Dyer house is among the largest and most elaborate. The one-and-a-half-story log house features multiple side gables at various heights, dormer windows and fieldstone chimneys. The walls of the house are exposed, rounded logs chinked with cement and joined at each corner with a saddle notch. Rustic Revival houses of more modest scale stand at 102 Scientific Street and 706 Rockford Road.

GLOSSARY OF ARCHITECTURAL TERMS

ANAGLYPTA: A heavy, textured wallpaper invented in 1877 and popularly used by Victorians, especially when featuring Asian scenes or patterns painted to resemble hand-tooled leather.

ARCADE: A sequence of consecutive arches supported on piers or columns, started by the Romans and often associated with Classical and Mediterranean architecture.

ARCH: A curved structure of masonry spanning an opening.

ARCHITRAVE: The lowest of three components of an entablature, the lintel that spans above columns in classical architecture. Often found as trim around windows and doors in classically inspired designs.

ART DECO: A style of design popularized by the Exposition Internationale des Arts Decoratifs et Industrials Modernes in Paris, 1925. The design used natural forms and geometric shapes in stylized form as inspiration for consumer goods, decorative style and architecture.

ASHLAR: Masonry of smooth-squared stones laid in horizontal courses.

BALLOON FRAME: A construction technique begun in the Midwest in the early nineteenth century that employs common studs that rise from the sill to the top of the wall in a manner that encapsulates the entire living space of a building at one time, like a balloon.

BALUSTER: A pillar or column supporting a handrail or coping.

BALUSTRADE: A railing supported by a series of small posts or balusters.

BANISTER: American alternative term for balustrade.

Glossary of Architectural Terms

BATTERED POST: A support that is tapered with height, often located atop a masonry pier as a contributing element of the Arts and Crafts style.

BAY: 1) A compartment of a building, as defined by columns, pillars, windows or other prominent vertical elements. 2) A projection from a building containing windows, often polygonal or semicircular in plan. Often associated with Colonial buildings.

BEAD, BEADED SIDING: A half-rounded and incised edge used to finish weatherboards, joists, sheathing or other finish material. Often employed to reduce splintering, the finish technique was found in the High Point area before 1850.

BEAD BOARD: Wood sheathing machined with a continuous bead set in pairs, or patterns, and employed for use as wall paneling, wainscoting or ceiling material in the late nineteenth and early twentieth centuries.

BELT COURSE: A projecting horizontal course of brick, stone or wood used on exterior walls, usually delineating stories.

BLIND ARCH: An arch that is not open, but affixed to a wall in relief form.

BOARD AND BATTEN: Vertically placed siding of boards with seams covered by narrow strips of wood.

BOND: The pattern in which bricks are laid. Popular bonds in the Piedmont include Common and Flemish.

BRACKET: A small supporting member projecting from a wall or vertical surface in the form of a horizontal support. Often found as an element of a cornice.

BUNGALOW: A house type named for low and open houses found in India, often featuring porches, a low roofline and an informal floor plan. Bungalows are most often associated with Craftsman- and Prairie-style residences.

BUTTRESS: A projection of masonry or brickwork from a wall to give additional strength, particularly for vertical load-bearing walls.

CAME: A slender strip or band of lead used to adhere two panes of glass, often stained glass.

CANTILEVER: A structural technique or member projecting outward beyond its point of support, often stabilized by weight on its inner end.

CAPITAL: The crowning feature placed atop the shaft of a column or pilaster.

CARTOUCHE: An oblong ornamental frame or crown.

CASEMENT: A hinged window frame that opens horizontally like a door.

CASTELLATED: Decorative features associated with castles, such as tooth-like crenellation and turrets.

CAST IRON: Iron features set into a desired shape by pouring into a form when semi-molten.

CENTER-HALL, CENTER-PASSAGE: A house plan that features a central passage or hallway that extends the depth of a house, flanked by rooms of equal size. Can be single pile or double pile.

CHAMFER: A beveled or forty-five-degree face cut into the edge of timber as a finish or design element, sometimes used to reduce splintering.

Glossary of Architectural Terms

CHIMNEY POT: Plain or decorated clay or terra cotta flue, often circular or oblong in section, located atop chimneys, particularly in English-inspired designs.

CLAMP: A temporary kiln used to fire bricks, often by burning wood, and resulting in variations of color of brick.

CLAPBOARD: Overlapping horizontal boards that cover the timber-framed wall of a building. Northern American term for weatherboard. Often of equal thickness from top to bottom.

CLASSICAL: The architecture originating in ancient Greece and Rome, and the associated principles and forms of aesthetics that were largely revived during the Renaissance and Neoclassical periods.

CLIPPED GABLE: Also called Jerkin Head roof. A type of roof with the gable-end rafter pair sloped inward well above the main slope's eaves to form a hip.

COLONETTE: A thin or attenuated column.

COLONNADE: A range of columns supporting an entablature or arches.

COLUMN: A vertical support of round section. In Classical architecture the column has three parts: base, shaft and capital. The Greek Doric column is exceptional in that it has no base.

CORBEL: A bracket or series of inverted steps projecting from a wall used to support an overhang.

CORNICE: In Classical architecture, the projecting upper portion of an entablature; also often identified atop a window, or as the top portion of a building or wall.

CRAB ORCHARD STONE: A durable, mottled sandstone with unusually high silica content known for its durability and color variation; used in construction of Rockefeller Center in New York.

CRENELLATED: A form given to medieval battlements and castles that incorporates alternating wall heights somewhat like squared teeth of a saw.

CRESTING: A decorative feature located atop buildings, often made of cast or wrought iron and associated with Victorian architecture. (see Ecker House)

CUPOLA: A diminutive dome or domed structure rising from a roof or tower.

DEMILUNE: Crescent moon, or half circular, in plan—i.e., a half-circular porch. (see Wilson House)

DENTILS: An element of Classical architecture that resembles small, tooth-like blocks, often located as a component of a cornice. Small version of modillion.

DORIC ORDER: The Classical order most readily distinguished by its simple, unornamented capitals, fluting and the absence of a base.

DORMER WINDOW: An upright window lighting spaces beneath a roof. When it is on the same plane as the wall, it is called a wall dormer; when it rises from the slope of the roof, it is a roof dormer.

DOUBLE PILE: Two rooms in depth.

DOVETAIL: A flared tenon, resembling a dove's tail, and a complementing mortise, used to secure two pieces (usually wood).

Glossary of Architectural Terms

DUKE STONE: A phyllite, or fine-grained, foliated metamorphic rock that was quarried and used to construct many of the buildings on the west campus of Duke University in Durham.

EAVE: The underside of a sloping roof projecting beyond a wall.

ECLECTIC: A focus in architecture that celebrated diversity, including period detail, craftsmanship, regional traditions and interesting materials.

EGLOMISE: The practice of decorating a mirror by painting the underside of the glass before the surface is given its reflective coating.

ELEVATION: The vertical face of a building, whether external or internal, or a drawn representation of this.

ELL: A wing or extension to the rear of a building, positioned at right angles to the main block and often containing a kitchen.

ENGAGED PORCH: A porch that is located within the structure of a building beneath the rafters of the main roof.

ENTABLATURE: The upper portion of a Classical order of architecture, the lintel that bridges columns or the top of a wall, consisting of architrave, frieze and cornice.

FAÇADE: The front face, or main elevation of a building.

FACHWERK: A building technique in which a wooden frame is filled by clay, brick or stone to create a solid wall.

FANLIGHT: A semicircular or semielliptical window with radiating muntins suggesting an open fan.

FENESTRATION: The arrangement of windows on a building.

FLUSH SHEATHING: Horizontally placed siding of boards placed flush, without overlap. Often found on walls not prone to weather, such as beneath porch roofs and interior spaces.

FLUTING: Vertical groves, as on a Greek column.

FOURSQUARE: Also American foursquare. A house type of cubical form, rising two stories and topped by a hipped roof. Popular during the early twentieth century, foursquares often are associated with Prairie-style residential architecture.

FRENCH DOOR: A door inspired by French prototypes that contains multiple glass panes and is often grouped in pairs.

FRENCH TILE: A flat ceramic tile featuring vertical grooves, often pigmented, used to cover roofs.

GABLE: The upper, triangular part of an exterior wall under the end of a ridged roof, or a wall rising above the end of a ridged roof.

GAMBREL ROOF: A roof with two slopes of different pitch on either side of the ridge.

GLAZED HEADER: The short end of a brick, exposed to direct flame when fired, causing the sand content of the brick to turn to dark glass. Used to distinguish bond patterns, or as decorative diagonal patterns on chimneys.

GRAINING: A decorative treatment (faux finish) often on wood or plaster that simulates the color and texture of wood using paint.

GREEN MAN: The facial features of a human face, often resembling greenery or foliage, placed over a main entry for supernatural protection or good luck.

Glossary of Architectural Terms

HALF-DOVETAIL: A log or corner timbering technique employing only the uppermost feature of a flared dovetail mortise and tenon to secure an above beam.

HALL-PARLOR PLAN: A plan that features a single large multi-purpose hall with a fireplace, including a smaller parlor, sometimes also with a fireplace, to one side. Popular in the region around High Point before the Civil War.

HIP ROOF: A roof with sloped instead of vertical ends.

I-HOUSE: A house type first described by geographer Fred Kniffen as being observed in Midwestern states beginning with the letter I, but existing throughout the Eastern United States. I-houses feature central hallways flanked by single, equal-size rooms and rise two stories. The houses also feature side-gabled roofs and often have chimneys rising from the sides, the rear or on the ridge of the house. Popular in the region around High Point between the Civil War and the Depression.

INDIANA LIMESTONE: A very fine, gray stone quarried in western Indiana valued for its regular tone and used on many monumental buildings such as the Pentagon in Arlington, Virginia, and the Empire State Building in New York.

IONIC ORDER: A Classical order distinguished by the form of the capital, with a spiral scroll, called a volute, on four corners.

JOIST: Structural horizontal framing members that support floorboards or ceiling material.

KEYSTONE: The central, wedge-shaped stone of a semicircular arch.

KNEE BRACE: A diagonal timber member that braces extended eaves against an exterior wall; often employed in Craftsman-style buildings.

LABEL MOULD: A square or rectangular molding above a doorway or window.

LINTEL: Horizontal supporting beam that spans an opening in a wall or between columns.

LOGGIA: A gallery with an open arcade or colonnade on one or more sides. (see Adams House)

LUNETTE: A semicircular window or wall panel framed by an arch. (see Albion Millis House)

MARBLING: A decorative treatment (faux finish) often on wood or plaster that simulates the color and texture of marble using paint.

MEDALLION: An oblong, oval or circular ornamental feature that adorns walls and ceilings of classically inspired architecture.

MODILLION: A small supporting block or bracket that projects from a wall or vertical surface in the form of a horizontal support. Often found as an element of a cornice.

MORTISE AND TENON: Means of securing two structural elements using a recess, notch or hole (mortise) cut into timber to receive a rectangular projection (tenon), secured by pegs (trenails).

MOUNT AIRY GRANITE: A fine, gray granite quarried near the city of Mount Airy noted for its fine texture, durability and even tone.

MULLION: Slender post or upright member dividing windows or other openings set in a series.

MUNTIN: A slender band of metal or strip of wood that provides support to panes of glass.

Glossary of Architectural Terms

NOGGING: A mix of brick, mortar, earthen material, grass, twigs or wooden slats used to infill between timber structural members.

OCULUS: A circular window prominently featured on the façade of a building that resembles an eye in form or function.

OGEE: An S-shaped double curve consisting of one concave and one convex part. Often incorporated into classically inspired moldings.

ORDER: An accepted mode of proportion and decoration for Classical architecture. The Greeks recognized three orders: Doric, Ionic and Corinthian. The Romans added Tuscan and the Composite.

ORIEL WINDOW: A small bay window, especially one projecting from an upper story.

OVOLO: A convex molding whose profile is a quadrant of a circle or ellipse. A Grecian ovolo is flatter or egg-shaped in profile.

PALLADIANISM: A style of architecture derived or inspired by the publications and buildings of Renaissance Italian architect Andrea Palladio (1508–1580). Palladian aesthetics inspired tripartite windows, known as Palladian windows, often with a higher arched window centered in the composition.

PANEL: A surface enclosed by a border or frame, or raised above or sunk beneath the plane of a wall.

PARAPET: A low screening wall alongside a roof, often a continuation of a primary exterior wall.

PATIO: Spanish term for courtyard, or a paved outdoor space in the United States.

PEBBLEDASH: A stucco parging featuring embedded pebbles or small stones, often found in gables of Craftsman-style buildings.

PEDIMENT: The triangular section of wall above the entablature, within a gable or a feature over a window or door.

PEN: A room, or interior space of a building, most often referred to in describing log buildings and barns.

PENDANT: The extended base of a corner post of a cantilevered overhang, often decoratively carved and synonymous with first period architecture of New England.

PENT ROOF: An eaves-like feature projecting from a wall to throw off rain and snow.

PERGOLA: A structure of posts or piers carrying beams and trelliswork for climbing plants.

PIER: A heavy masonry support as distinct from a column, often rectangular or square in plan.

PILASTER: A flattened, rectangular column, pier or half-column attached to a wall, often placed to support an overhead roof or to stabilize a load-bearing wall.

PLINTH COURSE: A course of molded or staged bricks that define the base of the façade of a building.

PORTE-COCHERE: An extended roofline that provides for covered passage for vehicles, most often associated with residential construction in the early twentieth century.

PORTICO: A large porch or covered entranceway, often with a pediment, supported by columns or pillars.

QUAKER PLAN: A plan in which three rooms exist: one large multipurpose room with two smaller rooms to one side, of equal size positioned to the front and rear.

Glossary of Architectural Terms

QUATREFOIL: A four-lobed shape or element often associated with medieval or Tudor period architecture.

QUOINS: A detail of stacked or staggered stones or bricks found on the outside corner of a building.

REJA: Spanish term for a metal window grille or lattice.

RETURN: The continuation of a building element, especially decorative components such as molding or a cornice.

RUSTICATION: Rough-surfaced stonework. (see Southern Railway Passenger Depot)

SADDLE NOTCH: A log or corner timbering technique employing a semicircular shape to accommodate a circular log above.

SADDLEBAG: A plan in which two rooms flank a single interior chimney, most commonly associated with log construction.

SASH: A window frame that opens by sliding up or down.

SEGMENTAL ARCH: A portion, or segment, of a semicircle; not a full rounded arch.

SHEATHING: Weatherproof material covering the exterior of a building, including weatherboards, brick, stone or other material.

SHED ROOF: A pitched roof without a gable and exhibiting straight eaves.

SHOULDER: A projection resulting from a sharp change in width or thickness, resembling a human shoulder, such as a chimney.

SIDELIGHT: One of a pair of long, narrow windows flanking a door, most often associated with Neoclassical architecture.

SILL: 1) The base or bottom element of a window, sometimes made of wood or stone. 2) A heavy horizontal structural member of a wood frame house, on which studs or posts are placed.

SINGLE PILE: A building one room deep.

SPANDREL: A panel or surface directly below an upper-story window.

SPANISH TILE: A rounded or half-circular ceramic tile, often pigmented, used to cover roofs.

STUCCO: A granular cement used to protect exterior walls or imitate decorative stonework.

SURROUND: The border or casing of a window or door opening.

TERRA COTTA: A ceramic material, often molded into decorative shapes, colored and glazed, used for exterior design of buildings. The style was most popular in the early twentieth century.

TRANSOM: A self-contained window located above a doorway or other window, often square in shape.

TREFOIL: A three-lobed shape or element often associated with medieval or Tudor period architecture.

TRIPARTITE: An element, object or building having three distinct parts.

TRIPLE-A: An I-house with a forward-facing gable centered upon the roofline so that two side gables and one center gable total three gables.

TURNED: An element fashioned on a lathe, most often with a circular cross section.

Glossary of Architectural Terms

TUSCAN ORDER: A Classical order most readily distinguishable by its simplicity. The columns are never fluted, the capitals are unadorned and the entablature lacks triglyphs that are part of the Doric order.

TYMPANUM: The triangular space within a pediment or gable, often decorated with a circular or semi-circular window.

VENEER: A thin sheet of material—such as a non-load-bearing sheathing of brick, stone or stucco—or a thin face of fine wood.

VILLA: A term used to describe houses of the Mediterranean.

V-NOTCH: A log or corner timbering technique employing an inverted V-shape to secure an above beam.

WAINSCOT: Wood sheathing or panel work used to line the interior walls of buildings.

WATER TABLE: The molded detail or sloping top of a plinth course in masonry buildings, located at the top of the foundation at the level of the primary floor.

WEATHERBOARD: Overlapping horizontal boards that cover the timber-framed wall of a building. Southern American term for clapboard. Often of increasing thickness from top to bottom.

WROUGHT: Iron features created, manufactured or forged by hand into a desired shape by striking when semi-molten.

PRESERVATION RESOURCES

GUILFORD COUNTY HISTORIC PRESERVATION COMMISSION
The Guilford County Historic Preservation Commission (GCHPC) was established in 1980 by Guilford County, High Point, Jamestown and Gibsonville. Its primary purpose is to help preserve and protect Guilford County's unique architecture, rich history and cultural heritage. The major activity of the commission is the designation of buildings as Guilford County local landmarks. Upon application by the property owner, the commission may recommend to the local governing body (for example, High Point City Council) that it pass an ordinance designating the property as a Guilford County Historic Property.

HIGH POINT HISTORIC PRESERVATION COMMISSION
The High Point Historic Preservation Commission is a nine-member body appointed by the City Council. Not more than one member may be appointed from each of the city's two existing locally designated historic districts, Johnson Street and Sherrod Park. The remaining members are appointed from throughout the city. A full-term appointment is three years. Historic districts are established in order to help maintain and preserve areas of the city that have significant historic or architectural value. Regulations are applied through the use of an overlay zoning district, which sets forth rules that require review of all building activity affecting the exterior of structures.

HIGH POINT HISTORICAL SOCIETY
The High Point Museum and Historic Society exists to encourage a sense of heritage, place and community for the enrichment of the public. The High Point Historic Society, a nonprofit organization, staffs the museum and historical park. It receives some financial assistance from the City of High Point and depends upon membership, donations, gifts and grants to preserve a variety of artifacts, items and material from High Point's past.

Preservation Resources

HIGH POINT PRESERVATION SOCIETY
The High Point Preservation Society is an incorporated, nonprofit organization chartered to support and encourage the preservation of High Point's historic buildings and sites. The organization has worked with other organizations in the past, resulting in the creation of the High Point Historic Preservation Commission and preservation of the Southern Railway Passenger Depot.

INTERNATIONAL COUNCIL ON MONUMENTS AND SITES
ICOMOS is an international non-governmental organization of professionals, dedicated to the conservation of the world's historic monuments and sites. ICOMOS provides a forum for professional dialogue and a vehicle for the collection, evaluation and dissemination of information on conservation principles, techniques and policies.

NATIONAL REGISTER OF HISTORIC PLACES
The National Register of Historic Places is the nation's official list of cultural resources worthy of preservation. Authorized under the National Historic Preservation Act of 1966, the National Register is part of a national program to coordinate and support public and private efforts to identify, evaluate and protect our historic and archaeological resources. Properties listed in the register include districts, sites, buildings, structures and objects that are significant in American history, architecture, archaeology, engineering and culture. The National Register of Historic Places is administered by the National Park Service, which is part of the U.S. Department of the Interior. The National Park Service also maintains the nation's parks, provides technical assistance for restoration and promotes preservation through tax credits.

NORTH CAROLINA STATE HISTORIC PRESERVATION OFFICE
The North Carolina State Historic Preservation Office assists private citizens, private institutions, local governments and agencies of state and federal government in the identification, evaluation, protection and enhancement of properties significant to North Carolina history and archaeology. The agency carries out state and federal preservation programs and is a component of the Office of Archives and History, North Carolina Department of Cultural Resources. The office administers, coordinates and assists state and federal tax incentives, technical support, publications, archaeology and the National Register of Historic Places.

PRESERVATION NORTH CAROLINA
Founded in 1939, Preservation North Carolina is North Carolina's only private, nonprofit, statewide historic preservation organization. Its mission is to protect and promote buildings, landscapes and sites important to the heritage of North Carolina. Preservation North Carolina's work with difficult properties has also raised the level of awareness about the value and promise of historic preservation to local communities. Among Preservation North Carolina's other activities are the operation of two major museum properties (the Bellamy Mansion in Wilmington and Ayr Mount in Hillsborough), awards, workshops, publications, legislative advocacy and preservation easements.

NOTES

Chapter 1 EARLY SETTLEMENT AND DEVELOPMENT
1. Sizemore, *Buildings and the Builders*, 6–7.
2. The Uwharrie River.
3. Lawson, *New Voyage to Carolina*, 55–56.
4. Merrell, "Indians' New World," 95–113.
5. Barden, "Historic Prairies," 149–52.
6. Hinshaw, *Carolina Quaker Experience*, 18–20; Levi, *Quakers and the American Family*, 241.
7. Oppermann, "Deep River Friends Meeting House and Cemetery."
8. A.M. Briggs, untitled essay, 1932, Briggs Family Papers.
9. Taylor, "History of the Phillip Hockett land"; Taylor, interview.
10. "History of Deep River Friends Meeting," Briggs Family Papers.
11. A.M. Briggs, "Untitled" 3, Briggs Family Papers.
12. Wells, "Haley House."
13. Quaker plan houses were named by Thomas Tileston Waterman, who observed their occurrence in association with members of the Society of Friends (Quakers). See Briggs, "Quaker Plan Houses," 3–42.
14. A.M. Briggs, "Untitled" 4, Briggs Family Papers.
15. A.M. Briggs, 5, Briggs Family Papers; North Carolina Friends Historical Collection.
16. A.M. Briggs, "Short History of Deep River Monthly Meeting and Community," Briggs Family Papers, 1–2.
17. Briggs, "Quaker Plan Houses."
18. Haworth, *Deep River Friends*, 70.
19. Tin mining has existed in Cornwall since the Stone Age, but mining reached its peak in the nineteenth century. Competition from Australia depressed the price of tin to a level that made Cornish ore unprofitable. At its height, the Cornish Tin Mining Industry had around six hundred steam engines working to pump out the mines. Hundreds of mines were established in the area around Redruth, Camborne and Newquay. Engine houses were often constructed of stone to encapsulate steam engines, and featured high smokestacks to ventilate exhaust.
20. Barnett and Brenner, "McCulloch's Gold Mill."
21. Klain, "Quaker Contributions to Education," 292.

Chapter 2 THE VILLAGE OF HIGH POINT
22. Lossing, *Pictorial Field-Book*, chapter 15, endnote 37.
23. Colonel William A. Blair, "Old Plank Road, High Point's Main Street, Followed Trail Indians Blazed," in Sizemore, *Buildings and the Builders*, 38.
24. Joyce, *Clarks' Collection*, 104.
25. Trelease, *North Carolina Railroad*, 25; A.M. Briggs, "Untitled" 4–7, Briggs Family Papers.
26. Joyce, *Clarks' Collection*, 162.
27. Ibid., 110.
28. Whatley, interview.
29. Joyce, *Clarks' Collection*, 98.
30. Pierce, *High Point Public Schools*, 15.
31. "Preparatory Schools—Seminaries and Institute," in Sizemore, *Buildings and the Builders*, 308. This building was later used as the High Point Female College in 1889, on which the description of the structure is based.

32. Mrs. Charles W. Perry in Sizemore, *Buildings and the Builders*, 50.
33. Sizemore, *Buildings and the Builders*, 249–56.
34. Joyce, interview. Note: Washington Street was changed to Washington Drive in the 1960s when the city standardized center-city road designations to reflect north-south "streets" and east-west "drives."
35. Oppermann, "Deep River Friends Meeting House and Cemetery."
36. Perry, "The Railroad Crosses the Old Plank Road and a Setting for a City is Laid," in Sizemore, *Buildings and the Builders*, 49. Mrs. Denny was the first interred in Oakwood Cemetery; however, two earlier remains, those of the seven-year-old son of Dr. Lindsay and those of Lizzie Denny, were reinterred in Oakwood after it opened.
37. The Bellview was known by a number of names as the property changed hands, including Piggott's Hotel, Barbee House, the Bellevue and the Biltmore Hotel.
38. Perry in Sizemore, *Buildings and the Builders*, 50.
39. Blair, "Characters, Incidents and Stories of Half a Century," in Sizemore, *Buildings and the Builders*, 65.
40. Perry in Sizemore, *Buildings and the Builders*, 47.
41. Joyce, *Clarks' Collection*, 112.
42. Ibid., 29. Camp Fisher was located where William Penn High School now stands.
43. John W. Cannon, "Old High Point Hotels Have Interesting History," in Sizemore, *Buildings and the Builders*, 33–35; John Gilchrist Barrett, *North Carolina as a Civil War Battleground*, 94–98.
44. Joyce, *Clarks' Collection*, 30, 104. Evidence from diaries and reports of the period indicate it is unlikely that Davis was a guest of the Barbee Hotel; however, it is possible that his wife Varina and their children stayed in the hotel, as they passed days before the railroad tracks were destroyed.
45. Joyce, *Clarks' Collection*, 105; Trelease, *North Carolina Railroad*, 260.
46. Whatley, interview.
47. Joyce, *Clarks' Collection*, 156.
48. Stockard, *History of Guilford County*, 89.
49. Joyce, *Clarks' Collection*, 39.
50. Sanborn Insurance map, 1885. In 2003, tobacco and molasses residue discovered on the fourth floor of the structure confirmed the manufacturing of plug tobacco in this building.
51. Joyce, *Clarks' Collection*, 40.
52. "Preparatory School-Seminaries and Institutes," in Sizemore, *Buildings and the Builders*, 308–09; Darr, "O. Arthur Kirkman House: Blair School Amendment."
53. Wilson, "One Hundred and One Years," 22–25.
54. Matthews and Sink, *Wheels of Faith*, 206; Joyce, *Clarks' Collection*, 51.
55. "Catalog of High Point Female College," in Sizemore, *Buildings and the Builders*, 309–12.
56. "The Development of Education in High Point and Surrounding Area," in McPherson, *High Pointers*, 98.
57. "St. Mary's Church Consecrated October 18, 1947," and "A Brief History of Central Friends Church," in Sizemore, *Buildings and the Builders*, 256–58.
58. Robinson and Stoesen, *History of Guilford County*, 77.
59. Thomas B. Smith, "Negroes of City Have Won and Retain Respect for Splendid Achievement," in Sizemore, *Buildings and the Builders*, 323.
60. Ibid., 323–24; Joyce, *Clarks' Collection*, 92–94.
61. A.M. Briggs, "Untitled" 12–13, Briggs Family Papers.
62. Cultural geographer Fred Kniffen named this type of house form the I-house in the 1930s for his initial observation of the type in Midwestern states of Iowa, Illinois and Indiana. See Kniffen, "Folk Housing," 549–77; Michael Southern, "The I-house as a Carrier of Style in Three Counties of the Northeastern Piedmont," in Swaim, *Carolina Dwelling*, 70–83.

Chapter 3 THE RISE OF INDUSTRY
63. Darr, "O. Arthur Kirkman House and Outbuildings."
64. Sanborn Insurance maps, 1885, 1890, 1896.
65. Hanchett, *Johnson Street*, 66.
66. Whiffen, *American Architecture*, 115–20.
67. Joyce, *Clarks' Collection*, 37.
68. Payne, interview.
69. Darr, "Application: Brown House."
70. Hanchett, *Johnson Street*, 35; "New Buildings," *High Point Enterprise*, September 23, 1908: 1.
71. Whiffen, *American Architecture*, 159–65.
72. "Mr. Kirkman Buys," *High Point Enterprise*, April 20, 1900: 1.
73. Guilford County Register of Deeds Office, Plat Maps, Deed Book 2, page 14; A.M. Briggs, 9, Briggs Family Papers.
74. S.C. Clark, "Residential Development has Provided a Romantic Chapter of Local History," in Sizemore, *Buildings and the Builders*, 288–92.
75. Guilford County Register of Deeds Office, Plat Maps, Deed Book 2, page 98.
76. Wilson, *One Hundred and One Years*, 23–24; Smith in Sizemore, *Buildings and the Builders*, 325.
77. Guilford County Register of Deeds Office, Plat Maps, Deed Book 91, page 267.
78. Joyce, *Clarks' Collection*, 58.
79. Cross, "William Penn High School."
80. Joyce, *Clarks' Collection*, 58.
81. Perry, *First Presbyterian Church*, 64–65; Farriss, *High Point North Carolina*.
82. "1886 and 1888 in High Point," in Sizemore, *Buildings and the Builders*, 104, 323.
83. J.J. Farris, "1900–1903 A Brief Summary of Manufacturing," in Sizemore, *Buildings and the Builders*, 123.
84. Robinson and Stoesen, *History of Guilford County*, 156.
85. Farris in Sizemore, *Buildings and the Builders*, 123.

Chapter 4 THE HOSIERY MANUFACTURING AND HIGH POINT'S GROWTH AS A CITY
86. Ibid., 156.
87. Ibid., 166.
88. Davis, *Southern Railway*, 22–28.
89. "New Passenger Depot," *High Point Enterprise*, April 18, 1906: 1.
90. Briggs, interview, September 14, 2000.

91. Robinson and Stoesen, *History of Guilford County*, 217; "High Point: The Industrial City of the South," in Sizemore, *Buildings and the Builders*, 142.
92. Manieri, "Tomlinson Chair Manufacturing Company Complex"; "A New Factory: Tomlinson Manufacturing Co. Will Make Chairs," *High Point Enterprise*, August 17, 1900.
93. "1916 to 1918," in Sizemore, *Buildings and the Builders*, 139.
94. Briggs, interview, September 14, 2000.
95. Dowdy, e-mail.
96. *Carolina Architect*.
97. "From a Single Mill 30 Years Ago Has Grown South's Hosiery Center," *High Point Enterprise*, January 20, 1935, 1.
98. Farriss, *High Point North Carolina*; "High Point: The Industrial City of the South," in Sizemore, *Buildings and the Builders*, 139–43.
99. Mellichampe, interview. Mellichampe served as secretary and treasurer of Pickett Cotton Mills, Inc.
100. "Evolution of the Mill Form," in Toole, *Cotton Mills*, 128–30.
101. Ibid., 103–05.
102. McPherson, *High Pointers*, 290.
103. "Oliver Causey Sowed Seeds of Important Manufacturing Line: Pickett, Highland and High Point Yarn Mill Afford Large Employment to Supply Yarn and Cloth," *High Point Enterprise*, January 20, 1935.
104. Ward, interview. Ward was a native of Highland Mill village and a "Cotton Classer" for Highland Cotton Mill, 1947–87.
105. "The Dynamic Decade 1920–1930," in Sizemore, *Buildings and the Builders*, 78; "City Loses Industries While Most Places Gain," *High Point Enterprise*, April 7, 1949: 1A.
106. "Stehli, with Roses and Landscaping, Sets a Standard and Ideal for Industry," *High Point Enterprise*, January 20, 1935: 1A.
107. Briggs, interview, July 27, 2004. Briggs is a native of High Point and son of Roy Briggs Sr., owner of High Point Buggy Company.
108. Robinson and Stoesen, *History of Guilford County*, 182.
109. Shipman, *High Point*, 64.
110. Robinson and Stoesen, *History of Guilford County*, 181–82.
111. Brown, *State Highway System*, 152; Sizemore, *Buildings and the Builders*, 302.
112. "Redding Building," *High Point Enterprise*, March 27, 1907: 1A.
113. "Officers and Board of Directors 'At Home,'" *High Point Enterprise*, February 5, 1908.
114. High Point City Directory, 1933. J.C. Penney subsequently relocated to a larger building across South Main Street, now destroyed.
115. "Sheraton Hotel Opens Today in High Point," *Greensboro Daily News*, November 23, 1921: 1A.
116. "High Point, The Industrial City of the South," in Sizemore, *Buildings and the Builders*, 139–43.
117. "Speakers Tell Why New Bank Building is Credit to City," *High Point Enterprise*, February 21, 1924: 1A.
118. Draper, "Building Zone Map." The plan is on display in the High Point Planning office lobby.
119. Smith in Sizemore, *Buildings and the Builders*, 322–27.
120. "Black People Have Contributed Much to the Development of High Point," in McPherson, *High Pointers*, 90–92.
121. Hart, "Aero View"; Williford, "Kilby Hotel."
122. Chavis, interview; "Lander Funeral Set Thursday," *High Point Enterprise*, February 10, 1965.
123. "The Dynamic Decade 1920–1930," in Sizemore, *Buildings and the Builders*, 78–86.
124. Robinson and Stoesen, *History of Guilford County*, 175.
125. Ibid., 178.
126. *Greensboro, High Point*.
127. Joyce, *Clarks' Collection*, 73.
128. McPherson, *High Pointers*, 16.
129. Phil Speaks, "Big Bureau City's Enduring Trademark," *High Point Enterprise*, January 25, 1985.
130. Joyce, *Clarks' Collection*, 78.
131. Robinson and Stoesen, *History of Guilford County*, 177.
132. "The Dynamic Decade 1920–1930," in Sizemore, *Buildings and the Builders*, 78–86.
133. Letter from Guilford County Superintendent Thomas R. Foust to State Agent N.C. Neubold, September 1915, in Browning, *Bending the Twigs*, 96–97.
134. Robinson and Stoesen, *History of Guilford County*, 233.
135. Ibid.
136. McCaslin, *Remembered Be Thy Blessings*, 21.
137. Perry, *First Presbyterian Church*, 141–42.
138. Jackson and Brown, *History of the N.C. Chapter of the AIA*, 98.
139. Hartsoe, e-mail.
140. S.C. Clark, "Residential Development Has Provided a Romantic Chapter of Local History," in Sizemore, *Buildings and the Builders*, 290.
141. A.M. Briggs 11, Briggs Family Papers.
142. Hanchett, *Johnson Street*, 9.
143. Clark in Sizemore, *Buildings and the Builders*, 288–92.
144. Guilford County Register of Deeds Office.
145. Little, "Sherrod Park Historic District."
146. Robinson and Stoesen, *History of Guilford County*, 195.
147. Foscue, interview. Foscue is the daughter of C.F. Tomlinson.
148. Campbell, "Lucy and J. Vassie Wilson House."
149. Briggs, interview, October 6, 2004; Johnston and Waterman, *Early Architecture*.
150. Briles, interview. Briles is the daughter of Lee Briles
151. Darr, interview. Darr is the current occupant of the O. Arthur Kirkman House.
152. Darr, "O. Arthur Kirkman House and Outbuildings."
153. Smith, *Architectural Resources*, 56.
154. Pond, interview; Smith, *Architectural Resources*, 56.
155. Shipman, *High Point*, 352–53.
156. Smith, *Architectural Resources*, 56.
157. Phillips, "John Hampton Adams House"; Smith, *Architectural Resources*, 36, 53. Smith speculates that the house was designed by Lorenzo S. Winslow, a draftsman for Greensboro architect Charles Hartmann, who later became architect to the White House during the Truman and Kennedy administrations.
158. Brown, *Maryfield USA*, 33.

159. Plans are in the possession of current owner of the Welch House, William Mangum.
160. Folger, interview.
161. Graybeal, "A.E. Taplin Apartment Building."
162. Phillips, "Jarrell Apartments."
163. Robinson and Stoesen, *History of Guilford County*, 193.
164. "Long Neglected Tate Park Turned to Beauty Spot," *High Point Enterprise*, June 12, 1949: 1A. After several years of debate concerning maintenance and upkeep costs, the park site was sold to neighboring First Baptist Church and paved for a parking lot in 1952.
165. Draper, "Building Zone Map." Also see "City of High Point Proposed Park and School Plan," by Morris Knowles Inc., Engineer of Pittsburgh, PA, 1928.
166. "Colored Cemetery," *High Point Enterprise*, January 25, 1910: 1.
167. Joyce, interview.
168. Joyce, interview; "Completing Plan for Burial Park," *High Point Enterprise*, July 14, 1935: 1.

Chapter 5 MODERN PERIOD AND CIVIL RIGHTS ERA
169. "Planning Director for City to Report Here on March 1," *High Point Enterprise*, February 12, 1950: 1.
170. Sharpe, *New Geography*, 820.
171. Orr and Stewart, *North Carolina Atlas*, 108.
172. "We're All-America," *High Point Enterprise*, March 18, 1963: 1A.
173. Smith, *Architectural Resources*, 68.
174. Trexler, interview.
175. "Shopping Center Opens Thursday," *High Point Enterprise*, November 11, 1959: 1A.
176. "New Shopping Center To Open On S. Main," *High Point Enterprise*, July 24, 1960: 1D.
177. Whiffen, *American Architecture*, 261–66, 279–92.
178. McPherson, *High Pointers*, 25–26.
179. Freeman, interview.
180. Mays, interview; "Electronics Firm to Hold Open House," *High Point Enterprise*, February 23, 1958: 1A.
181. Masonry blocks made with Northeast Solite aggregate were developed in 1947 as a lightweight alternative to traditional masonry units.
182. Conner, interview and tour.
183. Ibid.
184. Levy, interview. Levy is the daughter of architect Edward Loewenstein.
185. Mays, interview.
186. Robinson and Stoesen, *History of Guilford County*, 159.
187. Oppermann, "Guilford County Office and Court Building"; Smith, *Architectural Resources*, 68.
188. "Elimination of the Railroad Grade Crossings," in Sizemore, *Buildings and the Builders*, 86–87.
189. Robinson and Stoesen, *History of Guilford County*, 183.
190. Conner, interview and tour.
191. Freeman, interview.
192. Bishir and Southern, *Historic Architecture of Piedmont*, 110–11.

193. Mays, interview.
194. McPherson, *High Pointers*, 13.
195. "High Point School Board Awards Two Architects' Contracts at Meeting," *High Point Enterprise*, March 1, 1949: 1A.
196. Mays, interview.
197. Briggs, interview, July 27, 2004. Briggs was a member of the building committee for the new meetinghouse.
198. Joyce, interview.
199. Conner, interview and tour.
200. Bishir and Southern, *Historic Architecture of Piedmont*, 204–05. The Gamble House in Durham was erected in 1935 and closely resembles the Whitsell House.
201. Smith, *Architectural Resources*, 67.
202. Mays, interview.
203. Ibid.
204. Ibid.
205. Briggs, interview, October 6, 2004. Name of magazine has not been determined, but its existence is corroborated by Mays and others.
206. Conner, interview and tour.
207. Freeman, interview.
208. Coggin, interview.
209. "A New Apartment House and a New Suburban Home," *High Point Enterprise*, February 8, 1935: 1A.
210. Briggs, interview, October 6, 2004.
211. Plunz, *History of Housing*, 138.
212. "City Council Approves Building of Apartments," *High Point Enterprise*, May 10, 1949.
213. Marks, interview.
214. *Carolina Architect*.
215. Robinson and Stoesen, *History of Guilford County*, 193.
216. "Historic Jamestown Here is One of the Country's Outstanding Recreation Developments to Reflect Credit on Community," *High Point Enterprise*, January 20, 1935.
217. "Negro Park Will Prove Big Boon for Residents," *High Point Enterprise*, November 14, 1937: 1.

WORKS CITED

Amos, Robert T. Telephone interview. August 6, 2004.

Art Work of Piedmont Section of North Carolina. Published in Nine Parts. Chicago: Gravure Illustration Company, 1924.

Barden, Lawrence S. "Historic Prairies in the Piedmont of North and South Carolina, USA," *Natural Areas Journal* 17, no. 2 (1997).

Barnett, Angela, and James T. Brenner. "McCulloch's Gold Mill." National Register Nomination, 1978, Survey and Planning Branch, Historic Preservation Section, North Carolina Division of Archives and History, Raleigh.

Barrett, John Gilchrist. *North Carolina as a Civil War Battleground, 1861–1865*. Raleigh: Division of Archives and History, North Carolina Department of Cultural Resources, 1993.

Bishir, Catherine W. *North Carolina Architecture*. Chapel Hill: University of North Carolina Press, 1990.

Bishir, Catherine W., and Michael T. Southern. *A Guide to the Historic Architecture of Piedmont North Carolina*. Chapel Hill and London: University of North Carolina Press, 2003.

Briggs, Benjamin. "Quaker Plan Houses of Deep River Quarterly Meeting, Guilford County, North Carolina." *The Southern Friend* (Spring–Autumn 1999).

Briggs Family Papers. North Carolina Friends Historical Collection, Guilford College, Greensboro, NC.

Briggs, Roy. Personal interviews. September 14, 2000, July 27, 2004, October 6, 2004.

Briles, Ruth. Telephone interview. November 6, 1999.

Brown, Cecil Kenneth. *The State Highway System of North Carolina: Its Evolution and Present Status*. Chapel Hill: University of North Carolina Press, 1931.

Brown, Joe E. *Maryfield USA: A Success Story*. High Point: Maryfield Nursing Home, Incorporated, 1997.

Browning, Mary A. *Bending the Twigs in Jamestown: A History of Education in Jamestown, North Carolina 1755–1945*. Jamestown: Historic Jamestown Society, 2004.

Campbell, Nancy H. "Lucy and J. Vassie Wilson House." National Register Nomination, 2005, Survey and Planning Branch, Historic Preservation Section, North Carolina Division of Archives and History, Raleigh.

Works Cited

Carolina Architect and Allied Arts: A Pictorial Review of Carolina's Representative Architecture. Miami: Frederick Findeisen, 1942.

Chavis, Glenn. Personal interview. May 11, 2005.

Coggin, Dot. Telephone interview. August 2, 2004.

Conner, Robert. Personal interview and tour of projects. April 21, 2004.

Cross, Jerry L. "William Penn High School (High Point Normal and Industrial Institute)." National Register Nomination, 1978. Survey and Planning Branch, Historic Preservation Section, North Carolina Division of Archives and History, Raleigh.

Darr, Dorothy Gay. "Application for the Designation of an Historic Landmark: Brown House." Guilford County Preservation Commission Files. June 28, 2005. Guilford County Planning Department, Greensboro, NC.

———. "O. Arthur Kirkman House and Outbuildings." National Register Nomination, 1988, Survey and Planning Branch, Historic Preservation Section, North Carolina Division of Archives and History, Raleigh.

———. "O. Arthur Kirkman House: Blair School Amendment." National Register Nomination, 1989, Survey and Planning Branch, Historic Preservation Section, North Carolina Division of Archives and History, Raleigh.

———. "Oakwood Historic District." National Register Nomination, 1990, Survey and Planning Branch, Historic Preservation Section, North Carolina Division of Archives and History, Raleigh.

———. Personal interview. June 20, 2003.

Davis, Burke. *The Southern Railway, Road of the Innovators.* Chapel Hill and London: University of North Carolina Press, 1985.

Dowdy, Lee. E-mail correspondence. November 18, 2004.

Draper, Earl Sumner. "Building Zone Map for the City of High Point." City of High Point Planning Department, 1926.

Farriss, J.J. *High Point North Carolina.* High Point: Enterprise Printing Company, 1896, 1900, 1903, 6th ed. 1911, 8th ed. 1918.

Folger, Margaret Clinard. Personal interview. 1992.

Foscue, Sarah Lacy. Telephone interview. January 2004.

Freeman, William F. Telephone interview. June 21, 2004.

Graybeal, Kaye. "A.E. Taplin Apartment Building." National Register Nomination, 1995, Survey and Planning Branch, Historic Preservation Section, North Carolina Division of Archives and History, Raleigh.

Greensboro Daily News. Greensboro, NC.

Greensboro, High Point, Guilford County, Some Assets and Liabilities. Raleigh: State of North Carolina Planning Board, 1947.

Guilford County Deed Books. Guilford County Courthouse, Greensboro and High Point, NC.

Guilford County Preservation Commission Files. Guilford County Planning Department, Greensboro, NC.

Hanchett, Thomas W. *Johnson Street Historic District, High Point, North Carolina: Its History and Architecture.* City of High Point, 1987.

Hart, Charles. "Aero View of High Point, North Carolina: The Manufacturing Centre of the South." Lithograph published by J.J. Farriss, 1913.

Hartsoe, Colleen. E-mail correspondence. July 4, 2004.

Haworth, Cecil E. *Deep River Friends: A Valient People.* Greensboro: North Carolina Friends Historical Society, 1985.

Hayes, Helen Snow. *History of the First Presbyterian Church, High Point, North Carolina: 1859–1959.* High Point: Hall Printing Company, 1959.

Hicks, Robert F., Jr. "The Spirit of Enterprise: The History of High Point's Formative Period, 1851–1926." Master's thesis, University of North Carolina at Greensboro, 1989.

High Point City Directories, 1910–1970. North Carolina Collection, High Point, NC.

High Point City Plat Books. Guilford County Courthouse, High Point, NC.

High Point Enterprise. High Point, NC.

High Point Museum Files. High Point Museum, High Point, NC.

High Point Public Library, Vertical Files, North Carolina Collection. High Point, NC.

Hinshaw, Seth B. *The Carolina Quaker Experience, 1665–1985.* Greensboro: North Carolina Yearly Meeting and North Carolina Friends Historical Society, 1984.

Hinshaw, Seth B., and Mary Edith Hinshaw. *Carolina Quakers: Our Heritage, Our Hope; Tercentenary 1672–1972.* Greensboro: North Carolina Yearly Meeting, 1972.

Works Cited

Jackson, C. David, and Charlotte V. Brown. *History of the N.C. Chapter of the AIA, 1913–1998: An Architectural Heritage*. Raleigh: NC AIA, 1998.

Johnston, Frances Benjamin, and Thomas T. Waterman. *The Early Architecture of North Carolina, a Pictorial Survey*. Chapel Hill: University of North Carolina Press, 1941.

Jordan, Paula S. *Women of Guilford County, North Carolina: A Study of Women's Contributions, 1740–1979*. Greensboro: Women of Guilford, 1979.

Joyce, Mary Lib Clark, ed. *Clarks' Collection of Historical Remembrances (Collections and Recollections from Three Generations of Clark Historians)*. Privately printed, 1999.

Joyce, Mary Lib Clark. Personal interview. March 4, 2004.

Klain, Zora. "Quaker Contributions to Education in North Carolina." Master's thesis, University of Pennsylvania, 1924.

Kniffen, Fred. "Folk Housing: Key to Diffusion." *Annals of the Association of American Geographers* (December 1965): 549–77.

Lawson, John. *A New Voyage to Carolina*. Edited by Hugh Talmage Lefler. Chapel Hill: University of North Carolina Press, 1967.

Levi, Barry. *Quakers and the American Family: British Settlement in the Delaware Valley*. Oxford: Oxford University Press, 1988.

Levy, Jane L. Telephone interview. March 24, 2004.

Little, M. Ruth. "Sherrod Park Historic District." National Register Nomination, 1991, Survey and Planning Branch, Historic Preservation Section, North Carolina Division of Archives and History, Raleigh.

Little, M. Ruth, and Kaye Graybeal. "Dr. Charles S. Grayson House." National Register Nomination, 1993, Survey and Planning Branch, Historic Preservation Section, North Carolina Division of Archives and History, Raleigh.

Lossing, Benson J. *The Pictorial Field-Book of the Revolution*. Vol. II. New York: Harper & Brothers, 1852.

Ludlow, J.L. "Map of High Point, N.C. Showing the Property of the Central Improvement Co. as Developed by J.L. Ludlow of Winston, N.C." High Point Public Library, Vertical Files Collection, High Point, 1892.

Manieri, Ray. "Tomlinson Chair Manufacturing Company Complex." National Register Nomination, 1982, Survey and Planning Branch, Historic Preservation Section, North Carolina Division of Archives and History, Raleigh.

Marks, Edgar. Telephone interview. February 18, 2005.

Marks, Robert, and Janet Fox. *High Point: Reflections of the Past*. High Point: Community Communications, Inc., 1996.

Matthews, Mary Green, and Jewel Sink. *Wheels of Faith and Courage*. Privately published, 1952, reprinted 2002.

Mays, Clayton. Telephone interview. April 20, 2004.

McAlester, Virginia, and Lee McAlester. *A Field Guide to American Houses*. New York: Alfred A. Knopf, 1988.

McCaslin, Richard B. *Remembered Be Thy Blessings: High Point University The College Years, 1924–1991*. High Point: High Point University, 1995.

McPherson, Holt, ed. *High Pointers of High Point*. High Point: Hall Printing Company, 1976.

Mellichampe, J.H., Jr. Personal interview. March 16, 1998.

Merrell, James H. "The Indians' New World: The Catawba Experience." In *Material Life in America, 1600–1860*, edited by Robert Blair St. George. Boston: Northeastern University Press, 1988.

"Morgan, John Pierpont." Microsoft Encarta Online Encyclopedia 2004. http://encarta.msn.com 1997–2004 Microsoft Corporation. All Rights Reserved.

North Carolina Friends Historical Collection. Guilford College, Greensboro, NC.

Oppermann, Langdon Edmunds. "Deep River Friends Meeting House and Cemetery." National Register Nomination, 1995, Survey and Planning Branch, Historic Preservation Section, North Carolina Division of Archives and History, Raleigh.

———. "Guilford County Office and Court Building." National Register Nomination, 1988, Survey and Planning Branch, Historic Preservation Section, North Carolina Division of Archives and History, Raleigh.

Orr, Douglas M., Jr., and Alfred W. Stewart. *The North Carolina Atlas: Portrait for a New Century*. Chapel Hill and London: University of North Carolina Press, 2000.

Payne, Roger. Telephone interview. September 17, 2004.

Pegg, William Wesley, Sr. *Something of the Story of Deep River*. Privately published, 1980.

Perry, Octavia Jordan. *History of the First Presbyterian Church, High Point, North Carolina: 1859–1959*. High Point: Hall Printing Company, 1959.

Works Cited

Phillips, Laura A.W. "Jarrell Apartments (Hardee Apartments)." National Register Nomination, 1990, Survey and Planning Branch, Historic Preservation Section, North Carolina Division of Archives and History, Raleigh.

———. "J.C. Siceloff House." National Register Nomination, 1990, Survey and Planning Branch, Historic Preservation Section, North Carolina Division of Archives and History, Raleigh.

———. "John Hampton Adams House." National Register Nomination, 2000, Survey and Planning Branch, Historic Preservation Section, North Carolina Division of Archives and History, Raleigh.

Pierce, Michael G. *History of the High Point Public Schools 1897–1993*. High Point: High Point Public Schools, 1993.

Plunz, Richard. *A History of Housing in New York City: Dwelling Type and Social Change in the American Metropolis*. New York: Colombia University Press, 1990.

Pond, Stephen. Personal interview. September 24, 2004.

Recreation Division, Parks and Recreation Department, City of High Point, NC. Retrieved October 4, 2004, from http://www.high-point.net/pr/recreation_division.htm.

Robinson, Blackwell P., and Alexander R. Stoesen. *The History of Guilford County, North Carolina, U.S.A. To 1980, A.D.* Greensboro: The Guilford County Bicentennial Commission, 1980.

Sanborn Insurance Company. Map series: 1885, 1890, 1896, 1902, 1906.

Sharpe, Bill. *A New Geography of North Carolina*. Vols. 1–4. Raleigh: Sharpe, 1954–65.

Shipman, Roy J. *High Point, A Pictorial History*. High Point: Hall Printing Company, 1983.

Sizemore, F.J., ed. *The Buildings and the Builders of a City: High Point, North Carolina*. High Point: Hall Printing Company, 1947.

Smith, H. McKeldon. *Architectural Resources: An Inventory of Historic Architecture: High Point, Jamestown, Gibsonville, Guilford County*. Raleigh: Division of Archives and History, North Carolina Department of Cultural Resources, 1979.

Stockard, Sallie W. *The History of Guilford County, North Carolina*. Knoxville: Gant-Ogden, 1902.

Swaim, Douglas, ed. *Carolina Dwelling*. Raleigh: North Carolina State University School of Design Student Publication, 1978.

Tankard, Judith B. *The Gardens of Ellen Biddle Shipman*. Sagaponack, NY: Sagapress, Inc., 1996.

Taylor, Barbara E. "History of the Phillip Hockett land on Richland Creek and Mordecai's Creek in Guilford Co., N.C." High Point Museum Files, High Point, 2004.

———. Telephone personal interview. April 6, 2006.

Thomas, C. Yvonne Bell. *Roads to Jamestown: A View and Review of the Old Town*. Fredericksburg, VA: BookCrafters, 1997.

Toole, Debbie Curtis, ed. *Cotton Mills, Planned Communities, and the New Deal: Vernacular Architecture and Landscapes of the New South*. Athens, GA: Green Berry Press, 1999.

Trelease, Allen W. *The North Carolina Railroad 1949–1871 and the Modernization of North Carolina*. Chapel Hill and London: University of North Carolina Press, 1991.

Trexler, Robert. Telephone interview. August 18, 2004.

Ward, Charles H. Telephone interview. June 23, 2000.

Weatherly, A. Earl. *The First Hundred Years of Historic Guilford, 1771–1871*. Greensboro: Greensboro Printing Company, 1972.

Wells, John B., III. "Haley House." National Register Nomination, 1971, Survey and Planning Branch, Historic Preservation Section, North Carolina Division of Archives and History, Raleigh.

Whatley, L. Mac. Telephone interview. July 29, 2004.

Whiffen, Marcus. *American Architecture Since 1780: A Guide to the Styles*. Cambridge and London: MIT Press, 1996.

Williford, JoAnn. "Kilby Hotel." National Register Nomination, 1981, Survey and Planning Branch, Historic Preservation Section, North Carolina Division of Archives and History, Raleigh.

Wilson, Jeanette Ouren. "One Hundred and One Years: Solomon Isaac Blair's School, the High Point Normal and Industrial Institute, and William Penn High School." *The Southern Friend* (Autumn 1995).

Winslow, Margaret Davis. *A Gift from Grandmother*. Privately published, 1958.

INDEX

A

A.E. Taplin Apartment Building 71, 188
Abbott's Creek Baptist Church 35
Adams, Elizabeth Barnes 173
Adams, John Hampton 49, 145, 173
Adams-Millis Corporation 134, 145, 146, 173, 177, 199
Adamsleigh 173
Adams House 173, 232
Airplane Bungalow 222, 230
Alexander's Store 33
Alexander, Harrison 33
All-American City 73
Allen Brothers Department Store 54, 118
Allen Jay House 10, 101
Allen Jay School 149
Alma Desk 37, 124, 135, 140, 141, 210, 212
Altizer-Cole Fabric Company 127
Alvin S. Parker House 204
Ambler, J.N. 62, 182
American Business Club 226
American Friends Service Committee 101
Amos, Charlotte 199
Amos, Robert T. 199
Amos Hosiery Finishing Plant 77, 199
Amos House 199
Annettie McBain Brown House 127
Anvil Brands 191
Arabian style 71, 231
Archibald Sherrod House 67
Armentrout, Hirum M. 196
Armentrout, Winnifred 196
Armentrout House 69, 196
Armfield, Wyatt 29
Artisan Acres 62
Art Deco style 45, 59, 74, 77, 78, 80, 83, 86, 88, 107, 113, 114, 115, 117, 121, 122, 167, 169, 170, 180, 216, 237
Atlantic Bank and Trust 183
Austin, Dr. J.W. 182
Austin, Etta 182

B

B'Nai Israel Synagogue 61, 82, 218
Babcock, Fred 74, 85, 214
Baldwin, Rosetta Cora 162
Baltimore Association to Advise and Assist Southern Friends 36, 101, 148
Barbee, Louise 225
Barbee, William G. 225

Barbee Dairy 225
Barbee Hotel 132
Barbee House 31, 32
Barber, Arthur 130
Barber-Hall Printing 130
Barker, A.A. 33
Barthmaier, Herbert 141
Barton, Harry 45, 57, 59, 61, 64, 68, 168, 169, 174, 185, 189, 194, 206, 216
Battle of Bentonville 32
Baughman, Milo 214
Bauhaus 110, 211
Beard Hat Shop 23, 24
Beeson, Isaac 22, 99
Beeson, Richard 99
Beeson Brothers 34
Beeson Hardware 114
Beeson House 22, 99
Behr-Manning Corporation 214
Bell, Polly 99
Bellini, Mario 128
Bencini, Emery 179, 193, 206
Bennett's Mill 103
Bennett, Harold C. 181
Bennett Advertising Building 76, 181
Bennison, Tenor 149
Bernice Bienenstock Furniture Library 170
Best, Benjamin 136
Best Building 34
Big Bear food market 75
Bill Stronich House 226
Bivens, John 10, 94
Bivens and Caldwell Building 75, 181
Blair, Colonel W.A. 28
Blair, David H. 147
Blair, John J. 10, 105
Blair, Reverend and Mrs. Walter 160
Blair, Solomon 42, 159
Blair, William Allen 34
Blairwood Dairy 103
Blair Hoskins Shoe Company 188
Blair Park 71, 87, 147
Blair Park Clubhouse 233
Blandwood 28, 103
Bloomington 22, 30, 93, 137
Boone-Wilmington Highway 52
Borum, George 95
Bowman-Field farm 47
Bowne, Marie Antoinette Wood 208
Bowne, Reverend Henry Norwood 208
Bowne House 208

Index

Brentwood School 80
Briggs, A.M. 21, 61
Briggs, E.L. 64
Briggs, Henry Clay 233
Briggs, Isla Horney 233
Briggs, Joy R. 100
Brightwell 213
Briles, Bertie Wallace 172
Briles, Lee 172
Briles, Ruth 172
Briles House 65, 172
Broad Street freight depot 46
Brooks, Reverend Daniel 86, 132, 143, 152, 161
Brooks Memorial Methodist Church 143
Brown, Annettie McBain 40, 127
Browntown 22, 93
Brutalism style 75, 76, 81, 110
Bryan, S.T. 202
Buis (Bewes), William 97
Bullock, Reverend O.S. 152, 156
Burford, S.E. 156
Burford Auditorium 59, 80, 159
Burnett, W.G. 177
Burnett-McCain House 67, 177
Burris Memorial Hospital 177, 200
Burton, Criscilla Jane 100
Byrum House 224

C

Camp Fisher 32
Cannon, Ruth Coltrane 10, 23, 101
Cape Fear River 27
Cape Fear Road 102, 110, 117
Caraway Mountain 19
Carolina Veneer 195
Carr, Julian S. 124
Carrick, Dr. D.B. 40, 191
Carrickmoor 191
Carroway tribe 19
Carteret, John, second Earl Granville 20
Castle McCulloch 99
Catawba Town 20
Cates, Forrest 73
Causey, O.S. 33
Cecil House 136
Cedar Falls 32
Centennial Exposition of 1876 41
Central Friends. *See* High Point Friends Meeting
Central Highway 52
Central Savings Bank 109

Chamber of Commerce 58, 60, 71, 132, 133, 226
Charles F. Tomlinson School 80, 216
Chautauqua Club 39
Chernault-Proctor House 224
Chestnut Hill 23, 100, 101
Citizens Real Estate and Insurance Company 189
City Lake Park 10, 23, 87, 95, 232, 233
Civitan Club 226
Clara Cox Homes 87, 163
Clark, Daisy Ogburn 190
Clark, David 30, 32
Clark, F.H. 42
Clark, Stephen C. 9, 62, 72, 179, 182, 185, 186, 190, 193, 202, 215, 222
Clark House 190
Cloverdale 39, 51, 144
Cloverdale Dye Works 144, 173
Cloverdale School 58, 144
Coggin, Dot 85, 214
Coggin, Thayer 85, 214
Coggin House 214
Cole, Nat King 155
College Village Barber Shop 75
College Village Shopping Center 74, 75, 225
Collins, William 95
Colonial Revival style 39, 41, 42, 51, 55, 62, 63, 64, 82, 83, 87, 116, 124, 125, 131, 136, 143, 145, 146, 148, 160, 163, 167, 170, 171, 176, 177, 183, 185, 187, 188, 194, 195, 198, 201, 206, 208, 210, 222, 224, 235
Coltrane, John 160
Comer Covington House. *See* Hillbrook
Commercial National Bank 54, 117, 118, 119, 177, 198
Confederate Monument 31, 132
Conner, Robert 74, 76, 78, 82, 85, 134, 137, 153, 181, 218, 219
Conner House 219
Connor, J.O. 164
Consolidated Hosiery Mill 65, 177
Consolidated Mirror Company 197
Continental Furniture Company 47, 195, 198
corner-timbered (log) houses 21, 94, 236
Cornwall, England 25, 99
Cottam, Robert 202
Cottam-Wall House 202
Couch, Mary 233
County Building 78

Covington, Elizabeth Harriss 212
Covington, W. Comer 212
Cox, Bertha Snow 198
Cox, Clara Ione 86, 163
Cox, J. Elwood 33, 39, 41, 42, 118, 119, 130, 198
Cox, Joe D. 64, 118, 183, 185, 193
Cox, May 185
Cox House 41, 64, 185
Craftsman, The 66
Craftsman style 42, 45, 51, 62, 66, 67, 88, 126, 131, 136, 143, 144, 146, 160, 162, 170, 178, 180, 182, 183, 186, 187, 188, 194, 222, 223, 224, 225, 229, 230, 235, 241
Creelman family 132
Crouch family 179
Crouse, J.L. 115
Crown Hosiery 198, 205
Cummins, Claude J. 195
Cummins, Mecca 195
Cummins House 195

D

Dalton, Carter 178
Dalton, Frank 207
Dalton, Margaret Hayworth 207
Dalton, Mary Land 178
Dalton, Reverend P.H. 31
Dalton Building 34
Dalton Furniture Company 47, 183
Dalton House 66, 126, 178
Daniels, Josephus 45
Daniel Brooks Homes 86, 161, 163
Davis, A.J. 28, 103, 105
Davis, Dr. Murray 158
Davis, Jefferson 32
Davis, Margaret 103
Davis, O.E. 152
Davis, Stephen 98
Davis, Winslow 100
Deconstructivism style 109, 128
Deep River 19, 21, 28, 31, 40, 56, 94, 95, 97, 98, 99, 102, 103, 234
Deep River Cabin 95
Deep River Friends Meeting 21, 31, 93, 95, 98, 105, 234
Deitrick, William Henley 74, 80, 159, 217, 228
Denny, K.C. 204
Denny, Margaret 31
Denny House 204
Denny Roll and Panel Company 49

Index

Depot Square 29, 46, 61, 107, 108, 109, 110, 123
Diana Shop 75
Dick, Elizabeth 97
Donald W. Conrad Agency 94
Dowdy, D.A. 111, 161
Dowdy, David 108
Dr. Davis Office 158
Dr. Gaylord House 153
Dr. J.J. Cox Building 76
Draper, Earl Sumner 45, 54, 59, 62, 193, 194, 210, 216
Dutch Colonial style 57, 64, 136, 147, 175, 183, 187, 189, 190, 191, 205, 208, 214
Dyer, Dr. John Wesley 236
Dyer House 236

E

Eagle Furniture 37, 38
Early Architecture of North Carolina 64
East Green Service Station 222
Ecker, Ferdinand 41, 170, 176
Eckerd 75
Ecker Apartments 86, 170
Ecker Glass and Mirror 49, 176
Ecker House 41, 176
Eckstein, Billy 155
Edmunds, T.V. 182
Edwards, Alice 203
Edwards, Charles C. 203
Edwards Business College 203
Edwards House 70, 194, 203
Elihu Mendenhall House 28, 102
Elks Club 126
Ellis, Collier 209
Ellis, Ruth 85, 194, 209
Ellison House 224
Ellis House 209
Elm Street School 58
Emerywood 59, 61, 62, 63, 64, 67, 68, 71, 82, 83, 85, 86, 87, 161, 176, 182, 183, 193, 194, 195, 197, 198, 201, 202, 203, 205, 206, 207, 209, 210, 215, 232
Emerywood Court 86, 175
Emerywood Estates 194
Emerywood Forest 82, 194, 218
Emerywood Section 4 Showhouse 202
Emerywood West 63, 68, 69, 183, 194, 210, 213
Emma Blair School 58
English Cotswold style 212

Eubank and Caldwell 82, 116
Eunice and Ralph Parker House 210
Everette Hill House 226
Everhart, Eccles B. 61, 78, 174, 226

F

F.D.R. Canal 107
F.W. Woolworth's 75
Fairview 39, 56, 143
Fairview School 58
Farabee's Store 29, 34, 110, 111
Farriss, J.J. 9, 44, 48, 135, 141, 142, 176
Ferndale Junior High School 59, 80
Ferndale Middle School 216
Ferree, Tyson 74, 86, 114, 122, 161, 169
Field, E.H.C. 124
Finch, Meredith Slane 215
Fire Station Number 4 57, 175
First Baptist Church 31, 43
First Baptist Church, North Main Street 82, 116
First Baptist Church, Washington Drive 55, 71, 82, 116, 152, 155, 156
First Methodist Church 116
First Methodist Protestant Church. *See* First Methodist Church
First Presbyterian Church 31, 43, 61, 167, 168
First Reformed United Church of Christ 137
First Union National Bank 134
First United Methodist Church. *See* First Methodist Church
Fitzgerald, Ella 155
Floral Garden Park Cemetery 72
Florence Female Academy 25, 100, 103, 104
Florence School 59
Foor and Robinson Hotels 53, 54, 115
Forest Park 63, 229
Forsyth, Milton D. 97
foursquare type 66, 67, 131, 136, 156, 183, 184, 194, 222, 240
Foust, Thomas 149
Frank, E. Letitia 185
Frank, Julius 185
Frank Dalton House 192
Fraser, Alma 124
Fraser, Henry W. 124, 140, 141
Fraser, Ida Myrtle 125, 141
Freedmen's Bureau 42
Freeman, Peter 217
Freeman, William 74, 85, 119, 121, 123, 217, 219

Freeman and Associates 75, 120
Freeman House 219
Fries, Francis 29
Fries Warehouse 32
Froelich, Jake 10, 131
Froelich, Mazie 131
Froelich and Wall Veneer 202
Furniture City Upholstery 208

G

Gannaway family 144
Gantt, Rowland and Ella 86, 136, 169
garden city movement 87
Gardner, Penelope 103
Garron, Dr. 152
Gaylord, Dr. Cavessa J.H. 152, 153, 156
Gaylord, Sallie 153
Georgian Revival style 59, 82, 159, 174, 200, 204, 212, 217, 226
Giant Furniture 190, 205
Gibson, Geneva F. 197
Gibson, Sloan 85, 197
Gibson House 85, 197
Gibson Ice Cream 197
Glenn, Chalmers 109
Glenn, Governor Robert 109
Globe Furniture 37, 163
Godwin, Beulah 179
Godwin, Dr. Jason 179
Godwin House 179
Goldston Park 87
Gordon, Pegram & Company 114
Gordon-Van Tine 195
Gothic Revival style 25, 35, 39, 43, 158
Grant, W.T. 75
Granville District 20
Graylyn 212
Grayson, Bertha Crawford 169
Grayson, Dr. C.S. 169
Grayson House 169
Gray family 143, 144, 212
Great Fayetteville and Western Plank Road 15, 27, 28, 107, 110, 117, 137
Great Western Plank Road. *See* Great Fayetteville and Western Plank Road
Greek Revival style 28, 31, 102, 105, 132
Greenhill Cemetery 72, 162
Greensboro Daily News 117
Greensboro Daily News Building 76, 117
Greenway Place 63

Index

Griffin, Alfred J. 42, 152, 159
Griffin Park 63, 160
Grimes Street School 58
Gropius, Walter 75, 110
Guilford County 20, 22, 27, 29, 30, 35, 77, 86, 93, 94, 97, 98, 100, 142, 160, 236, 245
Guilford County Courthouse 120, 121, 122
Guilford County Office and Court Building 77, 78
Guilford General Hospital 58, 200
Guilford Hosiery Mills 177

H

H.A. Millis House 10
H.R. Welborn & Co. tobacco manufacturing company 114
Haley, John 94
Haley House 10, 22, 93, 94
Hall, W.B. (Will) 130
Hall Printing 130
Hammer, Lulu Blanche 125
Hardee, Constance Charles 171
Hardee Apartments 71, 171
Harmon House 42, 136
Harper, Peggy 231
Harper, Terry 231
Harper House 70, 231
Harrison Hall 80
Harriss, Julius Ward 212
Harriss and Covington Hosiery Mills 68, 212
Harris Building 34, 112
Hartmann, Charles 45, 54, 82, 119, 199, 218
Haverford College 34, 104
Haworth, Judge Byron 193
Haworth, Sarah C. 193
Hayes, Dr. William A. 196
Hayes, Helen 196
Hayes House 196
Hayworth, Charles E. 140
Hayworth, Judge Byron 85
Hayworth-Barthmaier, Myrtle 140, 141, 212
Hayworth Fine Arts Center 227
Hayworth Roll and Panel 212
Henry, Guy 202
Henry, Minnie 202
Henry Motor Sales 202
Highland Cotton Mill 50, 144, 145, 146, 173
Highland Cotton Mill Village 51, 145
Highland Methodist Church and Parsonage 145
Highland School 145

High Point's Housing Authority 86, 161
High Point, Randleman, Asheboro and Southern Railroad 34
High Point, Thomasville and Denton Railroad 58, 126, 141
High Point Buggy Company 52
High Point Central High School 84, 216
High Point Chair and Home Furniture 37, 170
High Point City Hall 129
High Point College. *See* High Point University
High Point Country Club 61, 63, 194, 199, 210
High Point Enterprise 34, 71, 73, 82, 108, 135, 146, 176, 183, 194, 202, 222
High Point Enterprise Building 74, 114
High Point Excelsior Company 48
High Point Female Academy 30, 35
High Point Fire Department 224
High Point Friends Meeting 82, 217
High Point Furniture Company 37
High Point High School 59, 61, 77
High Point Historical Society 10, 94, 245
High Point Hosiery Mill 49, 144, 182
High Point Ice and Coal Company 177
High Point Insurance and Real Estate Company 182, 223
High Point Machine Works 215
High Point Marble and Tile Building 128
High Point Meeting 35
High Point Memorial Hospital 58
High Point Metallic Bed Company 47
High Point Motor Company 125
High Point Museum 21, 94, 109, 245
High Point Normal and Industrial School 42, 159
High Point Preservation Commission 10, 11
High Point Preservation Society 10, 246
High Point Public Graded School 42, 43
High Point Public Library 78, 152, 153, 168
High Point Realty Investment Company 184
High Point Underwear Company 183
High Point University 60, 61, 80, 84, 222, 225, 226
Hill, Abigail 103, 104
Hill, Anna 102
Hill, Everette 85, 226
Hillbrook 68, 212, 213
Hillcrest Manor 86
Hill Veneer Company 49
Hinton, Willis 34, 132, 152
Hinton Hotel 34
Historic American Buildings Survey 10

Historic Jamestown Society 96
Hockett, Miriam 102
Hoffman, Joe F., Jr. 121
Hoggatt, Joseph 94
Hoggatt, Mahlon 94
Hoggatt, Mary 105
Hoggatt House 21, 94, 95
Holton, A. Julius 185
Holton, Charles 231
Holton, Nell 195
Holton, Roland T. 195
Holton House 22, 185
Holt McPherson Center 115
Hook, C.C. 43
Hoover, Dr. 156
Horace S. Haworth Hall of Science 81, 227
Horney House 224
Hoskins, Alice 189
Hoskins, Bascom 189
Hoskins House 187, 189
Hudson, Homer T. 191
Hudson, Lola 191
Hudson House 191
Hughes, Ethel Griffin 55
Hughes, Raleigh James 69, 232
Hunt, Nathan, Jr. 30, 137
Hunter, Herbert 60, 61, 148, 164, 174, 226, 227
Hunt Hotel 30, 136, 137
Hyndman and Hyndman 109

I

Immaculate Heart of Mary Church 82, 232
Independence Hall 60, 227
Indiana limestone 57, 77, 241
Ingram, Mary and Thural 162
International style 84, 86, 88, 129, 192, 210
Interurban Motor Line 126
Irish order of the Poor Servants of the Mother of God 232
Italianate style 25, 29, 30, 39, 40, 100, 103, 137, 173, 234
Italian Renaissance style 57, 69, 71, 119, 173, 194, 203, 205, 232

J

J.C. Penney 53, 118
J.H. Adams House 11, 70
J.H. Jenkins & Co. 114
J.N. Pease and Associates 76, 110
J. Ed Millis House 199

258

Index

J. Elwood Cox Manufacturing Company 130, 185
Jackson, Celeste 200
Jackson, Dr. Walter Leo 200
Jackson Hosiery Mills 200
Jackson House 200
Jamestown 22, 23, 27, 30, 31, 70, 87, 93, 96, 102, 103, 116, 120, 234
Jamestown Furniture Exposition Building 48, 120
Jamestown Indulged Meeting House 10, 23, 95
Jamestown Rifles 95, 101
Jarrell Apartments. *See* Hardee Apartments
Jarrell Building I 54, 117
Jarrell Building II 118
Jarrell Hotel 29
Jay, Allen 23, 101
Jay, Martha 101
Jefferson Medical College 104
Joe Cox Building 118
Johnson, Henry Lytle 100
Johnson House 100
Johnson Place 62, 67, 167, 176, 182, 223
Johnson Street 11, 39, 66, 87, 102, 176
Johnson Street School 58
Jonathan Harris House 97
Jones, Minnie 214
Jones, Wilber 214
Jones House 214
Joyce, Mary Lib 10, 94
Judge Haworth House 193
Julius Rosenwald Fund 58
Junior Order of Mechanics 31, 39, 58, 132

K

Kalte, Elizabeth 170
Kearns, Amos R. 198
Kearns, Gurney H. 205
Kearns, Kate Harmon 205
Kearns Furniture 47
Kearns House 70, 194, 205
Keen, Charles Barton 199, 206
Kendall, Solomon 29
Kephart, C.M. 222
Kerner, Israel 101
Kerner, Theodore 101
Kersey, Elizer 98
Keyauwees 19, 20
Kilby, John 55, 152, 155, 162
Kilby, Nannie 55, 152, 155, 162

Kilby Hotel 55, 152, 155
Kimball, Fiske 64, 214
King, Alice Carr 206
King, Annabella 206
King, Rufus 206
King Charles II 20
King House 206
Kinley, Grady Jacob 100
Kirk, Colonel George W. 32
Kirkman, Katherine 126
Kirkman, O. Arthur 37, 40, 66, 67, 125, 126, 127
Kirkman, O. Arthur, Jr. 126
Kirkman, Tom 41, 125
Kirkman Park Elementary School 87
Kiwanis Club 226
Klain, Zora 103
Klein, Fred B. 64, 208, 209
Klein House 209
Kroger 75

L

Lakewood par 3 golf course 100
Lamb, Jehu 100
Lambeth, Nannie 100
Lander, Fred 55, 160
Langdon, Reverend M.I. 30
Lashmit, Luther 68, 69, 212, 213, 215
Lassiter, R.G. 54
Lawson, John 19
Lebanon United Methodist Church 180
Ledbetter, Henry 101
Leonard Street School 58
Le Corbusier 75
Lincoln, Abraham 42
Lindley, J. Van 223
Lindsay, Andrew 97
Lindsay, Dr. R.C. 137
Lindsay, Frances Gordon 177
Lindsay, R. Odell 177
Lindsay, Robert 97
Lindsay Chair Company 47
Little Red Schoolhouse 228
Lockwood, Green & Company 50, 141
Loewenstein, Edward 74, 76, 117, 207
Long, Charles 48
Long, Charles F. 120
Long Street 180
Lords Proprietors 20
Lossing, Benson J. 27

Lyceum social club 34
Lynch's Select School for Boys 34, 126
Lynch, Major William Bingham 34

M

Mackey, Clarence 95
Mackintosh, Charles 232
MacMillan, Reverend Father Robert 232
Madison and Monroe Apartments 86
Mann Drugs 111
Margaret and Frank Dalton House 84, 207
Margaret and Henry D. Perry House 229
Market Square 10, 123, 124
Marklye's Grove 71
Marshall, David 23, 101
Marshall, Zelinda 23, 101
Marshall-Jay House 101
Marsh Furniture Company 47
Martin, Dr. 154
Martin, Ora Kilby 154, 155
Maryfield 232
Mary and H. Albion Millis House 10, 174
Mary L. and Charles F. Tomlinson House 189
Masonic Lodge 79, 123
Matton Drug Co. 34
Maupin, Lawrence 222
Maupin, Mamie 222
Mays, Clayton 74, 75, 168, 207
Mays and Parks, Associates 75, 85, 181, 193
McCain, Dr. H.W. 177
McCall's Magazine 224
McCulloch, Charles 23, 98
McCulloch Gold Mill 98
McCulloch Hall 60
McEwen, W.B. 183
McEwen Hall. *See* Women's Hall
McGary, R.A. 122
McJester, David 68, 202
McPherson, Holt 9, 194
McPherson Campus Center. *See* Slane University Center
Mechanicsville 39, 56, 139, 179
Mediterranean style 69, 70, 71, 167, 168, 182, 183, 184, 192, 194
Melrose House 124
Mendenhall, Elihu 28, 102, 104, 136
Mendenhall, Elihu Clarkson (Clark) 103
Mendenhall, Elijah 102
Mendenhall, James 102
Mendenhall, Nereus 104

Index

Mendenhall, Richard 96
Mendenhall Store 10, 23, 96, 233
Mercer, Greg 173
Miller, Albert 34
Millis, H. Albion 174
Millis, Helen Brooks 199
Millis, J. Ed 161, 199
Millis, J. Henry 49, 173, 174, 177, 199
Millis, Mary Lewis 174
Millis Square 10, 174
Minimal Traditional style 83, 183
Mission style 68, 70, 171, 172, 183, 194, 195, 229
Mitchell, R.E. 60, 226
Model Farm 36, 101, 147, 148
Modern style 75, 76, 79, 80, 81, 82, 83, 84, 85, 86, 110, 129, 134, 153, 158, 174, 187, 193, 197, 207, 209, 211, 214, 218, 226, 227
Modern Upholstery Company 74, 230
Montgomery family 179
Montlieu Avenue 62, 67, 68, 69, 82, 87, 222, 223, 225
Montlieu Avenue Elementary School 80, 228
Montlieu Dairy Farm 222
Moore, Alfred Abijah 176
Moravians 21
Morgan, J.P. 45
Morris Knowles Inc. 78
Morrow, Debbie 182
Morrow, Robert R. 182
Motsinger, S.L. 111, 114
Mount Zion Baptist Church 158
Municipal Building 57, 78, 79
Murray, Forest 190
Murray, Lucille 205
Murray, Marguerite 190
Murray, Walter L. 205
Murray House 70, 190, 205
Museum of Old Domestic Life 10, 105
Myrtlewood 212
Myrtle Desk 37, 124, 140, 141, 212

N

Nailer, Mose 144
Nailer family 144
Nathan Wright House 233
National Bank of High Point 34
National Civic League 73
National Furniture Mart 75

Native American 19, 110
Natuzzi Americas Building 128
Neo-Gothic style 59, 82, 88, 216, 218
Neoclassical Revival style 39, 53, 54, 56, 57, 63, 65, 111, 112, 113, 118, 119, 135, 154, 167, 191, 212, 213
New Formalism style 75, 76, 79, 80, 81, 88, 113, 133
New Garden Boarding School 101, 102, 104
New York Yearly Meeting 42, 159
Norman Revival style 68, 69, 212
Northup, Lamar 211
Northup and O'Brien 45, 68, 69, 190, 198, 199, 212, 213, 215
Northview Dairy Farm 103
North Carolina Chapter of the American Institute of Architects 61, 168
North Carolina Friends Yearly Meeting House 42
North Carolina Jaycees 133
North Carolina Methodist Protestants 60
North Carolina Railroad 9, 15, 27, 28, 29, 45, 103, 107, 117, 123, 137, 152
North Carolina Savings Bank and Trust Company Building 53, 65, 109, 111, 112, 119, 135, 172
North Carolina Society for the Preservation of Antiquities. *See* Preservation North Carolina
North Carolina State Historic Preservation Office 246
North Carolina State Legislature Building 78
North Carolina Yearly Meeting of the Society of Friends 135
North Side Hose Company Number 1/Old City Hall 10, 56, 131
North State Communications 134, 135

O

O. Arthur Kirkman Estate 125
O. Arthur Kirkman Manufacturing Company 125
Oaks, the 104
Oakview 235
Oakwood 11, 31, 86, 135
Oakwood Cemetery 31, 32, 72, 131, 132, 162, 223
Oakwood Court 86
Oakwood Garden Court Apartments 136
Oakwood Memorial Cemetery 72, 132

Oakwood Street 136
Oak Hill School 34, 35, 58, 142
Oddfellows Lodge 58, 152, 157
Odell, James 33
Odell and Associates 74, 76, 113, 124
Odell Hardware Company 33
Odell Lindsay House 177
Olive, Howard 82, 217
One Plaza Center 76, 108, 110
Oppermann, Joseph 97
Orange County 20
Own-A-Home Company 62, 222

P

Pardue, David L. 187
Pardue, Dora 187
Pardue House 187
Parish of St. Edward's 60
Parker, Deborah Tomlinson 204
Parker, Eunice 210
Parker, Ralph 140, 141, 210
Parks, Robert 75, 85
Parkway 61, 62, 70, 71, 87, 168, 182, 185, 186, 187, 188, 189, 190, 191, 192, 193
Park Street School 58
Parsons, Agnes Lowe 184
Parsons, David H. 184
Parsons residence 184
Payne, Isaac 40, 102
Peabody, George 96
Pease, Colonel J.N. 110
Pease, Norman 110
Penn-Griffin School of Performing Arts 160
Pennfield 22, 93
Pennsylvania State House 60
Penny, George 69, 232
Penny, Lena 232
Pennybyrn 69, 232
Penny brothers 113, 225
Penny Building 53, 113
Peoples Realty Company 42, 163
Perry, Henry 229
Perry, Margaret 229
Perry, Seborn 29
Perry Estate. *See* Margaret and Henry D. Perry House
Perry Plywood Corporation 224
Peter, Martha Custis 208
Peter, Thomas 208
Petty, J.H. 140

260

Index

Phebe and John Haley House 22
Philadelphia 20, 22, 60, 96, 217
Phillips, Charles 97
Phillips, Earl N. 213
Phillips, Lillian Jordan 213
Phillips-Davis 122, 213
Phillips Building 122
Pickett, Francis Marion 50, 141
Pickett Cotton Mills 50, 51, 141
Piedmont Hosiery Mills 49, 134, 173
Piggott's Hotel. *See* Barbee House
Piggott, Jeremiah 30
Pittsburgh Plate Glass Company 49, 176
Plaxico, Pat 10, 131
Powell, Annie Mae 141
Prairie style 62, 66, 67, 131, 156, 167, 170, 171, 172, 176, 177, 178, 179, 186
Preservation North Carolina 10, 246
Pretty Branch Creek 185, 210, 215
Primitive Baptist Church 180
Prince, Bessie 186
Prince, C.C. 186
Professional Building 74, 122
Pueblo Revival style 70

Q

Quakers 9, 20, 21, 22, 30, 31, 32, 33, 35, 36, 42, 59, 94, 96, 98, 99, 101, 102, 105, 159, 234
Quaker Woods 41, 42, 62, 135, 176, 182
Quality Shoe Store 224
Queen Anne style 35, 39, 40, 41, 42, 125, 127, 136, 144, 154, 163, 176, 180, 187

R

R.K. Stewart and Sons 116, 121, 174, 212, 232
R.K. Stewart House 136
R.O. Lindsay House 65
Ragsdale, William 87
Ranch style 83, 84, 183, 187, 194, 197, 224
Randleman 32, 232
Rankin, A.M. 140, 197
Rankin, Adele 197
Rankin, Alex M. 197
Rankin House 197
Raymond Veneer Company 49
Ray Street School 58, 222, 228
Redding, J.P. 52, 85, 140
Redding Flats 53, 71, 112, 135
Regency style 68, 83, 210, 211

Reverend Saulter House 156
Revolutionary War 27
Richardson, Henry Hobson 43
Richardsonian Romanesque style 42, 55, 108
Richard Mendenhall Plantation 104
Riddle, H.H. 182
Robbins Knitting Company 224
Roberts Hall 60, 226, 227
Robinson, John 34, 132, 152, 154
Robinson, William "Bill" 34, 154
Robinson House 154
Rock Gymnasium 80, 149
Roland Holton House 195
Roland Park 39, 62, 64, 67, 68, 69, 70, 182, 183, 185, 186, 193
Roland Park Company 182
Romanesque style 43, 155, 159
Rones, Dr. Max 113, 201
Rones, Fannie L. 201
Rones House 201
Roosevelt, Franklin Delano 80, 149
Rose, William P. 48, 120
Rosetta C. Baldwin House 162
Ross, L.S. 161
Rotary Club 226
Rowan County 20
Rowella Apartments 86, 169
Rustic Revival log style 236
Ruth, O.L. 161

S

S.H. Kress & Co. 54
Sampson, William A. 148
Sapona Side 40
Sapona tribe 19, 20
Sapp, Dr. A.J. 30
Saulter, Martha 156
Saulter, Reverend David S. 156
Sawyer, Sallie and Bill 35
Schute, Leon 74, 78, 79, 81, 129, 133, 227
Scott, Sarah 100
Scottish Bank 76, 134
Sears, Thomas 68, 213
Sears and Roebuck 53
Sechrest, Mont L. 85
Shadowlawn 198
Shelton, Mildred 211
Shelton, Roy 83
Shelton, Roy E. 211
Shelton House 211

Sheraton Hill 62, 71, 182, 186, 193
Sheraton Hotel 54, 58, 103, 115
Sherrod, Archibald 62, 67, 170, 223
Sherrod, Lizzie 170
Sherrod House 67, 170, 171
Sherrod Park 11, 62, 68, 87, 171, 223, 245
Sherrod Shirt Factory 170, 180
Shipman, Ellen Biddle 213
Shore, Mary and Jason 163
Showplace 109, 128
Siceloff, Jonathan Clarence 172
Siceloff, Mattie V. 172
Siceloff Hardware Company 172
Siceloff House 42, 172, 173
Silver, Milton 52, 165
Silver, Robert 52, 165
Silver Knit Hosiery Mills, Inc. 165
Six Associates 75, 120
Sizemore, Frank 9
Slane, Meredith Clark 215
Slane, Willis H. 164, 215
Slane Hosiery Mill 164, 215
Slane University Center 81, 227
Smallwood, Christopher 227
Smith, Bettie and Thomas 163
Smith, Henry 160
Smith, Reverend William Harry 158
Smith, Thomas B. 154
Smithdeal, Curtis 75, 86
Smith Dry Cleaners 75
Smith Furniture 47
Snow, "Capt" W.H. 33, 130
Snow, Ernest Ansel 40
Snow, R.E. 222
Snow Lumber Company 42, 130, 135, 179, 196, 204
Society of Friends. *See* Quakers
Southern Chair 37
Southern Furniture Exposition Building 48, 54, 75, 112, 119, 120
Southern Furniture Journal 186
Southern Railroad "Belt Line" 145
Southern Railway Passenger Depot 11, 46, 108, 246
Southgate Shopping Center 75
Spanish Eclectic style 184, 225
Spanish style 54, 68, 69, 70, 115, 126, 172, 173, 188, 192, 196, 203, 205, 222, 229, 231, 235
Spencer, Nathan 233
Spence Brothers 122

Index

Springfield Friends Fourth Meeting House 148
Springfield Friends Meeting 10, 31, 86, 93, 101, 163
Springfield Meetinghouse 31
Springfield Memorial Association 10, 105
Springfield School 101
St. Mark's Methodist Episcopal Church 43, 152, 156, 158
St. Mary's Episcopal Church 35, 61, 167, 174, 206, 208
St. Stephen AME Zion Church 55, 156, 158
St. Stephen Metropolitan Church 43
Stack, Levin 95
Stallings, Dr. J.N. 35
Stanton, Dr. D.A. 39
Stanton-Welch Building 39
Steele, E.D. 40
Steele Street 131, 132
Stehli, Emil 52
Stehli Silk Mill 52, 222
Stewart, R.K. 54, 116, 119, 136, 198, 199, 213, 232
Stoddard, W.L. 45, 54, 115
Stone, Edward Durell 74, 78, 80, 129, 133
Streamline Moderne style 74, 78, 157, 230
String and Splinter Club 52, 115
Stroud, Phebe 99
Stuart, Louisa 98
Sunnyside Ice and Fuel Company 172
Sydney Tomlinson House 224

T

Talmey, Rose 212
Taplin, A.E. 85, 122, 188, 192, 210, 223, 225, 229
Taplin, Ruth 192
Taplin House 192
Tate, Estelle Field 198
Tate, Fred N. 198
Tate Building 34
Tate Furniture Company 37, 210
Tate House/Kearnwood 198
Tate Park 58, 71, 82, 132, 133
Tedford, Clarence D. 70, 231
Terry, Nancy 183
Terry, Randall B. 183
Terry House 68, 183
Tesh, Dr. J.F. 222
Tesh, Ruth 222
Third Springfield Meeting House 28, 105

Thomas, Alice 191
Thomas, Frances C. 200
Thomas, Fred A. 200
Thomas, W.B., Jr. 164
Thomas, Walter B. 191
Thomas, William B. 164
Thomas Furniture Company 200
Thomas House 200
Thomas Mills, Inc. 164
Thompson, Mary and J.G. 163
Three Musketeers 69, 215
Tilden, Martha Robbins 96
Tillman, Dr. Otis 155
Tillson, R.D. 163, 169, 194, 210, 217
Tomlinson, Charles F. 189, 216
Tomlinson, Ethel Diffee 206
Tomlinson, Mary 189
Tomlinson, Sidney Halstead 206
Tomlinson Chair Manufacturing Company 47, 124
Tomlinson Furniture Company 123
Tomlinson Manufacturing Company 10, 124. *See also* Market Square
Tomlynhurst 68, 189, 193, 194, 206
Tom Kirkman House 125
Totera tribe 19
Trading Ford 19
Trexler, Ann E. 230
Trexler, John E. 230
Triangle Hosiery Company 212
Triangle Park 71
Tudor Place 64, 208
Tudor Revival style 62, 183, 187, 194, 195, 197, 198, 203, 204, 206, 207, 223, 224

U

Union Furniture 37, 191, 200
United States Post Office 29, 57, 121, 122, 176
Upjohn, Richard Hobart 45, 61, 168
Uwharrie Mountain 19, 30
Uwharrie tribe 19

V

van der Rohe, Mies 75, 110, 211
Venable, Floyd and Edna 103
Voorhees, Elizabeth Peyton 201
Voorhees, Everhart and Conner 174
Voorhees, Louis 45, 61, 64, 78, 174, 200, 201, 202, 208, 214, 228

Voorhees and Everhart 48, 76, 77, 82, 87, 120, 121, 163, 210, 217
Voorhees House 201
Vuncannon, Pearl M. 210
Vuncannon, S. Colon 210
Vuncannon House 210, 211

W

W. & J. Sloane 215
Wachovia Building 76, 109, 113
Wagoner, Harold E. 82, 218
Waldensian stonemasons 170
Wall, Elizabeth Bowne (Bonie) 202
Wall, Matt 202
Wall, Phebe 94
Wallace, William Roy 212
Walsh, Valette Harris 214
Walter Thomas House 191
Washington Drive 31, 39, 40, 54, 55, 58, 59, 143, 144, 151, 152, 154, 155, 156, 157, 158, 159, 160, 222
Washington Drive Branch 78, 79, 152, 153
Washington Street Methodist-Episcopal Church 31
Washington Terrace 87
Waters, Bishop Vincent S. 232
Waynick, C.M. 161
Waynick, Capus 10
Weaver, Elizabeth 182
Weaver, Joseph T. 182
Welborn's Crossroads 179
Welborn, David N. 188
Welborn, H.R. 33, 114
Welborn, Nancy P. 188
Welborn-Payne House 102
Welborn House 136, 188
Welch, J.C. 231
Welch, J.J. 39
Welch, Jonathan 94
Welch, William 29
Welch, Wilna 231
Welch Furniture 47
Welch House 70, 71, 231
Wesley Memorial Methodist Church 82, 218
Wesley Place 62
Westminster 22, 93
Westtown School 104
West End 34, 56, 71, 137, 139, 141
West High Street 29, 35, 37, 40, 47, 102, 123
West Locke Apartments 86

262

Index

Wheelen Swimming Pool, Chicago 233
Wheeler, Homer 42, 62, 135, 167, 176
Wheeler, James 94
Wheeler, R.A. 136
Wheeler, Runge and Dickey 53, 112
Wheeler Park 71
White, Alice N. 39
White, Gib 211
White, Mary and C.F. 163
White, Nancy 211
White House 211
White Oak 39, 42, 163
Whitsell, W.K. 84, 192
Whitsell House 192
Whitten, Dr. Clifford 157
Whitten Clinic 157
Willard, Ann Russell 184
Willard, R.M. 184
Willard House 184
Willet, Henry 82, 218
Williams, Marion Banner 235
Williams House 235
William and Mary Apartments 86
William F. Freeman, Associates 79
William Henley Deitrick 216
William Penn High School. *See* High Point Normal and Industrial School
Williard, Lewis Orville 230
Williard House 67, 230
Willoubar Terrace 63, 70, 225
Willowbrook Cotton Mill 33
Wilson, George F. 125
Wilson, J. Vassie 64, 208
Wilson, Lucy 64, 208
Wilson, Orianna 104
Wilson House 208
Wiltshire Avenue 70
Winn-Dixie 75
Winslow, Lorenzo S. 174
Woccon tribe 19
Women's Hall 60, 227
Woodruff, Bert 203
Woodruff, Dr. Fred 203
Woodruff House 203, 204
Workman, Everhart and Voorhees 71, 147
Works Progress Administration 71, 77, 147, 149, 233
World's Largest Bureau 58, 71, 132
World War Veterans Memorial 223
Worth, Governor Jonathan 148
Worth-Virdon mills 30

Wrenn, M.J. 227
Wrenn family 132
Wrenn Hall 81, 227
Wright, Frank Lloyd 67, 83, 171, 179, 226
Wright, John 143
Wright, Nathan 233
Wright family 144
Wyatt Early Harris Wheeler and Hauser 121

Y

Yadkin River 19
Yarborough Law Building 152, 154
YMCA 58
Yokley House 180
Young, Fred 222
Young, John 176
Young, Lee 146
Young, Lelia and Robert 163
Young, Lola 222
YWCA 79, 133, 173

Z

Zelinda and David Marshall House 23, 24
Zenke, Otto 212
Zollicoffer, Dallas 178, 179
Zollicoffer, Robah Bencini 178
Zollicoffer House 67, 178, 192

Visit us at
www.historypress.net